OECD ECONOMIC SURVEYS

# UNITED STATES

NOVEMBER 1985

ORGANISATION FOR ECONOMIC CO-OPERATION AND DEVELOPMENT

Pursuant to article 1 of the Convention signed in Paris on 14th December, 1960, and which came into force on 30th September, 1961, the Organisation for Economic Co-operation and Development (OECD) shall promote policies designed:

- to achieve the highest sustainable economic growth and employment and a rising standard of living in Member countries, while maintaining financial stability, and thus to contribute to the development of the world economy;
- to contribute to sound economic expansion in Member as well as non-member countries in the process of economic development; and
- to contribute to the expansion of world trade on a multilateral, non-discriminatory basis in accordance with international obligations.

The Signatories of the Convention on the OECD are Austria, Belgium, Canada, Denmark, France, the Federal Republic of Germany, Greece, Iceland, Ireland, Italy, Luxembourg, the Netherlands, Norway, Portugal, Spain, Sweden, Switzerland, Turkey, the United Kingdom and the United States. The following countries acceded subsequently to this Convention (the dates are those on which the instruments of accession were deposited): Japan (28th April, 1964), Finland (28th January, 1969), Australia (7th June, 1971) and New Zealand (29th May, 1973).

The Socialist Federal Republic of Yugoslavia takes part in certain work of the OECD (agreement of 28th October, 1961).

# CONTENTS

## TABLES

# DIAGRAMS

# BASIC STATISTICS OF THE UNITED STATES

## THE LAND

| | | | |
|---|---|---|---|
| Area continental United States plus Hawaï and Alaska (thous. sq. km) | 9 363 | Population of major cities, including their metropolitan areas (1.4.1980 estimates): | |
| | | New York | 9 120 000 |
| | | Los Angeles-Long Beach | 7 478 000 |
| | | Chicago | 7 104 000 |

## THE PEOPLE

| | | | |
|---|---|---|---|
| Population, July 1984 | 236 600 000 | Civilian labour force 1984 | 113 544 000 |
| No. of inhabitants per sq. km | 25 | *of which:* | |
| Population, annual net natural increase (average 1976-1981) | 1 486 000 | Employed in agriculture | 3 321 000 |
| | | Unemployed | 8 539 000 |
| Annual net natural increase, per cent, 1976-1981 | 0.6 | Net migration (annual average 1976-1981) | 487 000 |

## PRODUCTION

| | | | |
|---|---|---|---|
| Gross national product in 1984 (billions of US $) | 3 662.8 | Origin of national income in 1984 (per cent of national income[1]): | |
| GNP per head in 1984 (US $) | 15 481 | | |
| Gross fixed capital formation: | | Agriculture, forestry and fishing | 2.6 |
| Per cent of GNP in 1984 | 17.8 | Manufacturing | 22.3 |
| Per head in 1984 (US $) | 2 763 | Construction and mining | 5.9 |
| | | Government and government enterprises | 14.3 |
| | | Other | 54.9 |

## THE GOVERNMENT

| | | | | |
|---|---|---|---|---|
| Government purchases of goods and services, 1984 (per cent of GNP) | 20.4 | Composition of the 99th Congress: | | |
| Revenue of Federal, state and local governments, 1984 (per cent of GNP) | 33.5 | | House of Representatives | Senate |
| Federal Government debt as per cent of receipts from the public, 1984 | 186.3 | Democrats | 255 | 46 |
| | | Republicans | 180 | 54 |
| | | Independents | – | – |
| | | Undecided | – | – |
| | | Total | 435 | 100 |

## FOREIGN TRADE

| | | | |
|---|---|---|---|
| *Exports:* | | *Imports:* | |
| Exports of goods and services as per cent of GNP in 1984 | 9.9 | Imports of goods and services as per cent of GNP in 1984 | 11.7 |
| Main exports 1984 (per cent of merchandise exports): | | Main imports 1984 (per cent of merchandise imports): | |
| Machinery | 28.4 | Food, feeds and beverages | 6.4 |
| Transport equipment | 14.0 | Industrial supplies and materials | 37.7 |
| Food and live animals | 11.5 | Capital goods (excl. cars) | 18.3 |
| Crude materials (inedible) | 9.5 | Automobile vehicles and parts | 16.9 |
| Chemicals | 10.5 | Consumer goods (non-food) | 18.1 |
| Manufactured goods | 7.1 | All other | 2.5 |
| All other | 19.0 | | |

1. Without capital consumption adjustment.
*Note:* An international comparison of certain basic statistics is given in an annex table.

*This Survey is based on the Secretariat's study prepared for the annual review of the United States by the Economic and Development Review Committee on 23rd September 1985.*

*After revisions in the light of discussions during the review, final approval of the Survey for publication was given by the Committee on 22nd November 1985.*

## CONVENTIONAL SIGNS

| | | | |
|---|---|---|---|
| Q1, etc. | Calendar quarters | BEA | Bureau of Economic Analysis DoC |
| I,II | Calendar half years | BPEA | Brookings Papers on Economic |
| nsa | Not seasonally adjusted | | Activity |
| saar | Seasonally adjusted annual rate | CBO | Congressional Budget Office |
| COLA | Cost-of-living adjustment | CEA | Council of Economic Advisors |
| FY | Fiscal Year | DoC | Department of Commerce |
| NIPA | National Income and Product | DoL | Department of Labor |
| | accounts | FOMC | Federal Open Market Committee |
| NOW | Negotiable order of withdrawal | FRB | Federal Reserve Board |
| MMDA | Money market deposit account | NBER | National Bureau of Economic |
| MMMF | Money market mutual fund | | Research |
| | | OMB | Office of Management and the Budget |

6

# INTRODUCTION

The Administration's medium-term economic strategy, presented in the 1981 Program for Economic Recovery, contained a commitment to anti-inflationary monetary policy, tax and public expenditure reductions and regulatory reform. Expectations of sustained balanced economic growth were initially frustrated by the worst recession since the thirties (in 1981-1982) and post-war record high unemployment. But the subsequent cyclical upturn has also been very rapid. In the first two years of the recovery (1983/1984) output growth was stronger than in past upturns, inflation came down to one of the lowest rates in the OECD area, while unemployment also fell substantially. This situation stands in marked contrast to that in Europe, where disinflation has been accompanied by modest economic growth and rising unemployment. Business fixed investment in the United States has also risen strongly. Risks that the recovery may abort in the near future because of inflation and supply constraints have therefore been reduced. Since early 1985, however, activity has slowed down markedly and although prospects point to continued expansion, of the order of 2½-3 per cent over the next eighteen months or so, increasing signs of hesitancy have appeared.

Rising domestic and external imbalances are indeed imposing increasing risks for the sustainability of the recovery. These imbalances include continuing large budget deficits, rapidly rising government debt, a widening current external deficit and a rapid deterioration of the U.S. international investment position. In spite of recent declines, high real interest rates and the strong dollar remain sources of difficulty. Declining net exports have introduced a wedge between domestic demand and output. Industrial production has risen only slightly over the last year. By threatening the survival of some sectors of the economy poor external competitiveness also tends to fuel protectionist pressure. If left uncorrected, these imbalances could ultimately build up to unmanageable proportions, leading to a recession or to a rekindling of inflation, perhaps both. This situation raises fundamental issues for economic analysis and for policy, both in the United States and abroad. Major challenges will be to reduce the structural budget deficit and secure a smooth, orderly depreciation of the dollar, while sustaining the momentum of the recovery.

Part I of the Survey highlights the key features of the current recovery in relation both to past cyclical episodes and to developments elsewhere, notably in Europe. The monetary and fiscal policy stance is described in Part II. Short-term prospects are presented in Part III, with special emphasis being put on the potential risks and uncertainties which could blow the economy off course. Medium-term financial imbalances are examined in Part IV; the analysis deals with the impact of federal deficits on interest rates, government debt accumulation and activity. Problems related to the dollar and the sustainability of the external deficit are also reviewed in the context of medium-term financial imbalances. Section V assesses the impact of deregulation in the transport and telecommunications sectors. Conclusions are presented in Part VI.

# I. THE RECOVERY SO FAR

## A. Overview

The current recovery, now over two-and-a-half years old, followed the longest and deepest recession since the Great Depression. The three years between 1980 and 1982 were characterized by near stagnation of output and a sharp rise in unemployment and inflation to peaks of about 11 per cent. In many respects the upturn has followed a classic pattern. The recovery of output stemmed initially from a slowdown in the strong pace of inventory liquidation, and substantial increases in other interest-sensitive components of demand (particularly automobiles and housing). It quickly broadened to other demand components, especially business fixed investment. It has, however, been characterized by several distinctive features. Over the first ten quarters (late 1982 to early 1985), real domestic demand increased more rapidly than in comparable cyclical episodes (Diagram 1) but real GNP growth was more typical because of the strong deterioration in the current external balance. This pattern resulted from the strong cyclical position of the US economy in relation to that of its main trading partners and the marked real appreciation of the dollar. Real business fixed investment increased at roughly twice the rate experienced in earlier recoveries, with investment in high-tech areas being especially strong. The growth of employment has been rapid in sharp contrast to the European experience. But the large imbalance between domestic demand and output has been reflected in the disparity of sectoral growth; manufacturing output has stagnated over the past year while growth in the service sector has remained fairly buoyant. The inflation performance during the current recovery has also been better than at any time during the 1970s, with excessive wage demands and upward price pressures largely absent so far.

## B. Domestic demand and the external balance

During the first ten quarters of the current recovery personal consumption expenditures accounted for roughly 65 per cent of the increase in real GNP from the recession trough, a somewhat larger than typical share. Total consumer spending rose at an annual rate of 5 per cent, compared to the average rate of 4.6 per cent in past cyclical upswings (Table 1). Spending on durables – particularly automobiles and household furnishings – led the recovery, due both to the decline in interest rates (this category being relatively interest-sensitive) and to stock rebuilding following years of low sales. This was followed by a general broadening of consumer spending to non-durables and services as the expansion gained hold. Growth of consumption has been very uneven, however. In the first six months of 1984, real non-auto retail sales burgeoned at a 12 per cent annual rate but then showed little increase during the second half of the year. Similarly, real residential construction – which had declined by 36 per cent between 1979 and 1982 – rose nearly 50 per cent during the first year of the recovery, providing much of the early momentum of the expansion. Thereafter, housing starts flattened out, and by the beginning of the third year the housing sector's overall contribution to the expansion was only slightly larger than in earlier recoveries. Reflecting the strong employment performance as well as the final round of personal tax cuts effective 1st July 1983, real disposable income grew at a 5.0 per cent annual rate over the first ten quarters of the recovery. Federal government purchases of goods and services made a larger contribution to GNP growth than usual, as a result of higher defence outlays, but since that of state and local spending was somewhat smaller than in the past, the general government's contribution to demand was not out of line with previous recoveries[1].

8

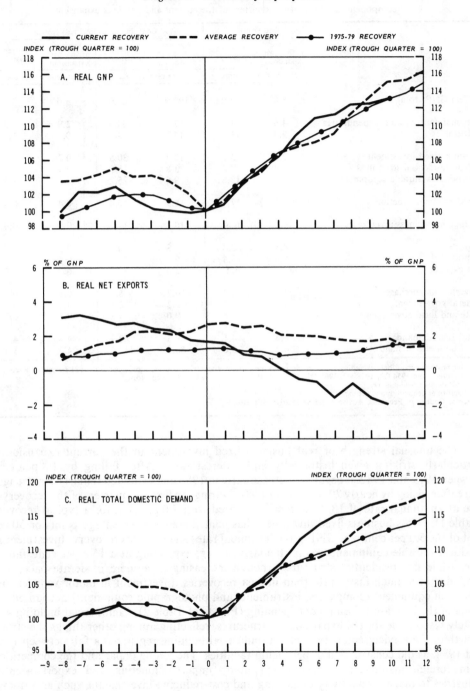

*Diagram 1.* **The recovery in perspective**

— CURRENT RECOVERY    – – – AVERAGE RECOVERY    —●— 1975-79 RECOVERY

A. REAL GNP

B. REAL NET EXPORTS

C. REAL TOTAL DOMESTIC DEMAND

*Source :* Secretariat calculations.

9

Table 1. **Contributions to GNP growth**

GNP components in the first ten quarters of the current and previous expansions[1]

| | Real growth | | Contribution to total real growth | | | |
|---|---|---|---|---|---|---|
| | Average of five past expansions | Current expansion | Average of five past expansions | Current expansion | Average of five past expansions | Current expansion |
| | Per cent, annual rate | | Per cent of total | | Per cent annual rate | |
| Real GNP, total | 5.0 | 5.0 | 100.0 | 100.0 | 5.0 | 5.0 |
| Personal consumption expenditures | 4.6 | 5.0 | 57.2 | 65.4 | 2.9 | 3.3 |
| Durables | 9.8 | 11.4 | 14.7 | 23.3 | 0.7 | 1.2 |
| Business fixed investment | 7.0 | 13.2 | 13.3 | 30.5 | 0.7 | 1.5 |
| Non-residential structures | 4.4 | 7.4 | 3.8 | 5.3 | 0.2 | 0.3 |
| Producers durable equipment | 8.6 | 15.8 | 9.6 | 25.2 | 0.5 | 1.3 |
| Residential construction | 11.1 | 17.4 | 8.9 | 10.4 | 0.4 | 0.5 |
| Change in business inventories | n.a. | n.a. | 10.7 | 17.1 | 0.5 | 0.9 |
| Exports | 8.1 | 0.4 | 9.8 | 0.6 | 0.5 | 0.0 |
| Imports | 6.8 | 18.4 | −6.5 | −30.8 | −0.3 | −1.5 |
| Net exports | n.a. | n.a. | 3.3 | −30.2 | 0.2 | −1.5 |
| Government purchases | 1.4 | 1.7 | 6.7 | 6.7 | 0.3 | 0.3 |
| Federal government | −0.7 | 1.6 | −2.3 | 2.5 | −0.1 | 0.1 |
| State and local government | 3.7 | 1.8 | 9.0 | 4.2 | 0.5 | 0.2 |
| Total final demand[2] | 4.4 | 4.1 | 89.3 | 82.9 | 4.4 | 4.1 |
| Final domestic demand[3] | 4.3 | 5.6 | 86.0 | 113.1 | 4.3 | 5.6 |

1. Five postwar expansions, excluding the expansion into the Korean War period and the short-lived 1980-1981 recovery. Recoveries measured from 1954 Q2, 1958 Q2, 1961 Q1, 1970 Q4, 1975 Q1 and 1982 Q4 recession troughs.
2. GNP minus stockbuilding.
3. Total final demand minus net exports.
Sources: Council of Economic Advisors and Secretariat estimates.

The unusual strength of real business fixed investment in the current expansion is particularly striking given historically high interest rates. After falling by 1.8 per cent between 1979 and 1982, it began to increase early in 1983 and exhibited remarkable strength thereafter, rising by nearly 20 per cent in 1984. During the first ten quarters of the recovery it rose at an annual rate of 13.2 per cent, compared with 7.0 per cent for a typical recovery (Table 1). Gross business fixed investment has contributed 1.5 percentage points or 30 per cent of the 5.0 per cent real GNP growth (annual rate) so far in this recovery. Investment in producer durable equipment was particularly strong, expanding at a 15.8 per cent annual rate, while non-residential structures, though increasing at a more moderate pace, also expanded at a much faster rate than in past recoveries. Investment in motor vehicles and high-tech equipment (computers, instruments and photographic equipment) accounted for much of the increase in equipment spending (Part C of Table 2). Commercial building was largely responsible for the expansion of structures, reflecting among other things the strong growth of the service sector. In contrast, industrial building registered a fall between 1982 and 1984, as did construction of petroleum facilities. The strong dollar and the competition from foreign manufactures encouraged many import-competing and export-oriented industries to make productivity-enhancing and cost-reducing investments, such as automation and computerisation, particularly of a labour-saving and material-saving nature.

## Table 2. Gross private domestic investment

### A. SHARE OF INVESTMENT IN GNP

| | Real business fixed investment | = | Real producers' durable equipment | + | Real non-residential structures | Ratio of structures to equipment |
|---|---|---|---|---|---|---|
| | As a per cent of real GNP | | | | | Per cent |
| 1945-1949 | 8.8 | | 5.5 | | 3.3 | 60.0 |
| 1950-1954 | 9.0 | | 5.4 | | 3.6 | 66.7 |
| 1955-1959 | 9.2 | | 5.3 | | 4.0 | 76.1 |
| 1960-1964 | 9.1 | | 5.1 | | 3.9 | 77.0 |
| 1965-1969 | 10.6 | | 6.4 | | 4.2 | 66.3 |
| 1970-1974 | 10.5 | | 6.7 | | 3.8 | 56.3 |
| 1975-1979 | 10.4 | | 7.3 | | 3.1 | 42.7 |
| 1980-1984 | 11.5 | | 8.1 | | 3.4 | 42.3 |

### B. GROWTH RATES OF REAL BUSINESS FIXED INVESTMENT OVER FIRST TEN QUARTERS OF RECOVERY
Per cent change, annual rate

| Business cycle trough quarter | Business fixed investment | = | Producers' durable equipment | + | Non-residential structures |
|---|---|---|---|---|---|
| 1954-II | 7.5 | | 7.2 | | 8.1 |
| 1958-II | 4.9 | | 4.6 | | 5.3 |
| 1961-I | 6.4 | | 10.0 | | 2.2 |
| 1970-IV | 9.5 | | 13.0 | | 3.6 |
| 1975-I | 6.5 | | 8.1 | | 2.7 |
| Average | 7.0 | | 8.6 | | 4.4 |
| 1982-IV | 13.2 | | 15.8 | | 7.4 |

### C. COMPOSITION OF GROSS REAL BUSINESS FIXED INVESTMENT

| | 1959 | 1982 | 1984 | 1984 | Growth rates Per cent annual rate | |
|---|---|---|---|---|---|---|
| | Per cent of total | | | $ 1972 billion | 1979-1982 | 1982-1984 |
| Total | 100.0 | 100.0 | 100.0 | 204.9 | −0.6 | 10.8 |
| Non-residential structures | 43.1 | 32.0 | 27.8 | 56.9 | 2.8 | 3.3 |
| Commercial | 10.4 | 9.8 | 9.9 | 20.3 | 7.6 | 11.4 |
| Industrial | 5.5 | 4.6 | 2.9 | 5.9 | −1.6 | −11.9 |
| Public utilities | 10.2 | 7.6 | 6.3 | 13.0 | −2.1 | 1.3 |
| Petroleum | 5.2 | 4.3 | 3.2 | 6.5 | 15.9 | −4.5 |
| Other | 11.8 | 5.7 | 5.4 | 11.1 | −0.3 | 8.1 |
| Producers' durable equipment | 56.9 | 68.0 | 72.2 | 148.0 | −2.0 | 14.2 |
| Instruments, photo equipment and computers | 4.0 | 22.9 | 25.4 | 52.1 | 14.8 | 16.8 |
| Communications | 3.8 | 8.7 | 8.1 | 14.0 | 3.0 | 6.8 |
| Motor vehicles | 10.7 | 10.1 | 14.4 | 24.6 | −11.0 | 32.8 |
| Aircraft | 1.9 | 1.4 | 1.2 | 2.4 | −7.0 | 2.2 |
| Other | 36.5 | 25.0 | 23.1 | 44.9 | −8.9 | 6.5 |

*Sources:* U.S. Treasury and Secretariat estimates.

Competition from foreign producers of capital equipment also helped to keep the cost of capital goods down compared to structures. Despite the buoyant recovery, costs of investment goods have been generally well-contained, with the business fixed investment deflator in the second quarter of 1985 only slightly above its late 1982 level.

In 1984 gross real business fixed investment was equivalent to roughly 12.5 per cent of real GNP, an increase from 9 per cent in the 1950s and 10.5 per cent in the 1970s (Table 2). While the share increase has been smaller on a net basis (see Table 19 below), due to a shift toward shorter-lived investment, the trend is encouraging. There has been a continuing substantial shift from investment in structures towards machinery and equipment, which accounted for around 55 per cent of business fixed investment in the late 1950s and early 1960s, but comprised over 70 per cent in the early 1980s. A larger share of investment has been going into high-tech components, such as computers, instruments, and communication equipment. Aided by relative price declines, these categories continued to expand strongly during the 1979-1982 period while other components recorded sharp declines. This is compatible with the observation that the high-tech manufacturing and service industries are more immune from cyclical downturns than the older and heavier manufacturing industries. It would also appear that much of the investment in these industries has been capital widening and labour using rather than simply capital deepening. This is reflected in the rapid growth of employment and output in the service sector – which tends to be relatively labour-intensive. Capital-widening investment would also be a consistent result of slow increases in real wage costs and high levels of real interest rates. A major exception would be the productivity-enhancing and labour-saving investments made in the older manufacturing industries (steel, auto, machinery), which are heavily unionised and have high labour costs in comparison with their main foreign competitors. It would appear that these industries have responded, like their European counterparts, by moving toward more capital-intensive techniques and shedding excess labour[2]. It is uncertain at this point what the shift to equipment and short-lived capital implies for prospective U.S. growth potential. On the one-hand it could mean a more flexible industrial structure, with an automatic upgrading of technology reducing the chance of large-scale obsolesence such as occurred in auto, steel, machinery and other large-scale U.S. manufacturing in the late 1970s. On the other hand, a shorter-lived capital stock could increase instability, especially if investment were to remain depressed for an extended period and the capital stock were quickly run down.

While it is usual for the trade balance to weaken somewhat during the first stages of an upturn – as the volume of imports normally rises more rapidly than that of exports – the deterioration during the current expansion has been well in excess of all previous experience (Table 3). During the first ten quarters of the current expansion the deterioration in the real net foreign balance amounted to 1.5 per cent of GDP a year on average. In contrast, during previous upswings the effect over the first two years was broadly neutral. This unusually large deterioration is largely attributable to exceptionally strong imports of goods and services. These rose at a 18.4 per cent annual rate in this recovery compared with a typical increase of 6.8 per cent. Imports of capital goods have been particularly strong (see Table 20 below), accounting now for roughly 30 per cent of investment in equipment compared with around 18 per cent in the late 1970s. Moreover, exports have also been weaker than usual. Total exports of goods and services in real terms increased at an annual average rate of 0.4 per cent during the current recovery, substantially less than in earlier upswings (8.1 per cent). Agricultural exports, in particular, have suffered. During the past four years, the volume of agricultural exports has stagnated while their value has fallen substantially. Overall, real net exports of goods and services on a national income accounts basis swung from a surplus of 1.6 per cent of GNP in the last quarter of 1982 to a deficit of 2.0 per cent in the second quarter

Table 3.  **Current account of the balance of payments**

$ billion

| | 1981 | 1982 | 1983 | 1984 | 1985[1] |
|---|---|---|---|---|---|
| Merchandise trade | | | | | |
| Total merchandise exports | 237.1 | 211.2 | 200.7 | 220.3 | 217.9 |
| Agricultural | 44.0 | 37.2 | 36.6 | 38.4 | 31.4 |
| Non-agricultural | 193.1 | 174.0 | 164.1 | 181.9 | 186.5 |
| Total merchandise imports | − 265.1 | − 247.6 | − 262.8 | − 328.6 | − 343.0 |
| Oil | − 77.8 | − 61.3 | − 53.8 | − 57.3 | − 49.7 |
| Non-oil | − 187.3 | − 186.3 | − 209.0 | − 271.3 | − 293.3 |
| Merchandise trade balance | − 28.0 | − 36.4 | − 62.0 | − 108.3 | − 125.1 |
| | | | | | |
| Services and transfers | | | | | |
| Net service transactions | 41.2 | 36.5 | 30.1 | 18.2 | 13.9 |
| Net investment income | 34.1 | 29.5 | 25.4 | 19.1 | 16.2 |
| Direct investment | 25.5 | 19.8 | 15.9 | 13.3 | n.a. |
| Other | 8.6 | 9.7 | 9.5 | 5.8 | n.a. |
| Net military | − 1.2 | − 0.3 | − 0.2 | − 1.8 | − 1.6 |
| Net other services | 8.3 | 7.3 | 4.9 | 0.9 | − 0.7 |
| | | | | | |
| Unilateral transfers | − 6.8 | − 8.1 | − 8.9 | − 11.4 | − 13.0 |
| Private | − 0.9 | − 1.2 | − 1.0 | − 1.4 | − 1.5 |
| U.S. Government | − 5.9 | − 6.9 | − 7.9 | − 10.0 | − 11.5 |
| Balance on services and transfers | 34.4 | 28.4 | 21.2 | 6.8 | 0.9 |
| | | | | | |
| Current account balance | 6.3 | − 8.1 | − 40.8 | − 101.5 | − 124.3 |
| (% GNP) | (0.2) | (− 0.3) | (− 1.2) | (− 2.8) | (− 3.2) |

1.  First half of 1985, annual rates.
*Sources:*  Department of Commerce, Bureau of Economic Analysis.

of 1985. The current account shifted from virtual balance to a deficit of around 3 per cent of GNP over the same period (Diagram 1).

The external deficit reflects in part weaker international competitiveness in the wake of the dollar appreciation. The dollar reached all-time highs against most currencies in early 1985 (Diagram 2). On a trade-weighted basis, the effective nominal appreciation from the third quarter of 1980 to the first quarter of 1985 amounted to around 58 per cent. Against the German mark and French franc, the dollar rose in value during the period by 83 per cent and 142 per cent, respectively, while against the Japanese yen it rose 17 per cent (or 25 per cent compared with its early 1981 low). Since March the dollar has lost some ground, and by the end of October its effective appreciation had fallen back to about 35 per cent of its 1980 value. Movements in the exchange rate are difficult to explain on the basis of historical relationships between real interest rate differentials or current account developments. Current account deficits have usually been associated with currency weakness. Though the real interest rate differential in favour of dollar denominated assets (see Diagram 16 below) may help to explain part of the appreciation between late 1980 and mid-1982, the dollar and interest rates have often moved inversely. To the extent that foreign investors have been attracted by higher interest rates in the United States, the Federal budget deficit may have contributed, but capital inflows may also have been due to increased confidence in the U.S. economy and the higher expected rates of return on U.S. physical assets resulting, among other things, from tax reductions. Unsettled economic and political conditions in certain regions abroad and pessimism over Western European growth prospects may also have played a role. (These issues are discussed in greater depth in Part IV).

### *Diagram 2.* **Exchange rate, international competitiveness and the current balance of payments**

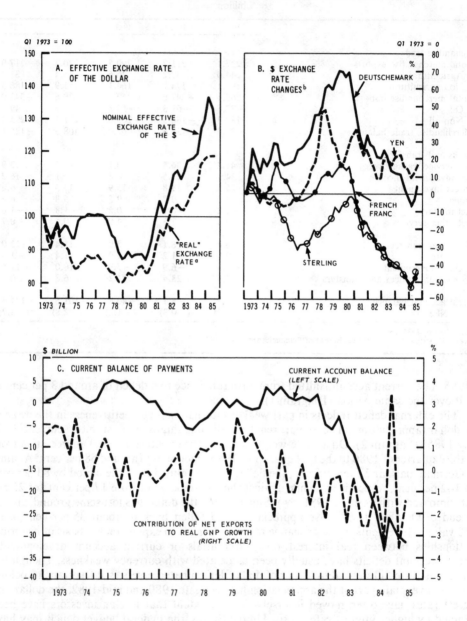

*a)* Relative unit labour costs expressed in a common currency.
*b)* Change in the dollar costs of foreign currency. Downward movements reflect an appreciation of the dollar against the currency concerned.
*Sources :* Federal Reserve Board ; Department of Commerce (Bureau of Economic Analysis); Secretariat estimates.

14

According to research at the Federal Reserve Bank of New York the impact of the dollar's appreciation since the end of 1980 could have been of some $45 billion in 1984[3]. The same order of magnitude is also suggested by Secretariat Interlink simulations. These attribute a further $40 billion of the $100 billion deterioration to the relatively buoyant cyclical position of the United States (measured as the deviation of actual total domestic demand growth from its historical trend of 2¾ per cent)[4]. The LDC debt situation has also had an impact. According to Administration estimates, the curent account balance deteriorated by about $25 billion between 1981 and 1984 because of lower LDC imports from the United States[5].

In the two years to 1984, the United States has accounted for around 70 per cent of the increase in aggregate demand in the OECD area, while contributing 55 per cent of output growth (compared with its 1982 share in area GNP of 40 per cent). The U.S. external deficit has thus imparted a demand stimulus to other countries. Interlink simulations suggest that the relatively strong U.S. recovery added 1 per cent to real GNP growth in the rest of the OECD area in 1984 (following a ¼ per cent contribution in 1983). The direct effect of the strong dollar on U.S. exports and imports could have been responsible for a further 1 per cent growth. However, the strength of the dollar has also had negative effects on the rest of the world. In many countries it has put upward pressure on import prices, although this has been attenuated to some extent by the weakness of commodity prices denominated in dollars. As a result, governments' disinflationary policies have been hindered, leading to higher levels of real interest rates than would otherwise have been the case (in order to moderate falls in the exchange rate).

Because of the drain of domestic demand into imports, the growth of U.S. industrial production and manufacturing employment has not been commensurate with that of domestic demand (Diagram 3). After bottoming out in November 1982, industrial production expanded at an annual rate of around 12 per cent through mid-1984; but then remained essentially flat until mid-1985, whereas final domestic demand continued to rise at an annual rate of 4½ to 5 per cent. Manufactures of business equipment, for example, exhibited some weakness, as purchasers turned increasingly to foreign suppliers and manufacturers shifted production to foreign facilities. Capacity utilization rates have consequently fallen back. During the recession, they fell below 70 per cent for most major manufacturing industries, from their previous highs of 87-91 per cent. They subsequently rose steadily to 82.5 per cent for all industries in 1984Q3, but then eased to 80.4 per cent in 1985Q2, as industrial production stagnated. This situation stands in marked contrast to past cyclical upswings when after ten quarters capacity utilization has usually been between 85 and 90 per cent.

## C. Inflation, employment and the labour market

Total civilian employment increased by 7.6 million (7.7 per cent) during the first ten quarters of the current upturn, compared to an average increase of 6.1 per cent in previous recoveries and 8.3 per cent following the 1974-75 recession (Table 4). Reflecting the atypically strong employment growth as well as some slowing of labour force growth, the unemployment rate declined sharply from a peak of 10¾ per cent in the fourth quarter of 1982 to around 7¼ per cent in mid-1984, where it has since stabilized. This represents a much greater decline than the 1.8 percentage point unemployment rate change which has been typical of other post-war recoveries. However, since the upturn has been from a base of relatively high unemployment, the unemployment rate remains 1½ points above its level at the previous cyclical peak (Diagram 3). Paralleling trends in industrial production, employment in some industries has failed to make a full recovery, while in others it has experienced rapid

*Diagram 3.* **Cyclical indicators**

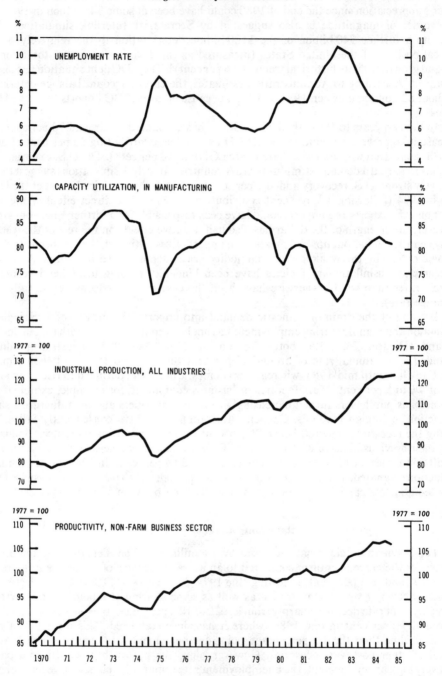

Source : Department of Commerce (Bureau of Economic Analysis).

## Table 4. Labour market indicators

### A. CHANGES IN PRODUCTIVITY, COMPENSATION AND RELATED MEASURES
Percent change at compound annual rate over first ten quarters of expansion

| Trough quarter | Productivity | Output | Hours | Employment | Hourly compensation | Unit labour costs |
|---|---|---|---|---|---|---|
| | | | Non-farm business | | | |
| 1949-IV | 4.0 | 7.8 | 3.6 | 3.4 | 7.6 | 3.4 |
| 1954-II | 2.3 | 5.3 | 2.9 | 2.7 | 5.0 | 2.7 |
| 1958-II | 2.3 | 6.0 | 3.6 | 3.2 | 4.3 | 1.9 |
| 1961-I | 4.0 | 5.7 | 1.6 | 1.5 | 3.6 | −0.3 |
| 1970-IV | 3.7 | 7.0 | 3.2 | 3.2 | 6.9 | 3.1 |
| 1975-I | 3.4 | 7.1 | 3.5 | 3.5 | 7.7 | 4.1 |
| 1980-III[1] | 2.0 | 3.8 | 1.8 | 2.0 | 9.5 | 7.4 |
| Average cycle | 3.5 | 6.6 | 3.0 | 2.9 | 6.2 | 2.6 |
| 1982-IV | 2.2 | 6.6 | 4.3 | 3.8 | 4.1 | 1.8 |
| | | | Manufacturing | | | |
| 1949-IV | 4.5 | 11.1 | 6.9 | 6.0 | 8.4 | 4.4 |
| 1954-II | 1.7 | 5.5 | 3.2 | 2.4 | 5.5 | 3.2 |
| 1958-II | 3.4 | 8.5 | 4.9 | 3.9 | 4.2 | 0.8 |
| 1961-I | 6.7 | 9.6 | 3.1 | 2.1 | 3.2 | −4.1 |
| 1970-IV | 6.2 | 10.2 | 4.1 | 3.1 | 6.2 | 0.3 |
| 1975-I | 5.5 | 8.3 | 4.0 | 2.9 | 8.2 | 3.9 |
| 1980-III[1] | 5.5 | 6.6 | 2.3 | 2.0 | 8.4 | 4.0 |
| Average cycle | 4.9 | 9.0 | 4.3 | 3.3 | 6.3 | 1.8 |
| 1982-IV | 3.5 | 8.1 | 4.1 | 3.1 | 3.7 | −0.2 |

### B. CHANGES IN EMPLOYMENT AND UNEMPLOYMENT

| Trough quarter | Change in civilian employment | | Change in civilian unemployment | | Unemployment rate 10 Qtrs | | | Employment to population ratio[3] |
|---|---|---|---|---|---|---|---|---|
| | Millions | Per cent[2] | Millions | Per cent[2] | Trough | Later | Change | |
| | | | | | Per cent | | | Per cent |
| 1949-IV | 2.40 | 4.2 | −2.47 | −57.1 | 7.0 | 3.0 | −4.0 | 57.2 |
| 1954-II | 3.93 | 6.6 | −0.95 | −25.7 | 5.8 | 4.1 | −1.7 | 57.3 |
| 1961-I | 2.26 | 3.4 | −0.82 | −17.2 | 6.8 | 5.5 | −1.3 | 55.4 |
| 1970-IV | 6.15 | 7.8 | −0.47 | −9.7 | 5.8 | 4.9 | −0.9 | 57.8 |
| 1975-I | 7.05 | 8.3 | −0.83 | −10.8 | 8.2 | 6.9 | −1.3 | 58.0 |
| Average | — | 6.1 | — | −24.1 | — | — | −1.8 | — |
| 1982-IV | 7.64 | 7.7 | −3.36 | −28.5 | 10.6 | 7.3 | −3.3 | 60.0 |

1. Per cent change over four post trough quarters.
2. Per cent change over period, not at annual rate.
3. Ten quarters after trough.
*Source:* Bureau of Labor Statistics.

### Diagram 4. **Employment performance**
Seasonally adjusted

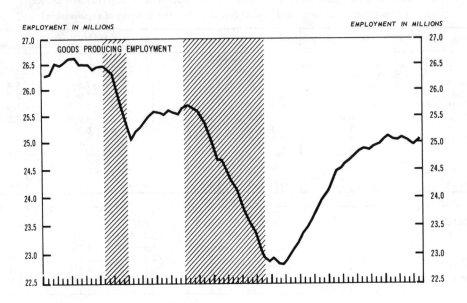

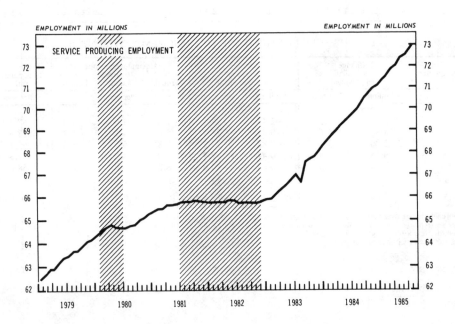

*Note:* Goods producing sector includes manufacturing, mining and construction.

growth. Following large cost-cutting layoffs in 1982, there was a rapid rehiring of production workers in the automobile and other durable industries, but since mid-1984 there has been a marked slowing in the growth of manufacturing employment (Diagram 4). Continuing employment declines in old, large-scale industries – such as steel – have been offset by rapid employment growth in some of the new, high tech industries (see Annex Tables A3 and A4). Electrical and electronic equipment has experienced the most rapid advance; lumber, furniture and construction have proved very resilient, reflecting the surge in housebuilding during the early part of the recovery; but primary metals, non-electrical machinery and textiles have regained only 50 per cent or less of their recession employment losses. Service sector employment, which has normally been relatively immune from overall job losses during recessions, has expanded strongly, led by business, professional and financial services and the leisure sector (travel, hotels, restaurants, etc.). (See Annex 1 for an elaboration of these trends.)

The unusually rapid growth of civilian employment during the first ten quarters of the current recovery was mirrored in a slower than average rate of productivity growth (Table 4). This is true for manufacturing as well as the non-farm business sector. Part of the lower productivity growth is due to the fact that during the current business cycle productivity turned up strongly in the quarter before the trough, reflecting in part cost-cutting measures taken by many businesses in mid-1982. The pick-up in productivity has typically coincided with the onset of output growth. However, in line with productivity growth, wage increases have been modest, with hourly compensation in manufacturing rising at a 3.7 per cent average rate in the current recovery versus a 7.6 per cent rate in the previous three upswings. As a result, unit labour costs in manufacturing remained essentially unchanged from the recession trough until mid-1985. Hourly compensation and unit labour costs in services, though increasing more rapidly than in manufacturing, have also been below typical recovery rates, so that even with relatively low productivity growth, the increase in unit labour costs in the private non-farm business sector has been between 1 and 2 per cent since 1983[6]. With the rise in the GNP deflator stabilizing in the somewhat higher 3.5-4 per cent range, corporate profits as a per cent of GNP have risen sharply, despite the stiff price competition from abroad[7]. After reaching a post-war low of 2.7 per cent in 1982, after-tax profits rebounded to 3.5 per cent of GNP in mid-1984, before falling back somewhat in late 1984 and 1985.

Although it is common for inflation to fall during the early stages of business cycle recoveries, its stability during the current upturn is remarkable. Diagram 5 suggests that there has been an improvement in the recent relationship between unemployment and price changes. This followed a deterioration from the mid-1960s to the end of the 1970s. Although inflation normally slowed during the first and second year of rising unemployment (e.g. 1975-76), this was not sufficient to offset the shifts associated with the early-1970s monetary disturbances and with the 1973-1974 and 1979-1980 oil price shocks. These resulted in a worsening of the short-term trade-off between higher inflation and lower unemployment with each new business cycle. Since 1980 the process of disinflation appears to have initially been consistent with labour market experience up to 1982, but in the second half of 1983 wage inflation was surprisingly low and there was no catch-up in 1984. This appears to be a significant shift although it may be premature to conclude that it is permanent. Some of this gain may be due to the appreciation of the dollar, which according to some estimates may have reduced the rate of inflation by 1-2 per cent a year over the past several years, but a key factor has been a dramatic decline in the wage bargaining power of the labour unions. Wage awards have involved substantial concessions on the part of labour (see Section III and Table 12 below). Union wage increases began falling before non-union wages and their deceleration has been greater. This has reflected cyclical pressures on certain industries as

*Diagram 5.* **Wage and price trends**

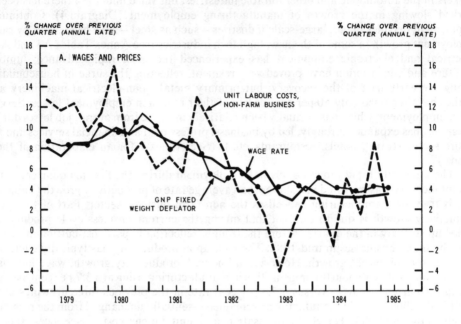

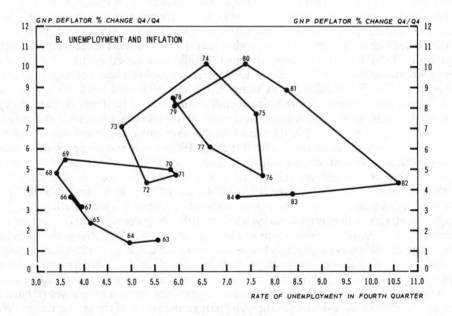

*Sources:* Federal Reserve Board; Department of Commerce (Bureau of Economic Analysis); Secretariat estimates.

well as longer-run market forces, including the impact of deregulation on key service industries (see Part V of the Survey). Some recent union wage settlements have involved an actual reduction in wages or fringe benefits or a relaxation of work rules. Concessions have occurred in previous recessions, but the scale of recent concessions is unprecedented.

The conjunction of rapid employment growth and low inflation in the United States has led observers to look to the functioning of the labour market and real wage-flexibility as explanations of differences between the United States and Europe. Since 1970, employment in the United States has grown by roughly 30 million, whereas in Western European there has been little if any increase. Despite the faster U.S. recovery, this contrast cannot be explained by differences in output growth, since both regions have grown by roughly 30 to 35 per cent since the early 1970s[8]. Consequently, productivity growth has been much higher in OECD Europe than in the United States, resulting in a significant narrowing of the gap in output per employee between the two regions. Better U.S. employment performance must therefore be attributable to labour market factors. In this respect, compared to most European countries the United States appears to have relatively few legal, regulatory or financial restrictions on hiring and firing, substantial labour mobility among occupations, industries and regions and a smaller proportion of unionised industries (See Annex 1). There also seems to have been a greater degree of real wage flexibility in the face of inflation and unemployment shocks. U.S. firms seem to have much greater ability to lay off labour during cyclical downturns and to rehire during ensuing upswings than their European counterparts, as evidenced by the much larger cyclical swings in US employment compared with the major Western European countries (Annex 1). Reflecting this, the United States has a much lower proportion of long-term unemployment than Western Europe.

Since the service sector has accounted for the bulk of new job entrants in recent years, it is natural to look to conditions in that sector as a partial explanation of employment growth as a whole. In this respect it is noteworthy that average wages are normally lower in services than in manufacturing, that part-time work is more common and that there is greater labour mobility in that sector. Small firms predominate, and easy entry and exit coincide with relatively low labour costs, a lower degree of unionisation and greater competition (enhanced by deregulation). Service industries dominate the most labour intensive sectors, though many of the high-technology and fast-growing industries also fall in the service category and employment here has been encouraged by capital widening. (Noteworthy are data processing, telecommunications, medical services, and scientific research.) Moreover, the service sector is also important as an entry point and training ground for young people and women. An industrial analysis of new job entrants indicates that nearly all new employees in the goods-producing sector had been employed previously in services. The flexibility of the labour force is enhanced by the large proportion of young people, singles and women in the labour force and the tendency for Americans to change jobs and occupations rather freely. The higher labour mobility in the U.S. is also reflected in the much lower average job tenure and greater employment turnover in the United States than in major Western European countries (Annex 1).

More generally, the labour force is relatively mobile and employment practices are flexible. This is evidenced by several factors (discussed more fully in Annex 1). Centres of growth have shifted from one region to another, as some types of industry have declined and others boomed. Mobility has been one factor facilitating the advance of "high-tech" manufacturing and service industries (particularly in California and the North-East), while many "old" manufacturing industries have successfully adjusted to price pressures, either by reducing real wages through geographic relocation or by shedding excess labour through labour-saving investment. Light manufacturing firms (textiles, apparel, leather, etc.) have been relatively successful in reducing real labour and other costs by shifting regionally (generally to the South in the past, but also increasingly to other areas such as New England, because of cheap – often immigrant – labour). In some cases, they have been able to retain or even increase their previous employment and output levels[9]. Because of their heavy plant investments and geographic requirements, it has been more difficult for heavy manufacturing (particularly auto, steel and heavy machinery) to escape union pressures and other cost disadvantages through regional relocation. Consequently, they have followed more the European model of "shedding" labour by making large labour-saving investments and closing down unprofitable plants and operations. For example, employment in the steel industry is currently about 300 000 – less than one-half the level of 15 years ago. Employment in the auto industry peaked in early 1979 with slightly more than 1.0 million jobs, but then it fell to 600 000 during the recession trough before rebounding to its current level of around 875 000 jobs.

There has been a steady decline in the importance of labour unions and collective bargaining agreements. Union members accounted for 16 per cent of the private work-force in 1982 compared with 25 per cent in 1966 (see Annex 1). The number of workers covered by major collective bargaining contracts now comprises less than 8 per cent of the labour force. Union membership and collective bargaining agreements have not protected workers from layoffs or wage reductions; nearly a half of workers so covered have been affected by wage and benefit concessions over the 1979-1982 period (Annex Table A-8 below). Concessions were concentrated in auto, steel, equipment manufacturing and meat packing, but workers in airlines, trucking and other transportation have also been affected, reflecting, among other things, the effect of deregulation. Real wage flexibility has thus operated in all sectors of the American economy, in contrast to the experience in Europe. While a real labour cost gap (i.e. an excess of wage increases over productivity changes) emerged in Europe after the first oil shock and persisted for many years, real labour costs and productivity have moved in line with one another in the United States[10]. Indeed, if real wage rigidity is measured by dividing the short-run elasticity of money wages with respect to inflation (which should be small) by the elasticity of money wages with respect to unemployment (which should be large), the United States (and Japan) appears to have enjoyed the lowest degree of labour market rigidity in the OECD area[11]. From cross-section analysis, this characteristic appears to be associated with relatively low unemployment rates, and must have helped U.S. employment to expand strongly long before the 1983-1984 upswing.

Further elements in the employment story are the growth of venture capital, small firms and self-employment[12]. New commitments to venture capital funds rose from $1.7 billion in 1982 to $4.5 billion in 1984. By end-1983 the total venture capital pool stood at $11.5 billion compared to an estimated $3.0 billion in the mid-1970s. Actual venture outlays rose to $3.0 billion in 1983. Reflecting these developments, the number of major venture capital firms has grown rapidly to 200 in 1983, with many of the largest commercial and investment banks providing funds in exchange for equity in the new firms. This has gone hand in hand with a surge in the market for new issues. The number of companies listed on the "over-the-counter" market rose from 2 600 to over 4 000 between the late 1970s and the early 1980s and the total amount raised in new issues expanded from $0.3 billion in the mid-1970s to $13.0 billion in 1983. This can be attributed to several factors. In 1974 pension funds were allowed to finance start-up companies and the maximum tax on long-term capital gains was subsequently cut to 28 per cent in 1978 and to 20 per cent in 1981. Moreover, the growth of "high-tech", particularly in computers, electronics and biotechnology, and, apparently, a resurgence of entrepreurship provided the investment opportunities. It is estimated that approximately 600 000 new companies are started each year, double the rate in the 1960s (see

Diagram 12D below). Although new firms have a high failure rate, they have also provided the bulk of new employment. The importance of new, small companies is further underscored by the fact that one-third of the Harvard University MBA (master of Business Administration) graduates are in companies with fewer than 100 employees. In recent years, there also appears to be a resurgence in self-employment which rose over 40 per cent between 1972 and 1984, with self-employment among women being particularly strong. Moreover, women have accounted for a large portion of new non-farm proprietorships started in recent years, taking their share of the total to an estimated 26 per cent in 1983. While the average enterprise owned by women is considerably newer and smaller than those owned by men – with net earnings being one third that of male-owned firms – it represents a significant form of new and part-time employment for women. As expected most of the growth has been in the service sector. The rapid growth of new firms reflect among other factors, the relative ease with which most individuals can start new businesses in the U.S. compared with the lengthy procedures required in many European countries. Moreover, since most licensing and franchise requirements are set at the state or local, rather than the national, level there is a certain built-in competition among states and communities to keep regulatory barriers, local taxation and other costs to a minimum in order to attract investment and employment opportunities.

## II. FISCAL AND MONETARY POLICIES

### A. Budgetary policy

The following paragraphs discuss three aspects of fiscal policy:
- The nature and legislative origin of the federal deficit, given the Administration's commitment to cutting both taxes and spending, and the lack of political consensus on where expenditure cuts should fall;
- The reforms introduced and proposed with respect to the structure of taxation, and their significance from a "supply-side" point of view;
- The impact of the federal deficit, and the state and local sector surplus, on the strength of the recovery.

### *The Federal budget deficit*

The main source of budgetary divergence between the United States and other OECD economies has lain in taxation policy. Because the emphasis in the rest of the OECD has been on reducing public sector indebtedness, priority has been given to cutting budget deficits, even though this has meant setting aside the aim of reducing tax burdens. In the United States, by contrast, "supply side" strategy has given precedence to lower tax rates over deficit reduction. Principally as a result of the Economic Recovery Tax Act of 1981 (ERTA), the effective household tax rate has fallen, by about 1½ per cent since 1980, after a small but gradual rise during the 1970s[13]. Corporate taxes have been more dramatically cut, halving as a proportion of corporate profits and falling by a third as ratio of federal income from 1980 to 1984. Total federal receipts declined by 1½ per cent of GNP over the same period (Diagrams 6 and 7). The objective of reducing public expenditure has not been achieved. The share of federal spending in GNP has risen by one percentage point since 1980. This increase is smaller than that experienced elsewhere in the OECD area (Table 5)[14]. But on a structural (i.e. cyclically-adjusted) basis, public expenditure growth has been nearer to the area average, since unemployment-related spending has not been as important an influence on outlays in the United States.

The 1981 Programme for Economic Recovery expected budget balance by FY 1984, whereas the outcome was a deficit of $175 billion (5 per cent of GNP). Table 6 examines the origins of the federal deficit, which may be traced to three basic sources:

- The automatic impact of the recession on budget revenues and unemployment-related outlays and (to a lesser extent) diminishing inflation-induced fiscal drag ("bracket creep");
- The "structural" excess of public spending over taxation, caused by the lack of political consensus as to what items of spending should be reduced[15];
- The growth of debt service expenditures, associated with the accumulation of government debt and high real interest rates.

At the trough of the recession, in 1982, nearly two-thirds of the federal deficit and almost all the general government deficit could be attributed to the cyclical weakness in the economy

Table 5. **General government expenditure and taxation**

Per cent of nominal GNP/GDP at market prices

| | 1979 | 1980 | 1981 | 1982 | 1983 | 1984[1] | 1985[1] | 1986[1] |
|---|---|---|---|---|---|---|---|---|
| **United States** | | | | | | | | |
| Direct taxes | 16.1 | 16.0 | 15.9 | 15.1 | 14.5 | 14.3 | 14.3 | 14.3 |
| Indirect taxes | 7.8 | 8.1 | 8.5 | 8.4 | 8.5 | 8.3 | 8.2 | 8.2 |
| Social security contributions | 7.7 | 7.7 | 8.0 | 8.2 | 8.3 | 8.4 | 8.4 | 8.5 |
| Total current receipts[3] | 33.3 | 33.8 | 34.4 | 34.0 | 33.7 | 33.5 | 33.7 | 33.7 |
| Purchases of goods and services | 19.6 | 20.4 | 20.2 | 21.2 | 20.7 | 20.4 | 21.0 | 21.3 |
| Current transfers | 10.1 | 11.1 | 11.2 | 12.0 | 12.0 | 11.1 | 10.9 | 10.8 |
| Interest on public debt (gross) | 2.9 | 3.3 | 3.9 | 4.4 | 4.6 | 5.0 | 5.3 | 5.4 |
| Total expenditure[3] | 32.7 | 34.9 | 35.3 | 37.8 | 37.7 | 36.8 | 37.4 | 37.5 |
| Cyclically-adjusted[2] | (32.0) | (33.0) | (33.3) | (33.6) | (33.9) | (34.8) | (35.6) | (35.7) |
| Budget balance | 0.6 | −1.2 | −0.9 | −3.8 | −4.1 | −3.4 | −3.7 | −3.8 |
| Cyclically-adjusted[2] | (1.2) | (−0.7) | (1.0) | (0.1) | (−0.6) | (−1.3) | (−2.0) | (−2.1) |
| **Other six major countries[4]** | | | | | | | | |
| Direct taxes | 10.9 | 11.6 | 12.0 | 12.3 | 12.5 | 12.7 | 12.9 | 13.0 |
| Indirect taxes | 11.4 | 11.5 | 11.7 | 11.8 | 11.8 | 11.9 | 11.9 | 11.9 |
| Social security contributions | 11.3 | 11.5 | 11.5 | 12.3 | 12.5 | 12.4 | 12.4 | 12.4 |
| Total current receipts[3] | 36.4 | 37.8 | 38.9 | 39.9 | 40.2 | 40.6 | 40.7 | 40.7 |
| Government consumption[3] | 15.5 | 15.8 | 16.3 | 16.5 | 16.5 | 16.4 | 16.2 | 16.0 |
| Current transfers | 15.0 | 15.2 | 16.1 | 16.9 | 17.2 | 17.1 | 17.0 | 17.0 |
| Interest on public debt (gross) | 3.1 | 3.6 | 4.0 | 4.4 | 4.6 | 4.9 | 5.1 | 5.1 |
| Gross investment | 4.0 | 4.1 | 4.0 | 3.9 | 3.7 | 3.6 | 3.4 | 3.3 |
| Total expenditure[4] | 40.4 | 41.4 | 43.1 | 44.3 | 44.7 | 44.9 | 44.5 | 44.1 |
| Cyclically-adjusted[2] | (39.8) | (40.6) | (41.4) | (41.6) | (41.7) | (42.1) | (41.8) | (41.5) |
| Budget balance | −4.0 | −3.6 | −4.2 | −4.4 | −4.5 | −4.3 | −3.8 | −3.4 |
| Cyclically-adjusted[2] | (−3.5) | (−3.0) | (−2.8) | (−2.3) | (−2.0) | (−1.8) | (−1.3) | (−0.9) |

1. *Economic Outlook,* 37, estimates and forecast for major six.
2. Per cent of potential GNP (GDP).
3. Components do not add to totals. For the United States, subsidies are not shown on the expenditure side and interest receipts on the revenue side. For the other six major countries, public entrepreneurial and property income are not shown on the receipts side, and nor are subsidies and net capital transfers on the expenditure side.
4. Japan, Germany, France, UK, Italy and Canada, weighted by 1982 GNP (GDP).
*Source:* Secretariat estimates (see *OECD Economic Outlook,* 37, Table 4).

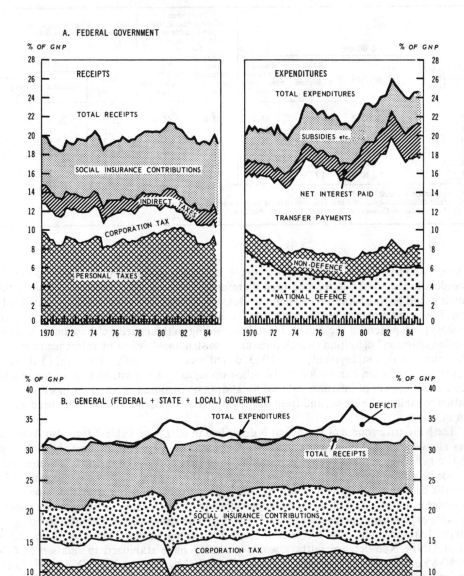

*Diagram 6.* **Government revenues and expenditures**

A. FEDERAL GOVERNMENT

RECEIPTS

TOTAL RECEIPTS

SOCIAL INSURANCE CONTRIBUTIONS

INDIRECT TAXES

CORPORATION TAX

PERSONAL TAXES

EXPENDITURES

TOTAL EXPENDITURES

SUBSIDIES etc.

NET INTEREST PAID

TRANSFER PAYMENTS

NON-DEFENCE

NATIONAL DEFENCE

B. GENERAL (FEDERAL + STATE + LOCAL) GOVERNMENT

TOTAL EXPENDITURES

DEFICIT

TOTAL RECEIPTS

SOCIAL INSURANCE CONTRIBUTIONS

CORPORATION TAX

PERSONAL TAXES

*Sources:* Department of Commerce (Bureau of Economic Analysis); Office of Management and Budget.

25

Table 6. **Sources of the federal deficit: structural and cyclical components**

| Calendar year national accounts basis | Deficit (+) $ Billion | | | Proportion of the actual deficit attributable to the business cycle Per cent | | Change in cyclically adjusted budget deficit (+) $ Billion | | |
|---|---|---|---|---|---|---|---|---|
| | Actual | Based on middle expansion GNP | Based on 6 % un-employment rate | Based on middle expansion GNP | Based on 6 % un-employment rate | Total | Due to | |
| | | | | | | | Inflation[2] | Policies and other factors |
| 1980 | 61.2 | 58.5 | 36.7 | 4.4 | 40.0 | 21.3 | − 26.0 | 47.3 |
| 1981 | 64.3 | 57.3 | 28.1 | 10.9 | 56.3 | 1.1 | − 27.1 | 26.0 |
| 1982 | 148.2 | 92.5 | 58.4 | 37.6 | 60.1 | 35.2 | − 7.1 | 42.3 |
| 1983 | 178.6 | 129.2 | 90.8 | 27.7 | 49.2 | 36.7 | − 7.2 | 43.9 |
| 1984 | 175.8 | 174.1 | 129.6 | 1.0 | 26.3 | 45.4 | − 10.0 | 55.4 |
| 1985[1] | 190.0 | 197.9 | 149.1 | 4.2 | 21.5 | 23.3 | − 8.2 | 31.5 |

1. Administration forecast.
2. Net effect of inflation-induced fiscal drag and indexed increases in government expenditures.
*Source:* Department of Commerce, Bureau of Economic Analysis.

(Tables 5 and 6). The influence of the cycle has since diminished as the recovery has proceeded, to the point where, measured by reference to peak-cycle (6 per cent) unemployment, it would be three-quarters structural. But, since the economy has recently stabilized at about 7 per cent unemployment, this may be an optimistic estimate of the cyclical (i.e. transitory) component of the deficit. Indeed, according to the Bureau of Economic Analysis' "middle expansion" definition (which measures the structural deficit by reference to average rather than peak employment), the 1985 deficit may be wholly structural (Table 6)[16]. Furthermore, inflation can no longer be relied upon, as in the past, to help restore budget balance. The impact of inflation-induced fiscal drag on income tax revenues has declined as inflation has fallen (Table 6), and from the beginning of 1985, indexation of tax brackets has been in force.

The legislative source of the deficit is described in part A of Table 7 (see also Annex 2). After allowing for subsequent tax increases and fiscal drag (part B of the Table), the total effective tax reduction has been much smaller than that announced in 1981; it amounted to just over 1½ per cent of GNP in 1985, compared with the original 4½ per cent effect of ERTA. Since the budget deficit has increased by nearly 3½ percentage points over the same period, this leaves just over a half of the budget deterioration (1¾ percentage points) to be explained by public expenditure increases (Table 7, part C). The expansion of defence spending has been partly responsible; from FY 1980 through FY 1985 it will have risen by just over 1 per cent of GNP. Non-defence outlays would probably have stabilized in relation to GNP in 1980-85 under pre-1981 policies, but are likely to fall by ½ per cent by FY 1985[17]. Cuts in other programmes have thus partially offset defence increases. But total budget outlays have grown by 1¾ per cent of GNP, because of the substantial rise in interest costs, amounting to 1¼ per cent of GNP.

During most of the 1960s and 1970s, gross interest payments[18] represented about 6 per cent of federal budget outlays (1¼ per cent of GNP). They began rising sharply from 1977 onwards, reaching 10.8 per cent of federal expenditures in 1984 (2½ per cent of GNP). Net interest payments have increased by 1½ per cent of GNP since 1979 (Table 15 below)[19]. This growth is attributable both to the expansion of government debt and to higher interest rates. Higher federal debt (see Diagram 14 below) has raised debt service by about ¾ per cent of

Table 7. **Sources of the federal deficit: effects of fiscal policy changes since 1981**
$ billion; Unified budget basis[1]

| Fiscal years | 1981 | 1982 | 1983 | 1984 | 1985 |
|---|---|---|---|---|---|
| **A.  DISCRETIONARY BUDGET CHANGES** | | | | | |
| Taxation[2] | | | | | |
| Economic Recovery Tax Act (1981) | — | − 41 | − 93 | − 137 | − 169 |
| Tax Equity and Fiscal | | | | | |
| Responsibility Act (1982) | — | — | 18 | 36 | 41 |
| Deficit Reduction Act (1984) | — | — | — | 1 | 9 |
| Social Security Amendments (1983) | — | — | — | 6 | 9 |
| Total discretionary tax cuts ( − ) | — | − 41 | − 73 | − 92 | − 106 |
| (% GNP) | | ( − 1.3) | ( − 2.3) | ( − 2.6) | ( − 2.7) |
| Government expenditure (increase = − )[3] | | | | | |
| Defence spending increases | | − 3 | − 16 | − 23 | − 35 |
| Non-defence spending cuts | | 40 | 48 | 50 | 38 |
| Effect of legislative actions on interest costs | | — | − 3 | − 10 | − 21 |
| Total expenditure increases ( − ) | | 36 | 30 | 18 | − 18 |
| (% GNP) | | (1.2) | (1.0) | (0.6) | ( − 0.5) |
| Budget balance | | | | | |
| Under policies in effect | | | | | |
| January 1, 1981 | − 58 | − 106 | − 152 | − 101 | − 86 |
| (% GNP) | (2.0) | (3.5) | (4.7) | (2.8) | (2.2) |
| Actual | − 58 | − 111 | − 195 | − 175 | − 210 |
| (% GNP) | ( − 2.0) | ( − 3.6) | ( − 6.0) | ( − 4.9) | ( − 5.4) |
| Net discretionary change[4] | 0 | − 5 | − 43 | − 74 | − 124 |
| (% GNP) | (0.0) | ( − 0.2) | ( − 1.3) | ( − 2.1) | ( − 3.2) |
| **B.  AUTOMATIC BUDGET CHANGES** | | | | | |
| Taxation (fiscal drag) ( + ) | | 26 | 5 | 14 | 40 |
| (% GNP) | | 0.9 | (0.2) | (0.4) | (1.0) |
| Government expenditure ( − ) | | − 70 | − 92 | − 45 | − 48 |
| (% GNP) | | ( − 2.3) | ( − 2.9) | ( − 1.3) | ( − 1.2) |
| Budget balance | | − 44 | − 86 | − 30 | − 7 |
| (% GNP) | | ( − 1.4) | ( − 2.7) | ( − 0.8) | ( − 0.2) |
| **C.  TOTAL CHANGE SINCE 1981[5]** | | | | | |
| Taxation (net reduction) ( − ) | | 15 | − 68 | − 78 | − 65 |
| (% GNP) | | (0.5) | ( − 2.1) | ( − 2.2) | ( − 1.6) |
| Expenditure (net increase) ( − ) | | − 34 | − 6.2 | − 26 | − 66 |
| (% GNP) | | ( − 1.1) | ( − 1.9) | ( − 0.7) | ( − 1.7) |
| *of which:* | | | | | |
| Defence | | ( − 0.6) | ( − 1.1) | ( − 0.9) | ( − 1.1) |
| Other | | (0.0) | ( − 0.2) | (1.0) | (0.6) |
| Debt interest | | ( − 0.5) | ( − 0.6) | ( − 0.9) | ( − 1.2) |
| Budget balance | | − 49 | − 129 | − 104 | − 131 |
| (% GNP) | | ( − 1.6) | ( − 4.0) | ( − 2.9) | ( − 3.4) |

1.  Excluding off-budget spending.
2.  Administration projections and estimates of tax reductions (FY 1986 Budget p. 4-4).
3.  CBO estimates of effects of expenditure changes (Economic and Budget Outlook, FY 1986-1990, p. 153).
4.  The discretionary change is the sum of discretionary tax cuts and expenditure cuts; the net automatic change is the sum of fiscal drag and built-in expenditure increases (i.e. increases already built into the 1981 baseline or resulting from changes in external parameters such as interest rates).
5.  The net overall change (A + B) is equal to the change since FY 1981 as listed under (C): e.g. the net change in the deficit in FY 1985 is the FY 1985 deficit (5.4) less the FY 1981 deficit (2.0) = 3.4 per cent of GNP.
*Sources:*  Bureau of Economic Analysis, Office of Management and Budget, Congressional Budget Office; Secretariat estimates.

GNP since 1979; higher interest rates have accounted for an increase of ½ per cent[20]. The sensitivity of the deficit to interest rates is such that a sustained one per cent rise in interest rates eventually increases outlays by nearly ½ per cent of GNP[21], of which nearly a half accrues by the second year. (The proportion of federal debt with a maturity of a year or less is 45 per cent). And if this additional spending were not offset by other spending cuts, the increase would eventually be ¾ per cent of GNP.

Against the background of a $200 billion deficit in 1983, and the prospect of similar deficits throughout the decade, the 1985 Budget (presented in February 1984 and covering the period from October 1984 to September 1985) proposed outlay reductions which were intended to set the deficit on a downward course (Table 8). This was recognised as a "downpayment", which needed to be followed by further action. Priority was still given to

Table 8.  **FY 1985 and FY 1986 budgets**

$ billion; Unified budget basis

| Fiscal years | 1982 | 1983 | 1984 | 1985 | 1986 | 1987 | 1988 | 1989 |
|---|---|---|---|---|---|---|---|---|
| Outlays under January 1, 1981 policies | 764 | 826 | 860 | 920 | 982 | 1 047 | 1 113 | 1 180 |
| **1985 BUDGET** | | | | | | | | |
| Baseline outlays | 728 | 796 | 854 | 945 | 1 019 | 1 094 | 1 163 | 1 230 |
| Proposed savings (−) | | | | −19 | −27 | −26 | −33 | −46 |
| Spending plan | 728 | 796 | 854 | 925 | 992 | 1 068 | 1 130 | 1 184 |
| Proposed revenue increases | | | | 8 | 12 | 14 | 18 | 23 |
| Revenues | 618 | 601 | 670 | 745 | 815 | 888 | 978 | 1 060 |
| Budget deficit (−) | −111 | −195 | −184 | −180 | −174 | −180 | −152 | −123 |
| (National accounts basis) | (−112) | (−185) | (−185) | (−169) | .. | .. | .. | .. |
| **1986 BUDGET** | | | | | | | | |
| Baseline outlays[1] | 746 | 808 | 852 | 960 | 1 024 | 1 109 | 1 200 | 1 263 |
| Proposed savings | | | | −1 | −50 | −83 | −105 | −125 |
| Spending plan | 746 | 808 | 852 | 959 | 974 | 1 026 | 1 095 | 1 137 |
| of which: | | | | | | | | |
| Spending ex. debt interest | 645 | 697 | 719 | 804 | 804 | 846 | 910 | 964 |
| Defence | 185 | 210 | 227 | 254 | 286 | 321 | 358 | 392 |
| Other | 460 | 487 | 492 | 550 | 518 | 525 | 552 | 572 |
| DEFRA revenue increases | | | 1 | 9 | 16 | 22 | 25 | |
| Revenues | 618 | 601 | 667 | 737 | 794 | 862 | 950 | 1 030 |
| Baseline deficit | −128 | −208 | −185 | −224 | −230 | −245 | −248 | −233 |
| Planned deficit (−) | −128 | −208 | −185 | −222 | −180 | −165 | −145 | −107 |
| (National accounts basis) | (−114) | (−189) | (−170) | (−190) | (−166) | .. | .. | .. |
| Congressional budget resolution (CBO estimate)[2] | −128 | −208 | −185 | −210 | −175 | −163 | −143 | −132 |
| Mid-session review[2] | −128 | −208 | −185 | −211 | −178 | −139 | −100 | −54 |

1.  Including off-budget spending, proposed to be included on budget, as follows:

| 1982 | 1983 | 1984 | 1985 | 1986 |
|---|---|---|---|---|
| 17 | 12 | 10 | 12 | 2 |

2.  The Mid-Session Review incorporated the Congressional compromise agreement on national defence, as embodied in the First Concurrent Resolution (Aug. 1st). For non-defence the Review restates the Administration's budget proposals, which incorporate cuts $ 10 to $ 54 billion larger than those implied by the First Concurrent Resolution.

Sources:   Office of Management and Budget, *FY 1985* and *FY 1986* Budgets; *Mid-Session Review of the 1986 Budget*, August 30 1985; CBO, *The Economic and Budget Outlook: an Update*, August 1985.

sely related to the useful economic lives of assets and take into account the impact [inf]lation on capital assets (increasing corporate tax bills by $15½ billion in 1990).

## Fiscal Stance and the Recovery

When trying to assess the contribution of fiscal policy to the recovery of activity[34], th[e fed]eral government deficit is probably the most relevant indicator (Diagram 8 and Table 5[). Th]e state and local surplus has been increasing and may be seen as an offset to federa[l bor]rowing[35]. In a development unprecedented since World War II, the per capita spending [of stat]e-local governments declined 6½ per cent in constant dollar terms between 197[9 and] 1983. This followed the so-called "tax revolt" (1978-1981), whereby state and local taxe[s fell] by 1½ per cent of personal income, and federal grants declined. The fact tha[t the] 1980-1982 recession exerted a strong negative influence on revenues also put downwar[d pres]sure on spending. The situation improved substantially in 1983, due to enacted ta[x in]creases and to the stronger-than-expected economic recovery, which raised state and loca[l re]ceipts relative to personal income[36]. As per capita real expenditures fell back, the overal[l sur]plus reached a post-war high of $44 billion (1½ per cent of GNP), compared wit[h $] billion in 1982 (Diagram 8). The budgetary situation further improved in 1984, the tota[l sur]plus widening to $51 billion. In contrast to 1983, when the improvement was in the "other [fun]ds", the bulk of the increase was in the social insurance fund surplus, though the buoyancy [of t]he economy still added enough revenues to increase the "other funds" surplus to nearly [$ ] billion.

Table 9. **Fiscal stance and the recovery**

|  | 1981 | 1982 | 1983 | 1984 | 1985 |
|---|---|---|---|---|---|
| **[UNI]TED STATES** | | | | | |
| [Ch]ange in structural budget balance[1] [negative = budget deficit expansion] (% of GNP) | −0.3 | 0.4 | −1.8 | −0.8 | −0.8 |
| [Appr]oximate effect of fiscal stance on real GNP growth (% p.a.)[2] | 0.4 | −0.5 | 2.5 | 1.1 | 1.3 |
| [Ac]tual GNP volume growth (% p.a.)[3] | 3.0 | −2.1 | 3.7 | 6.8 | 2.5 |
| [Pr]oportion of GNP volume growth "explained" by changes in changes in fiscal stance (%) | 13.0 | 24.0 | 67.0 | 16.0 | 50.0 |
| **[BIG] EUROPE[4]** | | | | | |
| [Ch]ange in structural budget balance[1] [negative = budget deficit expansion] (% of GNP) | 1.5 | −0.7 | 0.3 | −0.1 | −0.4 |
| [Appr]oximate effect of fiscal stance on real GNP growth (% p.a.)[2] | −1.1 | 0.5 | −0.3 | 0.1 | 0.3 |
| [Ac]tual GNP volume growth (% p.a.)[3] | 0.0 | 0.6 | 1.3 | 2.3 | 2¼ |
| [Pr]oportion of GNP growth "explained" by changes in fiscal stance (%) | neg. | 80.0 | neg. | 4.0 | 13.0 |

[1] [Th]e general government structural budget deficit adjusted for inflation.
[2] [Th]e effect of changes in the inflation-adjusted deficit on real GNP growth, calculated from a regression of the reduced [for]m $\#g = a + b \#B_{t-1}$, over the period 1970-1983, where g is the real growth rate, B is the inflation-adjusted structural budget deficit [and] # represents year-to-year changes. For the United States $\#g = 2.94 + 1.36 \#B_{t-1}$ [SE. = 0.58; R² = 0.30] (a positive shift in [B being] stimulatory). This relationship also exists, in differing degrees in most major European economies.
[3] [O]CD forecasts for 1985.
[4] [Ma]jor four European economies (Germany, France, U.K. and Italy).
Secretariat calculations.

defence spending, which despite certain proposed "savings" was planned to increase by an average of 7 per cent per annum in real terms from FY 1984 to FY 1989. Other spending was to be virtually frozen in real terms. With some small tax-raising proposals the package was estimated to be worth $27 billion in FY 1985 (giving a budget deficit of $180 billion). Agreement with the Senate (the "Rose Garden" downpayment agreement) was followed by a stalemate with the House over defence spending (the House also favouring tax increases)[22]. But the enactment of the Deficit Reduction Bill (DEFRA) gave the Administration most of what it wanted on non-defence programmes and taxation, though leaving the defence issue unresolved. It is expected to raise $16 billion in FY 1986, through various tax base and compliance measures (Table 8), and through spending cuts (chiefly in entitlement programmes) which reduced spending by around $11 billion. The Senate and House later reached agreement on defence totals some way below the "Rose Garden" figures, but these were not endorsed by the Administration.

Because of time lags in realising savings, the effects of the Budget cuts in FY 1985 and 1986 were expected to be relatively modest. But in any case, by the time the FY 1986 Budget was being drawn up, the 1985 deficit had risen to $222 billion[23], with deficits of $220-240 billion foreseen through the 1986-1990 period. This was partly due to lower inflation prospects (cutting receipts), and partly to higher interest rate assumptions. This brought a new urgency to the budget cutting process. With the proposal for tax increases meeting a negative electoral response during the Presidential campaign, a greater consensus on the need to cut expenditures emerged. Excluding debt service costs the 1986 Budget proposed to hold federal spending to the same level as in 1985 (Table 8)[24]. No changes were proposed in social security benefits and, though defence spending was to be reduced from planned levels, this was still intended to grow by 12½ per cent (8¼ per cent real) in FY 1986[25]. As in 1984, the pattern of proposed expenditure cuts favoured by Congress differed from the Administration (though since the debate has focused on spending cuts rather than tax increases there has been a significant degree of convergence).

The compromise budget guidelines adopted by Congress at the beginning of August eventually incorporated cuts of $55 billion from the Administration's $230 billion baseline deficit for FY 1986, giving a projected $175 billion deficit according to CBO estimates (Table 8)[26]. Defence authority is to be frozen in real terms in 1986 (with 2 per cent real growth thereafter), with spending on entitlement programmes such as Medicare, and farm price support also reduced. The freeze on social security increases and a wide range of programme terminations demanded by the Administration were not included. Given the past record of overspending by the committees which implement the (non-binding) resolution, some doubt has been expressed as to whether the cuts will materialise[27]. Indeed, the Administration estimates that there is little chance of meeting the Congressional deficit target for FY 1986 and forecasts a deficit of $185 billion or so, unless further cuts are made. The mid-session Review (Table 8) restated the Administration's proposals for non-defence programme cuts which would be needed to bring the deficit below $180 in FY 1985. Moreover, since the Administration and CBO estimates are based on growth of 4 and 3½ per cent respectively in 1986, it is evident that the projected deficits do not allow any margin for safety. If the economy performs worse than expected deficits could rise above $200 billion again. (On a 2¾ per cent real growth assumption for 1986 the OECD projects a federal deficit of $188 billion on a national accounts basis, even if the spending plans are implemented.) To forestall the possibility of high deficits persisting, the Senate and House have each adopted "balanced budget" bills, which would – if agreement can be reached by a joint conference committee – require across-the-board spending cuts in "controllable items" in order to balance the federal budget by FY 1991[28].

The 1981 tax reductions proceeded from the view that the tax system discouraged household savings and work incentives. Personal tax rates were therefore cut, in three stages, by 23 per cent. However, the effects have been limited and partial. After allowing for the fact that many tax payers have automatically moved into higher tax brackets as their incomes have risen, the reforms have effectively reduced personal tax rates (marginal and average) by just over 10 per cent since 1980 (Diagram 7, Annex 2). This may not have have been enough to improve the flow of resources into their most productive uses nor to remove the perception that the income tax is complicated and unfair. Because much saving is now exempt from tax, while interest on borrowing is tax deductible, this may have increased "arbitrage" between savings outlets without necessarily raising the supply of total saving. The household saving ratio has fallen below its historical average, and buoyant investment has had to be financed by capital imports, so the reforms do not seem to have had much effect on savings incentives[29]. Effective tax rates on financial investments vary significantly from asset to asset[30], with some earnings, such as those on municipal bonds, being free of tax and others being subject to negative rates. These distortions, and the erosion of the income tax base by a proliferation of special exclusions[31], have given a new impetus to tax reform. Furthermore, though the growth of venture capital and risk taking have probably been linked to tax rate reductions, the small rise in the labour force participation rates since 1981 does not suggest any marked shift in incentives to work[32].

The effects of tax reform on capital expenditure seem to have been more marked than on savings and labour supply, though the impact of tax cuts *per se*, are difficult to disentangle from the effects of lower inflation, falling relative prices of capital goods and changing real interest rates on the costs of capital (see Section IV). Average rates of corporate income have been halved since 1980 (Diagram 7C) and effective marginal rates, which are probably most relevant to investment decisions, have fallen from 35 to 15 per cent (see Annex 2). Rates on machinery and equipment have fallen furthest, and have recently been close to zero or even negative; rates on structures, at about 40 per cent, remain close to the statutory rate of 46 per cent. The tax bias in favour of machinery and against industrial building has, however, been reduced, since some classes of assets, such as office equipment, trucks and construction machinery seem to have actually faced a higher tax rates after the 1981-1982 reforms[33] (see Section IV). Moreover, despite the reforms, the tax system has remained diverse in its treatment of different investments, so that its overall economic impact is difficult to discern. To achieve a more uniform tax treatment of income which would minimise the impact of the tax structure on resource allocation, the Treasury introduced a new tax reform proposal in November 1984, aimed at reducing the complexity of the system. Designed to be "revenue neutral" this had intended to simplify the personal tax system by closing tax loopholes (thus expanding the tax base), reducing the 11 tax brackets to three and setting marginal rates (currently 11-50 per cent) at 15-35 per cent. The corporate tax rate was to be lowered, the investment tax credit eliminated and depreciation schedules lengthened. Less sweeping proposals were made in May 1985, the opportunities for exploiting tax loopholes being less rigorously curtailed. However, the aim of transferring a greater part of the tax burden to companies has been maintained, since the household tax burden would be cut by 5¼ per cent while company taxes would be raised 23 per cent. A reduction in the basic corporation tax rate from 46 to 33 per cent would partly offset the removal of corporate tax breaks, with the intention of reducing the after-tax cost of corporate equity capital relative to bonds (thus lessening bond market pressures and long-term interest rates). Repeal of the investment tax credit would increase tax revenues by $37½ billion by 1990. Depreciation would be more

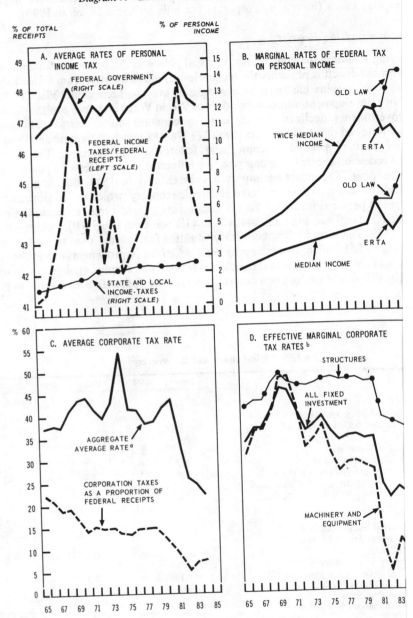

Diagram 7. **Effective rates of income tax and corporation tax**

a) The average tax rate is the ratio of domestic corporate tax liabilities to domestic corporate pro with the capital consumption and inventory valuation adjustments, less profits earned Reserve.

b) Marginal tax rates are based on the following assumptions: assets are financed 100 pe corporations earn a 4 percent real after-tax return, and all deductions or credits can be used in Expected inflation in each year is calculated as a function of prior inflation rates.

*Sources :* Congressional Budget Office ; Council of Economic Advisors ; Federal Reserve Board

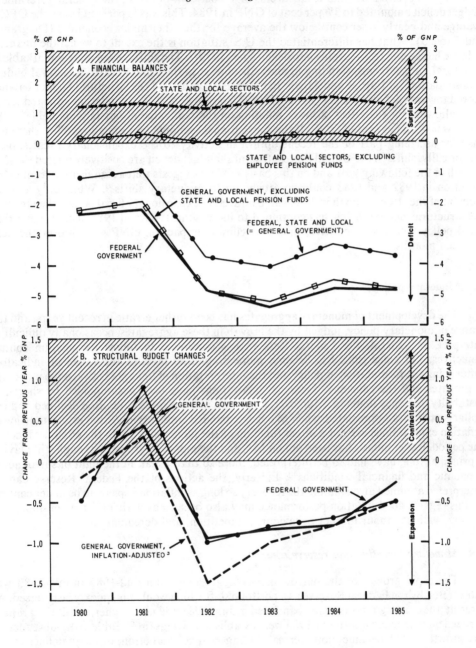

*Diagram 8.* **Budget indicators**

**A. FINANCIAL BALANCES**

STATE AND LOCAL SECTORS

STATE AND LOCAL SECTORS, EXCLUDING
EMPLOYEE PENSION FUNDS

GENERAL GOVERNMENT, EXCLUDING
STATE AND LOCAL PENSION FUNDS

FEDERAL, STATE AND LOCAL
(= GENERAL GOVERNMENT)

FEDERAL
GOVERNMENT

**B. STRUCTURAL BUDGET CHANGES**

GENERAL GOVERNMENT

FEDERAL GOVERNMENT

GENERAL GOVERNMENT,
INFLATION-ADJUSTED [a]

*a)* The general government structural balance, less the net real change in outstanding government debt. (See
OECD *Economic Outlook,* May 1985).

*Sources:* Department of Commerce (Bureau of Economic Analysis); Secretariat estimates.

Allowing for a state and local surplus of 1¼ per cent of GNP, the general government budget deficit amounted to 3½ per cent of GNP in 1984. This was ½ per cent below the OECD average and nearly 1 per cent below the average for the other major economies (Diagram 8 and Table 5). What has differentiated the U.S. situation is the extent to which the financial balance has swung from surplus into deficit since 1979[37]. The shift is even more remarkable in structural budget terms, standing in marked contrast to the trend towards structural budget "consolidation" in Europe and Japan. Between 1980 and 1984 the structural budget balance moved towards deficit by 2 per cent of GNP (Diagram 8, part B). In inflation-adjusted terms – i.e. allowing for the effect of lower inflation on the real value of outstanding debt[38] – the swing was – 2½ per cent of GNP. If the conventional spending lags are allowed for, there is a case for ascribing part of the recent upturn in activity to the expansionary fiscal stance. Historically, shifts in the United States structural budget deficit are positively related to GNP growth in the following year and on this basis Table 9 suggests that a significant part of GNP variation in 1982 and 1983 could be attributed to budgetary shifts[39]. While only a small element of the strong growth in 1984 can be traced to expansionary fiscal policy, the fact that the structural budget deficit has continued to increase in 1984 and 1985 should mean that fiscal policy will have a positive, though declining, impact on GNP growth over the next eighteen months.

## B. Monetary policy

The development of monetary aggregates has been rather erratic in recent years, and the stance of monetary policy, judged by the growth in these aggregates, occasionally difficult to interpret. In general, the Federal Reserve has continued to follow its inflation control objectives, but since 1982 has become more pragmatic in both the range of indicators influencing the formulation of policy and the interpretation of linkages between the monetary aggregates and the economy. Financial innovations have been accompanied by short-run instability in money demand. Moreover, long-term interest rates have often declined and the dollar sometimes appreciated when M1 has expanded most rapidly, suggesting that lower inflation expectations are not a direct function of the money supply. In the circumstances of the period, less emphasis has been put on M1, and the money aggregates, though still playing a principal role, have had to be interpreted, more so than usual, in the light of surrounding economic and financial conditions[40]. Latterly, the actions of the Federal Reserve can be interpreted as aimed at sustaining the recovery so long as inflation appears to be under control. In this regard, good inflation performance may also be seen as deriving from non-monetary factors, such as labour market behaviour, competition, and deregulation.

### Monetary targeting and reserve control

The rapid growth of the narrow money aggregates from mid-1982 to mid-1983 was interpreted by the Federal Reserve as a portfolio shift which would not quickly be reversed. As a result, the existing targets were abandoned in July 1983 and new, higher, monitoring ranges rebased on the second quarter of 1983 were established (Diagram 9, Table 10). Subsequently the growth of M1 became more normal, falling near to the bottom of its guidelines in the second half of 1984, but reviving towards the end of the year, to grow at an average annual rate of 7 per cent from the first quarter of 1983 to the last quarter of 1984. This compared with a growth rate of 9 per cent a year in nominal GNP over the same period. M2, which also overshot in early 1983 grew at a fairly consistent rate of just over 8 per cent a year after being

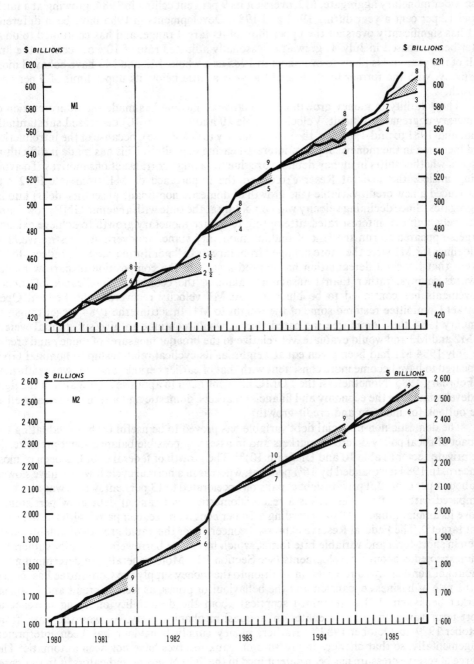

*Diagram 9.* **Monetary trends and targets**

*Source :* Federal Reserve Board.

rebased in early 1983, ending 1984 exactly in the centre of its 6-9 per cent monitoring range. The wider monetary aggregate, M3, overshot its 9 per cent ceiling in 1984, growing at a fairly rapid 12 per cent a year during 1983 and 1984. Developments in 1985 have been different. M1 has significantly overshot the upper limit of its target range, and has continued to do so after being rebased in July. It grew at a seasonally adjusted rate of 10½ per cent in the first half of the year and is likely to overshoot in 1985 as a whole. M2 and M3 have behaved more normally, with the former likely to end the year a little below its upper limit of 9 per cent growth.

The volatility in money growth rates relative to income has made the interpretation of monetary aggregates difficult. Velocity (Table 10 and Diagram 10) decreased substantially from mid-1981 to mid-1983 (i.e. the ratio of money to GNP rose), because of the introduction and inclusion in the money supply of interest-bearing deposits[41]. This has made it difficult to discern whether shifts in money demand are due to savings or transactions motives. To avoid being misled, the Federal Reserve reduced the importance of M1 from late 1982 and introduced a new credit variable (the growth of domestic non-financial sectors' debt) into its aggregates. Since declining velocity was coinciding at the time with anaemic GNP growth and relatively high real interest rates, attempting to reduce monetary growth to achieve existing targets appeared to run the risk of making monetary stance inadvertently restrictive. The guidelines for M1 were therefore changed from targets to "monitoring ranges". Indeed, to the extent that financial deregulation has caused a shift in the composition of narrow money towards savings, rather than transaction balances, the economic significance of money movements has continued to be blurred[42]. As M1 velocity recovered, the Federal Open Market Committee restored some of the weight to M1. In setting the 1984 target ranges in January 1984 the Committee indicated that it would continue to give substantial weight to M2 and M3 and would evaluate M1 relative to the broader measures of money and credit. By July 1984 M1 had been given equal weight, as its cyclical relationship to nominal GNP appeared to have become more consistent with that of earlier periods, and this was reaffirmed in February 1985. Nonetheless, the FOMC has continued to appraise aggregates in the light of developments in the economy and financial markets, domestic and international, as well as the outlook for inflation and credit growth[43].

The domestic non-financial debt variable has proved to be useful both in evaluating the impact of fiscal policy on credit markets and in assessing possible balance sheet pressures in the private sector (Table 10 and Diagram 10)[44]. The growth of federal debt has been of most concern. In 1984 it expanded by 16½ per cent, whereas in a normal cycle it would have slowed to about 4 per cent. But private debt expansion accelerated to 13 per cent, which was also high compared with past recoveries. As a result, domestic non-financial debt grew persistently above its annual range in 1984, recording a 14 per cent increase, compared with the 8-11 per cent target[45]. The Federal Reserve expressed concern over this rapid growth of indebtedness, often in short-term and variable rate forms, which has made borrowers especially vulnerable to unexpected economic developments (see Section III). More generally, in determining the amount of non-borrowed reserves, in addition to the money supply the Committee has looked at the rate of business expansion and the behaviour of prices, as well as credit and financial market behaviour. It has remained sceptical about the desirability of trying to react to short-term variations in aggregates in a quasi-mechanical way, as was the case from October 1979 to October 1982[46]. Rather, money supply behaviour has been interpreted judgementally, so that changes in pressure on bank reserves have not been automatic. The degree of reserve pressure has been determined in the light of several indicators[47]. In this case, the level of discount window borrowings, excluding extended credit, may be a more useful indicator of deliberate tightening or easing than the Federal funds rate[48].

defence spending, which despite certain proposed "savings" was planned to increase by an average of 7 per cent per annum in real terms from FY 1984 to FY 1989. Other spending was to be virtually frozen in real terms. With some small tax-raising proposals the package was estimated to be worth $27 billion in FY 1985 (giving a budget deficit of $180 billion). Agreement with the Senate (the "Rose Garden" downpayment agreement) was followed by a stalemate with the House over defence spending (the House also favouring tax increases)[22]. But the enactment of the Deficit Reduction Bill (DEFRA) gave the Administration most of what it wanted on non-defence programmes and taxation, though leaving the defence issue unresolved. It is expected to raise $16 billion in FY 1986, through various tax base and compliance measures (Table 8), and through spending cuts (chiefly in entitlement programmes) which reduced spending by around $11 billion. The Senate and House later reached agreement on defence totals some way below the "Rose Garden" figures, but these were not endorsed by the Administration.

Because of time lags in realising savings, the effects of the Budget cuts in FY 1985 and 1986 were expected to be relatively modest. But in any case, by the time the FY 1986 Budget was being drawn up, the 1985 deficit had risen to $222 billion[23], with deficits of $220-240 billion foreseen through the 1986-1990 period. This was partly due to lower inflation prospects (cutting receipts), and partly to higher interest rate assumptions. This brought a new urgency to the budget cutting process. With the proposal for tax increases meeting a negative electoral response during the Presidential campaign, a greater consensus on the need to cut expenditures emerged. Excluding debt service costs the 1986 Budget proposed to hold federal spending to the same level as in 1985 (Table 8)[24]. No changes were proposed in social security benefits and, though defence spending was to be reduced from planned levels, this was still intended to grow by 12½ per cent (8¼ per cent real) in FY 1986[25]. As in 1984, the pattern of proposed expenditure cuts favoured by Congress differed from the Administration (though since the debate has focused on spending cuts rather than tax increases there has been a significant degree of convergence).

The compromise budget guidelines adopted by Congress at the beginning of August eventually incorporated cuts of $55 billion from the Administration's $230 billion baseline deficit for FY 1986, giving a projected $175 billion deficit according to CBO estimates (Table 8)[26]. Defence authority is to be frozen in real terms in 1986 (with 2 per cent real growth thereafter), with spending on entitlement programmes such as Medicare, and farm price support also reduced. The freeze on social security increases and a wide range of programme terminations demanded by the Administration were not included. Given the past record of overspending by the committees which implement the (non-binding) resolution, some doubt has been expressed as to whether the cuts will materialise[27]. Indeed, the Administration estimates that there is little chance of meeting the Congressional deficit target for FY 1986 and forecasts a deficit of $185 billion or so, unless further cuts are made. The mid-session Review (Table 8) restated the Administration's proposals for non-defence programme cuts which would be needed to bring the deficit below $180 in FY 1985. Moreover, since the Administration and CBO estimates are based on growth of 4 and 3½ per cent respectively in 1986, it is evident that the projected deficits do not allow any margin for safety. If the economy performs worse than expected deficits could rise above $200 billion again. (On a 2¾ per cent real growth assumption for 1986 the OECD projects a federal deficit of $188 billion on a national accounts basis, even if the spending plans are implemented.) To forestall the possibility of high deficits persisting, the Senate and House have each adopted "balanced budget" bills, which would – if agreement can be reached by a joint conference committee – require across-the-board spending cuts in "controllable items" in order to balance the federal budget by FY 1991[28].

*Reforming the tax structure*

The 1981 tax reductions proceeded from the view that the tax system discouraged household savings and work incentives. Personal tax rates were therefore cut, in three stages, by 23 per cent. However, the effects have been limited and partial. After allowing for the fact that many tax payers have automatically moved into higher tax brackets as their incomes have risen, the reforms have effectively reduced personal tax rates (marginal and average) by just over 10 per cent since 1980 (Diagram 7, Annex 2). This may not have have been enough to improve the flow of resources into their most productive uses nor to remove the perception that the income tax is complicated and unfair. Because much saving is now exempt from tax, while interest on borrowing is tax deductible, this may have increased "arbitrage" between savings outlets without necessarily raising the supply of total saving. The household saving ratio has fallen below its historical average, and buoyant investment has had to be financed by capital imports, so the reforms do not seem to have had much effect on savings incentives[29]. Effective tax rates on financial investments vary significantly from asset to asset[30], with some earnings, such as those on municipal bonds, being free of tax and others being subject to negative rates. These distortions, and the erosion of the income tax base by a proliferation of special exclusions[31], have given a new impetus to tax reform. Furthermore, though the growth of venture capital and risk taking have probably been linked to tax rate reductions, the small rise in the labour force participation rates since 1981 does not suggest any marked shift in incentives to work[32].

The effects of tax reform on capital expenditure seem to have been more marked than on savings and labour supply, though the impact of tax cuts *per se,* are difficult to disentangle from the effects of lower inflation, falling relative prices of capital goods and changing real interest rates on the costs of capital (see Section IV). Average rates of corporate income have been halved since 1980 (Diagram 7C) and effective marginal rates, which are probably most relevant to investment decisions, have fallen from 35 to 15 per cent (see Annex 2). Rates on machinery and equipment have fallen furthest, and have recently been close to zero or even negative; rates on structures, at about 40 per cent, remain close to the statutory rate of 46 per cent. The tax bias in favour of machinery and against industrial building has, however, been reduced, since some classes of assets, such as office equipment, trucks and construction machinery seem to have actually faced a higher tax rates after the 1981-1982 reforms[33] (see Section IV). Moreover, despite the reforms, the tax system has remained diverse in its treatment of different investments, so that its overall economic impact is difficult to discern. To achieve a more uniform tax treatment of income which would minimise the impact of the tax structure on resource allocation, the Treasury introduced a new tax reform proposal in November 1984, aimed at reducing the complexity of the system. Designed to be "revenue neutral" this had intended to simplify the personal tax system by closing tax loopholes (thus expanding the tax base), reducing the 11 tax brackets to three and setting marginal rates (currently 11-50 per cent) at 15-35 per cent. The corporate tax rate was to be lowered, the investment tax credit eliminated and depreciation schedules lengthened. Less sweeping proposals were made in May 1985, the opportunities for exploiting tax loopholes being less rigorously curtailed. However, the aim of transferring a greater part of the tax burden to companies has been maintained, since the household tax burden would be cut by 5¼ per cent while company taxes would be raised 23 per cent. A reduction in the basic corporation tax rate from 46 to 33 per cent would partly offset the removal of corporate tax breaks, with the intention of reducing the after-tax cost of corporate equity capital relative to bonds (thus lessening bond market pressures and long-term interest rates). Repeal of the investment tax credit would increase tax revenues by $37½ billion by 1990. Depreciation would be more

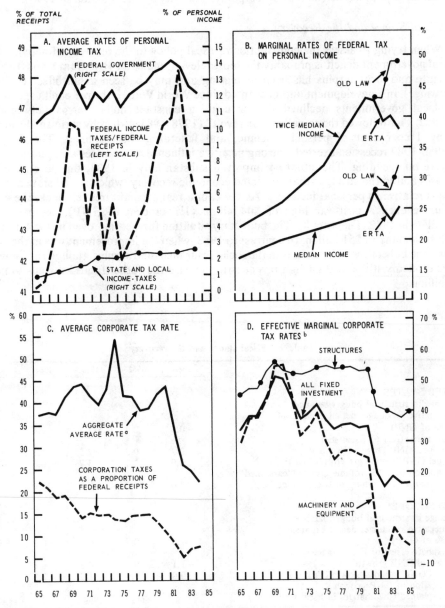

*Diagram 7.* **Effective rates of income tax and corporation tax**

% OF TOTAL RECEIPTS

% OF PERSONAL INCOME

**A. AVERAGE RATES OF PERSONAL INCOME TAX**

FEDERAL GOVERNMENT (RIGHT SCALE)

FEDERAL INCOME TAXES/FEDERAL RECEIPTS (LEFT SCALE)

STATE AND LOCAL INCOME-TAXES (RIGHT SCALE)

**B. MARGINAL RATES OF FEDERAL TAX ON PERSONAL INCOME**

OLD LAW

TWICE MEDIAN INCOME

ERTA

OLD LAW

ERTA

MEDIAN INCOME

**C. AVERAGE CORPORATE TAX RATE**

AGGREGATE AVERAGE RATE*a*

CORPORATION TAXES AS A PROPORTION OF FEDERAL RECEIPTS

**D. EFFECTIVE MARGINAL CORPORATE TAX RATES** *b*

STRUCTURES

ALL FIXED INVESTMENT

MACHINERY AND EQUIPMENT

*a)* The average tax rate is the ratio of domestic corporate tax liabilities to domestic corporate profits (NIPA basis) with the capital consumption and inventory valuation adjustments, less profits earned by the Federal Reserve.

*b)* Marginal tax rates are based on the following assumptions: assets are financed 100 percent by equity, corporations earn a 4 percent real after-tax return, and all deductions or credits can be used in the year earned. Expected inflation in each year is calculated as a function of prior inflation rates.

*Sources :* Congressional Budget Office ; Council of Economic Advisors ; Federal Reserve Board.

closely related to the useful economic lives of assets and take into account the impact of inflation on capital assets (increasing corporate tax bills by $15½ billion in 1990).

### Fiscal Stance and the Recovery

When trying to assess the contribution of fiscal policy to the recovery of activity[34], the general government deficit is probably the most relevant indicator (Diagram 8 and Table 5). The state and local surplus has been increasing and may be seen as an offset to federal borrowing[35]. In a development unprecedented since World War II, the per capita spending of state-local governments declined 6½ per cent in constant dollar terms between 1978 and 1983. This followed the so-called "tax revolt" (1978-1981), whereby state and local taxes fell by 1½ per cent of personal income, and federal grants declined. The fact that the 1980-1982 recession exerted a strong negative influence on revenues also put downward pressure on spending. The situation improved substantially in 1983, due to enacted tax increases and to the stronger-than-expected economic recovery, which raised state and local receipts relative to personal income[36]. As per capita real expenditures fell back, the overall surplus reached a post-war high of $44 billion (1½ per cent of GNP), compared with $33 billion in 1982 (Diagram 8). The budgetary situation further improved in 1984, the total surplus widening to $51 billion. In contrast to 1983, when the improvement was in the "other funds", the bulk of the increase was in the social insurance fund surplus, though the buoyancy of the economy still added enough revenues to increase the "other funds" surplus to nearly $10 billion.

Table 9.  **Fiscal stance and the recovery**

|  | 1981 | 1982 | 1983 | 1984 | 1985 |
|---|---|---|---|---|---|
| **UNITED STATES** | | | | | |
| Change in structural budget balance[1] | | | | | |
| [negative = budget deficit expansion] | | | | | |
| (% of GNP) | −0.3 | 0.4 | −1.8 | −0.8 | −0.8 |
| Proximate effect of fiscal stance | | | | | |
| on real GNP growth (% p.a.)[2] | 0.4 | −0.5 | 2.5 | 1.1 | 1.3 |
| Actual GNP volume growth (% p.a.)[3] | 3.0 | −2.1 | 3.7 | 6.8 | 2.5 |
| Proportion of GNP volume growth "explained" | | | | | |
| by changes in changes in fiscal stance (%) | 13.0 | 24.0 | 67.0 | 16.0 | 50.0 |
| **OECD EUROPE[4]** | | | | | |
| Change in structural budget balance[1] | | | | | |
| [negative = budget deficit expansion] | | | | | |
| (% of GNP) | 1.5 | −0.7 | 0.3 | −0.1 | −0.4 |
| Proximate effect of fiscal stance | | | | | |
| on real GNP growth (% p.a.)[2] | −1.1 | 0.5 | −0.3 | 0.1 | 0.3 |
| Actual GNP volume growth (% p.a.)[3] | 0.0 | 0.6 | 1.3 | 2.3 | 2¼ |
| Proportion of GNP growth | | | | | |
| "explained" by changes in fiscal stance (%) | neg. | 80.0 | neg. | 4.0 | 13.0 |

1.  The general government structural budget deficit adjusted for inflation.
2.  The effect of changes in the inflation-adjusted deficit on real GNP growth, calculated from a regression of the reduced form # g = a + b # $B_{t-1}$, over the period 1970-1983, where g is the real growth rate, B is the inflation-adjusted structural budget deficit and # represents year-to-year changes. For the United States # g = 2.94 + 1.36 # $B_{t-1}$ [SE. = 0.58; $R^2$ = 0.30] (a positive shift in B being stimulatory). This relationship also exists, in differing degrees in most major European economies.
3.  OECD forecasts for 1985.
4.  Major four European economies (Germany, France, U.K. and Italy).
*Source:*  Secretariat calculations.

## Diagram 8. Budget indicators

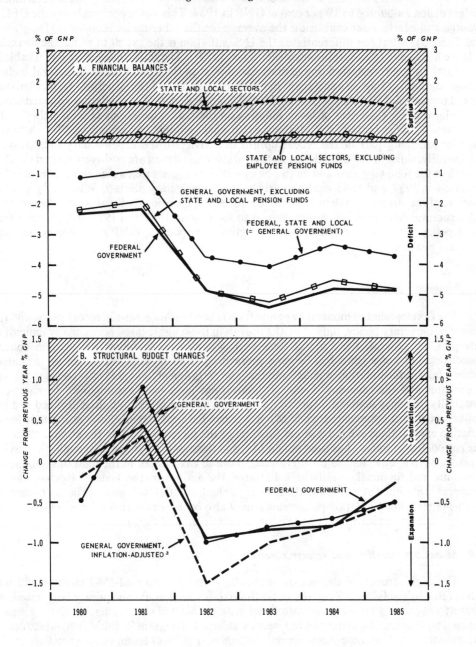

a) The general government structural balance, less the net real change in outstanding government debt. (See OECD *Economic Outlook*, May 1985).

*Sources:* Department of Commerce (Bureau of Economic Analysis); Secretariat estimates.

Allowing for a state and local surplus of 1¼ per cent of GNP, the general government budget deficit amounted to 3½ per cent of GNP in 1984. This was ½ per cent below the OECD average and nearly 1 per cent below the average for the other major economies (Diagram 8 and Table 5). What has differentiated the U.S. situation is the extent to which the financial balance has swung from surplus into deficit since 1979[37]. The shift is even more remarkable in structural budget terms, standing in marked contrast to the trend towards structural budget "consolidation" in Europe and Japan. Between 1980 and 1984 the structural budget balance moved towards deficit by 2 per cent of GNP (Diagram 8, part B). In inflation-adjusted terms – i.e. allowing for the effect of lower inflation on the real value of outstanding debt[38] – the swing was – 2½ per cent of GNP. If the conventional spending lags are allowed for, there is a case for ascribing part of the recent upturn in activity to the expansionary fiscal stance. Historically, shifts in the United States structural budget deficit are positively related to GNP growth in the following year and on this basis Table 9 suggests that a significant part of GNP variation in 1982 and 1983 could be attributed to budgetary shifts[39]. While only a small element of the strong growth in 1984 can be traced to expansionary fiscal policy, the fact that the structural budget deficit has continued to increase in 1984 and 1985 should mean that fiscal policy will have a positive, though declining, impact on GNP growth over the next eighteen months.

## B. Monetary policy

The development of monetary aggregates has been rather erratic in recent years, and the stance of monetary policy, judged by the growth in these aggregates, occasionally difficult to interpret. In general, the Federal Reserve has continued to follow its inflation control objectives, but since 1982 has become more pragmatic in both the range of indicators influencing the formulation of policy and the interpretation of linkages between the monetary aggregates and the economy. Financial innovations have been accompanied by short-run instability in money demand. Moreover, long-term interest rates have often declined and the dollar sometimes appreciated when M1 has expanded most rapidly, suggesting that lower inflation expectations are not a direct function of the money supply. In the circumstances of the period, less emphasis has been put on M1, and the money aggregates, though still playing a principal role, have had to be interpreted, more so than usual, in the light of surrounding economic and financial conditions[40]. Latterly, the actions of the Federal Reserve can be interpreted as aimed at sustaining the recovery so long as inflation appears to be under control. In this regard, good inflation performance may also be seen as deriving from non-monetary factors, such as labour market behaviour, competition, and deregulation.

### Monetary targeting and reserve control

The rapid growth of the narrow money aggregates from mid-1982 to mid-1983 was interpreted by the Federal Reserve as a portfolio shift which would not quickly be reversed. As a result, the existing targets were abandoned in July 1983 and new, higher, monitoring ranges rebased on the second quarter of 1983 were established (Diagram 9, Table 10). Subsequently the growth of M1 became more normal, falling near to the bottom of its guidelines in the second half of 1984, but reviving towards the end of the year, to grow at an average annual rate of 7 per cent from the first quarter of 1983 to the last quarter of 1984. This compared with a growth rate of 9 per cent a year in nominal GNP over the same period. M2, which also overshot in early 1983 grew at a fairly consistent rate of just over 8 per cent a year after being

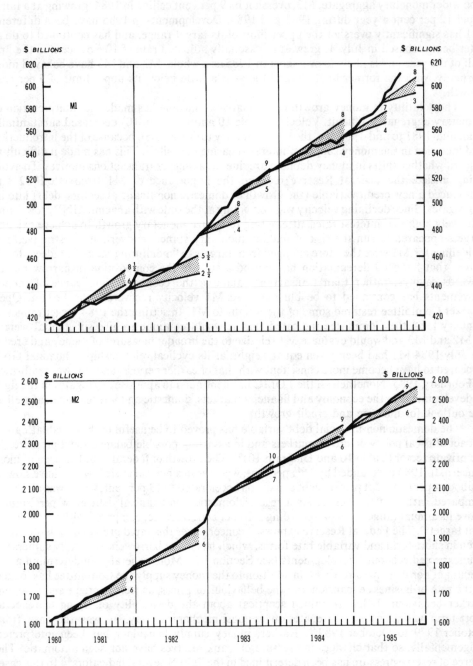

*Diagram 9.* **Monetary trends and targets**

*Source:* Federal Reserve Board.

rebased in early 1983, ending 1984 exactly in the centre of its 6-9 per cent monitoring range. The wider monetary aggregate, M3, overshot its 9 per cent ceiling in 1984, growing at a fairly rapid 12 per cent a year during 1983 and 1984. Developments in 1985 have been different. M1 has significantly overshot the upper limit of its target range, and has continued to do so after being rebased in July. It grew at a seasonally adjusted rate of 10½ per cent in the first half of the year and is likely to overshoot in 1985 as a whole. M2 and M3 have behaved more normally, with the former likely to end the year a little below its upper limit of 9 per cent growth.

The volatility in money growth rates relative to income has made the interpretation of monetary aggregates difficult. Velocity (Table 10 and Diagram 10) decreased substantially from mid-1981 to mid-1983 (i.e. the ratio of money to GNP rose), because of the introduction and inclusion in the money supply of interest-bearing deposits[41]. This has made it difficult to discern whether shifts in money demand are due to savings or transactions motives. To avoid being misled, the Federal Reserve reduced the importance of M1 from late 1982 and introduced a new credit variable (the growth of domestic non-financial sectors' debt) into its aggregates. Since declining velocity was coinciding at the time with anaemic GNP growth and relatively high real interest rates, attempting to reduce monetary growth to achieve existing targets appeared to run the risk of making monetary stance inadvertently restrictive. The guidelines for M1 were therefore changed from targets to "monitoring ranges". Indeed, to the extent that financial deregulation has caused a shift in the composition of narrow money towards savings, rather than transaction balances, the economic significance of money movements has continued to be blurred[42]. As M1 velocity recovered, the Federal Open Market Committee restored some of the weight to M1. In setting the 1984 target ranges in January 1984 the Committee indicated that it would continue to give substantial weight to M2 and M3 and would evaluate M1 relative to the broader measures of money and credit. By July 1984 M1 had been given equal weight, as its cyclical relationship to nominal GNP appeared to have become more consistent with that of earlier periods, and this was reaffirmed in February 1985. Nonetheless, the FOMC has continued to appraise aggregates in the light of developments in the economy and financial markets, domestic and international, as well as the outlook for inflation and credit growth[43].

The domestic non-financial debt variable has proved to be useful both in evaluating the impact of fiscal policy on credit markets and in assessing possible balance sheet pressures in the private sector (Table 10 and Diagram 10)[44]. The growth of federal debt has been of most concern. In 1984 it expanded by 16½ per cent, whereas in a normal cycle it would have slowed to about 4 per cent. But private debt expansion accelerated to 13 per cent, which was also high compared with past recoveries. As a result, domestic non-financial debt grew persistently above its annual range in 1984, recording a 14 per cent increase, compared with the 8-11 per cent target[45]. The Federal Reserve expressed concern over this rapid growth of indebtedness, often in short-term and variable rate forms, which has made borrowers especially vulnerable to unexpected economic developments (see Section III). More generally, in determining the amount of non-borrowed reserves, in addition to the money supply the Committee has looked at the rate of business expansion and the behaviour of prices, as well as credit and financial market behaviour. It has remained sceptical about the desirability of trying to react to short-term variations in aggregates in a quasi-mechanical way, as was the case from October 1979 to October 1982[46]. Rather, money supply behaviour has been interpreted judgementally, so that changes in pressure on bank reserves have not been automatic. The degree of reserve pressure has been determined in the light of several indicators[47]. In this case, the level of discount window borrowings, excluding extended credit, may be a more useful indicator of deliberate tightening or easing than the Federal funds rate[48].

Table 10. **Monetary indicators**

## A. MONEY, CREDIT AND VELOCITY
Percentage change from a year earlier

| | Annual average | | | Fourth quarter | | | | |
|---|---|---|---|---|---|---|---|---|
| | 1970-1980 | 1980-1982 | 1982-1984 | 1981 | 1982 | 1983 | 1984 | 1985 |
| Monetary and credit target[1] | | | | | | | | |
| M1 | | | | 6.2 | 4.0 | 7.0 | 6.0 | 5.5 |
| M2 | | | | 7.5 | 7.5 | 8.5 | 7.5 | 7.5 |
| M3 | | | | 8.0 | 8.0 | 8.0 | 7.5 | 7.8 |
| Debt | | | | .. | .. | 10.0 | 9.5 | 10.5 |
| Monetary and credit growth | | | | | | | | |
| M1 | 6.6 | 6.9 | 9.1 | 5.2 | 8.7 | 10.6 | 5.2 | 12.4[4] |
| M2 | 10.0 | 9.5 | 10.1 | 9.3 | 9.5 | 12.1 | 7.5 | 9.5[4] |
| M3 | 11.5 | 11.6 | 9.9 | 12.4 | 10.6 | 9.4 | 10.4 | 8.1[4] |
| Debt total | 10.6 | 9.2 | 12.0 | 9.7 | 8.9 | 10.9 | 13.6 | 12.7[5] |
| Federal | | | | 11.8 | 19.4 | 18.3 | 16.5 | n.a. |
| Non-federal | | | | 9.0 | 6.4 | 9.0 | 12.8 | n.a. |
| Velocity change[2] | | | | | | | | |
| M1 | 3.4 | 1.2 | 0.3 | 5.2 | -5.5 | -0.2 | 4.1 | -6.1[4] |
| M2 | 0.2 | -1.3 | -0.7 | 1.2 | -6.2 | -1.5 | 1.9 | -3.5[4] |
| M3 | -1.1 | -3.1 | -0.5 | -1.5 | -7.1 | 0.9 | -0.8 | -2.3[4] |

## B. INTEREST RATES
Per cent

| | Annual average | | | Fourth quarter | | | | |
|---|---|---|---|---|---|---|---|---|
| | 1982 | 1983 | 1984 | 1981 | 1982 | 1983 | 1984 | 1985[6] |
| Federal funds | 12.3 | 9.1 | 10.2 | 13.6 | 9.3 | 9.4 | 9.3 | 7.9 |
| Discount window borrowing | 11.0 | 8.5 | 8.8 | 13.0 | 9.0 | 8.5 | 8.5 | 7.7 |
| 3-month Treasury bills[3] | 10.6 | 8.6 | 9.5 | 11.8 | 7.9 | 8.8 | 8.8 | 7.5 |
| 10-year Treasury notes and bonds | 13.0 | 11.1 | 12.4 | 14.1 | 10.7 | 11.7 | 11.7 | 10.8 |
| AAA corporate bonds | 13.8 | 12.0 | 12.7 | 14.6 | 11.9 | 12.4 | 12.4 | 11.6 |

1. Average of target ranges.
2. GNP divided by monetary aggregate (percentage rate of change).
3. Secondary market.
4. 1985 Q3/1984 Q4.
5. June 1985/1984 Q4.
6. Second quarter.
*Source;* Federal Reserve Board.

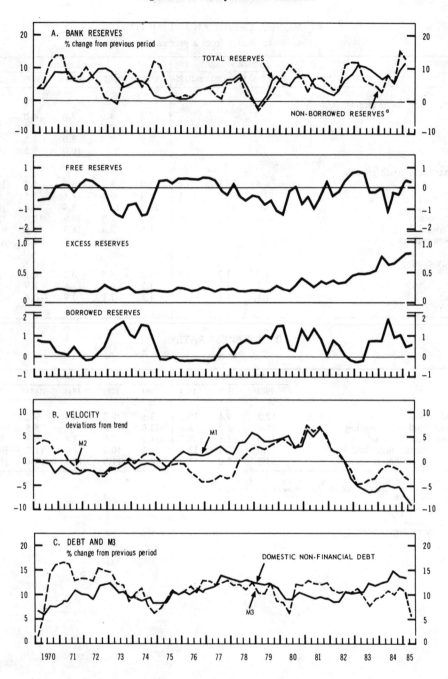

*Diagram 10.* **Money and debt indicators**

A. BANK RESERVES
% change from previous period

TOTAL RESERVES

NON-BORROWED RESERVES [a]

FREE RESERVES

EXCESS RESERVES

BORROWED RESERVES

B. VELOCITY
deviations from trend

M2

M1

C. DEBT AND M3
% change from previous period

DOMESTIC NON-FINANCIAL DEBT

M3

1970   71   72   73   74   75   76   77   78   79   80   81   82   83   84   85

*a)* Including extended credit.
*Source:* Federal Reserve Board.

*The conduct of monetary policy in 1984 and 1985*

At the beginning of 1984 money was growing rapidly and there was concern that the economy was expanding at an unsustainably rapid pace, so that the FOMC sought to increase pressure on reserves. The discount rate was raised to 9 per cent in April and the Federal Reserve moved to drain reserves, forcing the depository institutions to rely increasingly on borrowing at the discount window (Diagram 10). The concern at the time was that the strong pace of expansion would lead to price and wage pressures. The Federal funds rate was on a rising trend from then on (going from 9½ per cent in the early part of the year to 11.6 per cent in August) as the funding problems of Continental Illinois cast a shadow over financial markets and banks sought to reduce their borrowing at the discount window[49]. This, together with continuing concerns about international debt problems, for a time contributed to uneasiness in financial markets, and interest rates on short-term private credit instruments rose appreciably above those on government securities. Policies became more accommodating in late summer, as the FOMC began to respond to sluggish monetary and economic growth. This move was reinforced by a desire to temper a further strengthening of the dollar and by good inflation news (including optimism about the price of oil)[50]. The Federal Reserve discount rate was lowered in November and December to 8 per cent, and the federal funds rate dropped to 8.4 per cent by year end, reflecting reduced reserve pressure (Diagram 10). This resulted in a revival of M1 and M2 growth in the final months of 1984.

Money targets for 1985 were set in anticipation that they would "support another year of satisfactory expansion" of activity without an acceleration of inflation. The range for M1 was narrowed to 4-7 per cent and the 1984 targets for M2 (6-9 per cent) carried forward, in anticipation of 7-8 per cent nominal GNP growth. However, faltering GNP growth has been a factor conditioning the response of the Federal Reserve to the growth of money and credit. Despite the continuing rapid expansion in credit (at a 13 per cent annual rate in the first quarter) and an overshooting in M1 and M2, the Federal Reserve eased in the spring, supplying the market with reserves[51]. The Federal funds rate fell a full point between the end of March and the end of May, a shift reinforced by a cut in the discount rate to 7½ per cent. Short-term rates generally fell towards their cyclical lows. This relaxation appears to have reflected an increasing concern about the real growth of the economy. It was also influenced by the need to moderate the overvaluation of the dollar so as to assist import competing sectors and restore incentives to invest domestically[52]. These considerations were dominant in the July decision of the FOMC not to allow the overshooting of M1 to lead to a tightening of monetary stance. The sharp drop in the velocity of M1 was seen as reminiscent of the 1982-1983 experience, when the fall in interest rates was also accompanied by a decline in velocity. In re-examining its M1 range for 1985 the Committee expected much of the velocity decline to be permanent, so that the base for the range of M1 was shifted forward to the second quarter of 1985 and the range widened to 3-8 per cent. This change implied a willingness to see relatively slow monetary growth should the velocity decline be reversed and economic growth satisfactory, but was conditioned by increased uncertainty concerning the economy. With considerable slack in the economy the Federal Reserve has seen more leeway to let the money supply expand without once more igniting inflation.

*Money, interest rates and the recovery*

The pattern of short and long-term interest rates resulting from the interaction of the economy and monetary policy is shown in Diagram 11. Long-term rates on AAA commercial borrowing averaged 12.7 per cent in 1984, about ¾ per cent above the 1983 average (Table 10). They ended the year at 12.1 per cent, compared with a peak of 13¾ per cent in

*Diagram 11.* **Interest rates**

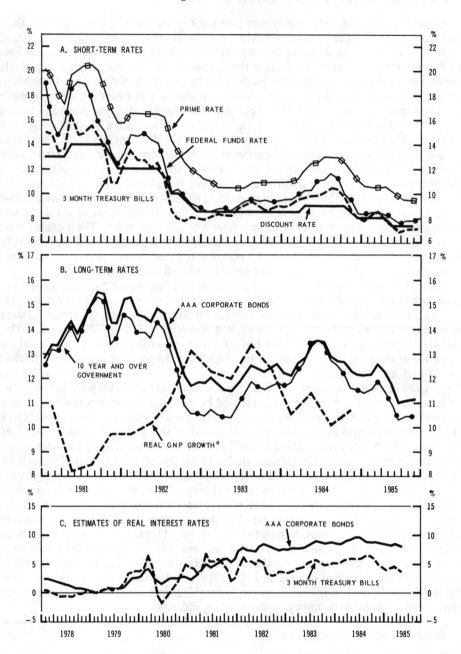

a) Quarterly rate of growth of GNP in 1972 prices (at annual rates), two quarters ahead. The correlation between the AAA rate in quarter t and the growth rate in quarter t+2 is .78 over the period 1981 Q1 and 1984 Q4.

*Sources:* Federal Reserve Board; Secretariat estimates.

40

mid-year and a low of 11½ per cent in mid-1983. From May 1983 bond prices were on a falling trend, but rallied in response to slowing economic growth and good inflation news from the end of June 1984. At the shorter end, three month treasury bills reached 9.6 per cent, nearly one point higher on average than in 1983. They began easing – in response to Federal Reserve action – somewhat later than long rates, ending 1984 at 8 per cent. After a slight firming in the early months of 1985, they fell a further percentage point up to mid-June. Real interest rates reached historically high levels in 1984. As measured by current inflation, long rates averaged about 9 per cent for corporations and 8-8½ per cent for the federal government. (For a discussion of the reasons for this see section IV.) As measured by *expected* inflation both short and long rates rose to peaks of 7 per cent in mid 1984, from lows of 3 and 4 per cent respectively at the end of 1982[53]. By year-end they had fallen back somewhat, to 5 per cent on three-month Treasury Bills and 6 per cent on 10 year government bonds, as nominal rates and inflation expectations declined. By historical standards the persistently high level of real rates has been one of the most unusual features of the recovery.

Historical relationships between monetary aggregates and macro-economic variables have become less reliable in recent years. In the past, monetary growth typically tended to be too expansionary too late in the cycle, and there was a very close relationship between money growth and inflation two years later[54]. This relationship did not hold in the 1982-84 period, when the real output/price split has been unusual. Past relationships between M1 growth and price changes, suggest that inflation should have been at 6-8 per cent rather than under 4 per cent. Monetary aggregates have thus been inadequate indicators of inflationary pressure during the recovery. (Indeed, overshooting of aggregates in 1983 went hand in hand with a strengthening of the dollar). Similarly, conventional St. Louis-type equations linking nominal GNP growth rates with lagged monetary growth (and a fiscal variable) dramatically overpredict growth early in the recovery and underpredict it in 1984[55]. This suggests that portfolio shifts in money demand have been important and that, given these and high real interest rates, fluctuations in monetary growth over the period cannot easily be interpreted in terms of their impact on aggregate demand.

Although the high level of real interest rates has not forestalled recovery or impeded the growth of private sector debt to record levels, a loose correlation would seem to exist between nominal (and even real) interest rate variations and ensuing swings in activity, via housing and consumer durable demand, and via the strength of the dollar and import penetration (see Diagram 11B). High interest rates have been, to some extent, a function of the strength of the recovery and of the large federal deficit, so they cannot be a direct indicator of monetary stance (and may even mislead if not interpreted with care). But in view of the problems in interpreting monetary growth, nominal and real interest rate changes, as well as exchange rate developments, may provide useful supplementary information for assessing the role of monetary policy in the recovery. The monetary easing in 1982 is clearly apparent in both interest rate and money supply indicators. The restriction applied from early 1983 to mid-1984, when the aim was to contain the pace of the upturn, is apparent from the non-borrowed reserve figures (Diagram 10) and reflected in rising interest rates (nominal and real). But M1 growth was in the upper half of the target range until mid-1984 (Diagram 9), by which time the preceding restraint seems to have showed through in an unexpectedly rapid deceleration in real GNP growth. The greater short-term emphasis on indicators other than monetary aggregates does not, of course, imply that monetary targeting has been, or should be, superseded by interest rate or exchange rate targets. Nor does it imply that a "flexible" approach to overshooting in the aggregates could not eventually result in the former links between monetary and price changes re-asserting themselves, particularly via a falling dollar. These inflationary dangers are discussed in Section III below.

## III. SHORT-TERM PROSPECTS, TENSIONS AND RISKS

### A. Policy stance and the short-term outlook

Considerable uncertainty surrounds the short-term outlook. As the economy approaches the fourth year of the cyclical upswing, some of the initial expansionary forces are losing their momentum. OECD projections point to near-term expansion at, or just below, the three per cent long-term growth potential of the economy up to the end of 1986 (Table 11). While recognizing the possibility of a more marked slowdown, following the hesitant growth from mid-1984 to mid-1985, the risks and tensions associated with imbalances in the economy are expected to be outweighed by forces making for continuing growth. Indicators on capacity utilisation and unemployment suggest that there is still considerable room for the U.S. economy to grow before meeting supply constraints. Moreover, employment, especially in the service sector, is continuing to grow at a robust rate which should help boost personal income and consumption. Inflationary pressures – which have contributed to the premature ageing of previous recoveries – are expected to remain subdued, despite the fall in the dollar. And with the ratio of inventories to sales currently at historically low levels, any further

Table 11. **Demand and output forecasts**

Per cent changes from previous period, s.a.a.r., 1972 prices

| | 1982 Current price $ billion | 1984 | 1985 | 1986 | 1984 I | 1984 II | 1985 I | 1985 II | 1986 I | 1986 II |
|---|---|---|---|---|---|---|---|---|---|---|
| Private consumption | 1 984.9 | 5.3 | 4 | 2¼ | 6.0 | 3.2 | 4.7 | 3¾ | 1¼ | 2½ |
| Government expenditure | 650.5 | 3.5 | 5¼ | 2¾ | 3.8 | 8.6 | 2.5 | 7¾ | ½ | 2¾ |
| Gross fixed investment | 440.9 | 18.0 | 5¼ | 1½ | 20.2 | 9.9 | 4.3 | 3 | 1¼ | ¾ |
| Final domestic demand | 3 076.3 | 6.8 | 4½ | 2½ | 7.7 | 5.2 | 4.2 | 4¼ | 1¼ | 2¼ |
| Stockbuilding[1] | −26.1 | 1.9 | −1 | ½ | 2.8 | −0.3 | −1.2 | −1 | 1½ | ¼ |
| Total domestic demand | 3 050.2 | 8.7 | 3½ | 2¾ | 10.6 | 4.9 | 3.0 | 3¼ | 2¾ | 2½ |
| Exports of goods and services | 348.4 | 4.7 | −4¼ | 3¼ | 5.0 | 3.4 | −8.6 | −3 | 5¼ | 6 |
| Imports of goods and services | 329.4 | 27.0 | 7 | 3½ | 32.5 | 17.2 | 5.4 | 1 | 4 | 4¾ |
| Foreign balance[1] | 19.0 | −1.8 | −1 | 0 | −2.2 | −1.3 | −1.3 | −¼ | 0 | 0 |
| GNP at constant prices | | 6.8 | 2½ | 2¾ | 8.3 | 3.6 | 1.7 | 2¾ | 2¾ | 2½ |
| GNP price deflator | | 3.8 | 3¾ | 3¾ | 4.1 | 3.5 | 4.0 | 3 | 4 | 4 |
| GNP at current prices | 3 069.3 | 10.8 | 6¼ | 6½ | 12.8 | 7.2 | 5.7 | 6 | 7 | 6½ |
| *Memorandum items:* | | | | | | | | | | |
| Private consumption deflator | | 3.2 | 3 | 3¼ | 3.0 | 3.3 | 2.9 | 2¾ | 3½ | 3½ |
| Breakdown of gross fixed private investment | | | | | | | | | | |
| Residential | 91.3 | 12.2 | 2½ | 4¼ | 11.4 | −3.4 | 2.7 | 8½ | 3½ | 1½ |
| Non-residential | 349.6 | 19.8 | 6¼ | 1 | 23.1 | 14.1 | 4.8 | 1½ | ¾ | ½ |
| Total employment | | 4.1 | 2 | 1½ | 4.5 | 2.4 | 2.1 | 1¼ | 1¾ | 2 |
| Unemployment rate (%) | | 7.5 | 7¼ | 7¼ | 7.7 | 7.3 | 7.3 | 7¼ | 7¼ | 7¼ |
| Stockbuilding at 1972 prices (annual rates) $ billion | | 24.8 | 9.2 | 18.9 | 26.0 | 23.7 | 13.7 | 4.8 | 17.6 | 20.3 |

1. The yearly and half-yearly rates of change refer to changes expressed as a percentage of GNP in the previous period.
*Source:* Secretariat projections.

inventory correction also appears unlikely. While reduced stockholding is partly the result of high interest rates and improved inventory management techniques – such as computerization – it also reflects conscious efforts by management to avoid undesired inventory accumulation due to sales fluctuations[56].

Fiscal and monetary policies are supporting a continuation of the recovery. With inflation remaining under control, and uncertainty continuing to attach to velocity changes in M1, it is assumed that the Federal Reserve will continue to give considerable weight to the performance of the real economy in evaluating movements in the money aggregates. Monetary growth is therefore expected to remain close to the upper end of the target ranges in 1986, which have been provisionally set at 4-7 per cent for M1 and 6-9 per cent for M2[57]. Consequently, interest rates are likely to move upwards only in reaction to a significant strengthening of demand. A weakening of the economy or a renewed surge in the dollar could induce the Federal Reserve to ease further, but the OECD forecast embodies the usual technical assumption of an unchanged dollar exchange rate. At the same time, budgetary policy has remained moderately expansionary through 1985 because of the impetus stemming from defence spending, but may become less so in 1986. Implementation of the Congressional agreement on budget cuts should be a positive factor, since any negative demand impact would be slow to be felt, while some of the possible benefits of lower interest rates could accrue immediately to the extent that bond markets are forward-looking. Although the forecast envisages long-term interest rates (AAA) in the 11 per cent range, trading could consolidate at a lower range if the Congressional agreement actually leads to declining federal borrowing requirements.

The short-term outlook for consumer spending seems fairly good. While fiscal policy is largely neutral with respect to after-tax incomes[58], employment growth is expected to continue to give momentum to the expansion of purchasing power. The recent easing of interest rates should help to avoid any abrupt correction to the rather low saving ratio and maintain demand for consumer durables and other interest-sensitive components of demand. The housing sector is expected to be reasonably buoyant, contributing moderately to real growth over the next eighteen months[59]. Business fixed investment, having been extremely strong in 1984, is expected to taper off, increasing at a rate of about 6 per cent (year-on-year) in 1985 followed by little real growth in 1986. Weakening corporate profits and the flattening of manufacturing orders and shipments, reflecting the strong dollar, have probably been factors behind the recent downward revision of investment intentions, while high office vacancy rates will probably make for continuing slack demand for commercial structures. Moreover, though the Administration's proposal to increase company taxes may give a short-run impulse to bring forward capital spending, there remains a concern about selected sectors – e.g. agriculture, energy, and some areas of real estate and banking – which are experiencing severe financial strains. Any adverse fallout is expected to be contained and not generalised to the rest of the economy, so that the projection is still based on an investment/GNP ratio (machinery and equipment in particular) which is historically high (see Table 19 below).

The external account is expected to deteriorate further, with the current account deficit reaching $130 billion this year and nearly $150 billion in 1986. Despite the depreciation of the dollar, reaccelerating real growth will continue to depress net exports, though to a lesser extent than in 1984. The growth in real imports of goods and services is expected to slow from the 27 per cent rate reached in 1984, to 7 per cent this year and below 4 per cent next. Export volume growth, though likely to recover from its 1985 trough, is projected to increase only gradually, because of the lagged effects of the strong dollar and relatively sluggish growth abroad. As a result, the growth of manufacturing output and employment may continue to be rather weak. At around 80 per cent, capacity utilization in manufacturing remains well below rates associated in the past with inflationary pressure (Diagram 3). There is therefore little danger of capacity constraints emerging in the near future. Moreover, though employment growth is expected to continue at a significant rate, the labour force is also projected to grow fairly strongly, so that the unemployment rate is not likely to decline much below its current level of around 7¼ per cent. Outside certain selected occupations, such as engineers, this should not imply demand pressure in the labour markets. Indeed, a sizeable segment of the manufacturing labour force laid off between 1974 and 1982 has not yet been rehired during this upswing. In such circumstances, gains made on the inflationary front over the past four years should be maintained.

The persistent strength of the dollar has played a major role in keeping imported commodity prices down and in exerting competitive pressures on export-oriented and import-competing industries – many of which tend to be highly unionized, such as auto, steel and machinery. However, wage moderation has not been confined to these sectors; it has been a feature of the manufacturing and service sectors alike (Table 12). Wage adjustments agreed under major private sector collective bargaining agreements signed in 1984 averaged 2.4 per cent – the lowest increase in the 17 year history of the series, while those signed during January-September 1985 averaged 2.9 per cent. For the private non-farm sector as a whole, hourly compensation in the third quarter of 1985 was only 4½ per cent higher than a year earlier. While compensation in the non-export sector might pick up somewhat and productivity growth diminish – to about 1 per cent per annum for the economy as a whole – the increase in unit labour costs should remain moderate, leading to inflation rates of 3½-4 per cent on current exchange rate assumptions (Table 13). Unlike 1984, however, profits are not expected to increase relative to labour income, and margins may be somewhat reduced under the projected price increases.

## B. Risks and imbalances

Monetary and fiscal conditions, together with good inflation performance, thus point to the continuation of the recovery after its recent pause. But account needs to be taken of possible risks and tensions in the forecast. These relate to:

i)  Developments in the household and corporate sectors;
ii)  The wedge which has emerged between domestic demand and GNP growth, because of the impact of the high dollar on export and import competing-industries. Certain sectors have not shared in the recovery and remain unusually vulnerable to an economic slowdown;
iii)  The problems of sustaining anti-inflation gains if the dollar should fall further.

### The debt position of the private sector

The surge in personal debt during 1983-84 has taken household financial liabilities to 82 per cent of personal income (Table 14). Greater debt repayments and interest burdens could therefore inhibit consumer spending. Consumer installment credit, in particular, has risen by nearly 2½ per cent of personal income since 1982. This has been well above the growth path of any other upswing since 1955, despite lower inflation and higher real interest rates. However, though total liabilities are significantly above the 1976-1982 average, so are household assets (Table 14). Household liquid assets have also increased relative to income, liquid net worth (liquid assets less credit liabilities) rising by 3 per cent of disposable income since 1982. Moreover, studies at the Federal Reserve Board have concluded that indebtedness

44

## Table 12. Negotiated wage settlements[1]

### I. AVERAGE EFFECTIVE WAGE ADJUSTMENTS IN 1984

In percent at annual rate

|  | For workers receiving a change[2] | For all workers (prorated) |
|---|---|---|
| All adjustments | 4.4 | 3.7 |
| From new settlements in 1984 | 3.0 | 0.7 |
| From deferred adjustments in previous settlements | 4.0 | 2.0 |
| From COLA adjustments | 2.7 | 0.9 |

### II. WAGE ADJUSTMENTS IN MAJOR COLLECTIVE BARGAINING SETTLEMENTS MADE IN 1984

Percent of workers affected

|  | First year adjustment | | | Over life of contract | | |
|---|---|---|---|---|---|---|
|  | All industries | Manu-facturing | Non-manu-facturing | All industries | Manu-facturing | Non-manu-facturing |
| A. All settlements (shares) | 100 | 100 | 100 | 100 | 100 | 100 |
| No wage increases | 17 | 13 | 20 | 12 | 7 | 15 |
| Decreases | 5 | 1 | 8 | 4 | 1 | 7 |
| Increases[3] | 77 | 86 | 72 | 84 | 93 | 78 |
| Under 2 per cent | 15 | 6 | 20 | 30 | 68 | 8 |
| 2-6 per cent | 48 | 77 | 32 | 44 | 22 | 56 |
| Over 6 per cent | 14 | 3 | 21 | 10 | 4 | 13 |
| B. Mean adjustment (per cent)[3] | 2.4 | 2.3 | 2.5 | 2.3 | 1.4 | 2.9 |
| Mean increase (per cent) | 3.8 | 2.7 | 4.5 | 3.1 | 1.6 | 4.2 |
| Mean decrease (per cent) | −9.6 | −10.9 | −9.6 | −6.2 | −4.1 | −6.3 |
| C. Number of workers (in millions) | 2.26 | 0.83 | 1.43 | 2.26 | 0.83 | 1.43 |

1. Settlements covering 1,000 workers or more. Average hourly earnings excluding overtime.
2. In 1984 6.2 million workers received wage changes averaging 4.4 per cent (which when prorated over 7.3 million workers covered by major agreements averaged 3.7 per cent). Of these, 2.5 million received COLA adjustments averaging 2.7 per cent (or 0.9 per cent when prorated over 7.3 million workers). Consequently, the sum of individual components do not equal "all adjustments" in this column.
3. Annual rate of adjustment.
4. Less than 0.5 per cent.
*Source:* U.S. Department of Labor.

## Table 13. Costs and prices

Percentage changes at annual rates

|  | 1984 | 1985 | 1986 | 1984 II | 1985 I | 1985 II | 1986 I | 1986 II |
|---|---|---|---|---|---|---|---|---|
| Hourly earnings[1] | 3.4 | 3.1 | 3.4 | 3.2 | 3.3 | 2.6 | 3.6 | 3.8 |
| Total compensation | 9.5 | 6.8 | 6.0 | 7.0 | 7.3 | 5.7 | 6.2 | 5.9 |
| Productivity | 2.6 | 0.5 | 1.0 | 1.2 | −0.5 | 1.7 | 0.9 | 0.7 |
| Unit labour costs | 2.5 | 4.3 | 3.2 | 3.3 | 5.6 | 2.8 | 3.4 | 3.2 |
| GNP deflator | 3.8 | 3.7 | 3.8 | 3.5 | 4.0 | 3.1 | 4.0 | 3.9 |
| Consumption deflator | 3.2 | 3.0 | 3.3 | 3.3 | 2.9 | 2.8 | 3.5 | 3.5 |
| Real disposable income | 6.5 | 1.8 | 1.8 | 4.0 | 1.5 | 0.4 | 2.4 | 2.0 |
| Personal savings ratio[2] | 6.3 | 4.2 | 3.9 | 6.4 | 4.9 | 3.4 | 4.0 | 3.8 |

1. Private non-farm, adjusted for overtime and sectoral shifts.
2. OECD National Accounts basis; as per cent of disposable incomes.
*Source:* Secretariat projections.

is probably not yet a serious problem, and the ratio of consumer installment debt to disposable income could rise further[60]. When adjusted for the "convenience" use of credit cards, the "debt burden" appears to be close to the 1976-1980 average[61]. Other special factors may have added further to the debt ratio: the average maturity on loans appears to have increased, perhaps adding $\frac{1}{4}$ point[62]; demographic factors – the relative increase in the younger age groups which use credit most – may have added a further $\frac{1}{2}$ point. Moreover, the growth of credit was supply constrained during 1980-1981 when ceilings on rates reduced the profits on consumer lending[63]. In earlier periods (1977-1978 for example), individuals seem to have used mortgage borrowing to finance consumption spending, but this has been less the case during the current upturn: total household debt (including mortgage liabilities) has increased slightly less than consumer debt (from 79 per cent of disposable income in 1982 to 81.7 per cent in 1984). These factors, together with the fact that the bulk of consumer borrowing has been accounted for by high income households[64], suggest that the household sector is not yet overburdened with debt. The growth of employment is thus likely to remain the chief influence on consumption, though the household savings ratio is likely to recover somewhat from its abnormally low third quarter level.

There may be more reasons to be worried about non-financial corporate sector debt. Despite higher pre-tax profits, lower tax rates and improved company cash flow, (which meant that company income exceeded capital expenditures in 1982-1983 (Diagram 12A and B), company financial positions have continued to deteriorate, judged by the traditional balance sheet yardsticks. The trend towards dependence on short-term debt, relative to long-term, has continued, the debt/equity ratio has worsened, and the ratio of liquid assets to short-term liabilities has fallen (Diagram 12C). These have all made for a corporate financial

Table 14.  **Household financial positions**

Percent of disposable income

|  | 1976-1980 | 1981 | 1982 | 1983 | 1984 | 1985 I |
|---|---|---|---|---|---|---|
| Saving |  |  |  |  |  |  |
| Personal saving ratio | 6.1 | 6.7 | 6.2 | 5.0 | 6.1 | 4.8 |
| Financial saving[1] | 2.3 | 4.4 | 5.1 | 2.7 | 3.2 | 1.6 |
| Outstandings, end of period[2] |  |  |  |  |  |  |
| Financial assets | 225.8 | 227.6 | 240.3 | 249.4 | 248.0* | 254.4* |
| Liquid assets[3] | 114.3 | 116.0 | 118.2 | 120.1 | 125.9* | 128.6* |
| Total liabilities | 77.8 | 79.4 | 79.5 | 81.4 | 83.5* | 86.3* |
| House mortgages | 50.0 | 49.6 | 49.0 | 49.4 | 50.6 | 51.7 |
| Total consumer credit | 22.0 | 19.6 | 19.7 | 20.3 | 22.3 | 23.4 |
| Consumer installment debt | 16.6 | 14.9 | 14.7 | 15.5 | 17.1 | 18.8 |
| ( – Adjusted for credit cards) | (16.3) | (14.3) | (14.1) | (14.7) | (16.2) | n.a. |
| *Memorandum Items:* |  |  |  |  |  |  |
| Financial net worth | 147.9 | 148.2 | 160.8 | 168.0 | 164.5* | 168.1* |
| Liquid net worth[3] | 39.4 | 38.4 | 41.7 | 42.4 | 45.6* | 45.8* |
| Household financial assets/liabilities[4] | 2.26 | 2.20 | 2.29 | 2.32 | 2.24* | 2.24* |

1. Saving *less* expenditure on owner-occupied housing, net of depreciation.
2. Households, personal trusts and non-profit organisations.
3. Liquid assets equal holdings of deposits and credit market instruments (except corporate equities). Liquid net worth equals liquid assets minus outstanding credit market liabilities.
4. Ratio of credit market instruments *plus* equities to credit market debts. This excludes life insurance and pension fund reserves.
*Sources:* Federal Reserve Board (*Flows of Funds and Federal Reserve Bulletin*, June 1985) and Secretariat estimates (*).

*Diagram 12.* **Company finances**

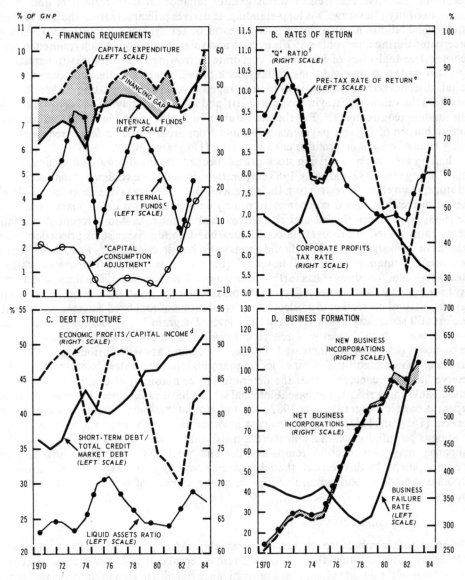

a) Financing gap = difference between capital investment and internal funds.
b) Internal finance = domestic undistributed profits, plus inventory valuation and capital consumption adjustments, plus capital consumption allowances and foreign earnings.
c) External finance = credit market funds, trade debt and direct foreign investment in the United States.
d) Capital income includes economic profits plus net interest paid.
e) Rate of return = corporate pre-tax profits plus interest, divided by the replacement cost of corporate capital (equipment, structures, land and inventories) at the start of the year.
f) Ratio of market value to asset replacement cost for non-financial corporations.
*Sources:* Congressional Budget Office; Council of Economic Advisors; Federal Reserve Board; Secretariat estimates.

structure which may be vulnerable both to short-run monetary conditions and to fluctuations in economic activity. The trend towards greater reliance on short-term debt and on debt relative to equity ("leverage") is long-standing. It derives principally from the bias in the tax system which allows nominal interest on loans to be set against corporation tax. This was exacerbated during much of the 1970s by high and volatile inflation, which resulted in zero or even negative real rates of interest on corporate borrowing. Since returns to capital were depressed by the same conditions, falling stock prices, relative to the replacement cost of capital, discouraged new stock issues, encouraged investment in existing rather than new assets (see the valuation ratio in Diagram 12B), and led to firms relying on borrowing to meet their funding requirements[65]. But the end result of higher company indebtedness has been a growing burden of interest payments being met from gross profits, a factor reflected in the falling ratio of economic profit to capital income (Diagram 12C)[66].

Falling inflation and a rising stock prices checked the trend towards debt finance for a while. During late 1982 and early 1983 corporations issued large volumes of long-term bonds and stock, in an effort to restructure their finances. But the process was short-lived[67]. Higher rates of interest dissuaded companies from relying on long-term credit markets and from late 1983, bond issues slowed and short-term debt again rose. More recently, the fall in interest rates has led to a recovery of bond issues, but despite a rise in stock prices debt/equity ratios have risen sharply, and the liquid assets ratio has deteriorated[68]. Part of the debt has been used to finance "leveraged buyouts" (borrowing to finance takeovers) which by substituting debt for equity[69] has further accentuated balance sheet distortions. These trends may have a positive dimension, reflecting the pursuit of greater rationalisation, insofar as they may be a natural correction to a selective undervaluation of real fixed assets – "the valuation ratio" is still some way below its early 1970 level (Diagram 12B). They may also reflect a re-evaluation of banks' asset preferences in favour of domestic lending at a time when the international debt problem increased the risks of lending abroad. Furthermore, short-term borrowing has avoided the danger of locking into high interest rates. However, the Federal Reserve has been concerned that the deteriorating composition of company liabilities has caused bankruptcy risks to increase. Financial strains have eased since the record number of corporate bond downgradings in 1982, but the rate of business failures has continued to increase (Diagram 12D). Though business incorporations also remain at a high level, the situation is potentially volatile, and there is a risk that in view of vulnerable balance sheets companies may over-react to temporary demand weakness by sharply curtailing their investment plans. In this respect, though financial crowding out may have been avoided by corporate short-term borrowing, this may be at the expense of storing up future financing troubles.

### Sectoral imbalances

Among other imbalances that could increase the risk of a marked economic slowdown or a reacceleration of inflation, the widening current external deficit is of particular concern, not only because of the danger of increased protectionism but also in view of its associated sectoral imbalances. The decline in agricultural income and the relatively poor performance of export and import-competing industries is indeed a potential source of instability. While the strong dollar has helped to contain inflationary pressures by depressing the prices of agricultural, petroleum, and other commodities, and by restraining wages and prices in import-competing industries, it has imposed heavy adjustment costs on some sectors. Moreover, the agricultural and energy sectors, in particular, have experienced severe financial problems, with ripple effects on certain other sectors, such as agri-business and banking (including thrift institutions) in the agricultural areas and commercial real estate in the energy-rich states. So

48

far, these problems have been largely contained with only minor spill-overs into other sectors. There is, however, a danger that an economic slowdown would exacerbate financial difficulties of distressed sectors. Many of the troubled areas have improved significantly with the recovery, but there are serious questions about whether they are as yet well prepared for an economic downturn. These problems have been exacerbated by swings in inflationary expectations, real interest rates, exchange rates and trade flows.

America's agriculture enjoyed strong export demand and relatively high domestic prices during most of the 1970s, against the background of a weak dollar and supply constraints abroad. However, the rise of the dollar over the last four years has reduced the international competitiveness of American agricultural products – many of which, as in many other countries, are artificially supported by domestic price support schemes. As foreign sales have fallen, domestic surpluses have risen and exerted downward pressure on domestic prices. US agricultural exports have plummeted in value terms over the past two and a half years as both volume and dollar prices have fallen. The adjustment from high to low inflation has also severely affected land values. Many farmers had gone heavily into debt in the late 1970s to buy "overvalued" land or machinery on the expectations that foreign demand for US agricultural goods would remain strong, that high inflation would continue and that negative real interest rates would prevail. They have therefore found it difficult to cope with depressed farm product prices, high debt service payments and operating expenses, in addition to declining land values. Little relief is in sight barring a substantial decline in the dollar or major crop failures in other parts of the world that would reduce the surplus stocks of farm products.

Similarly, the boom in commercial real estate in the energy-rich states came to an abrupt end with the softening of the oil market and the collapse of oil drilling activities, with the result that cities such as Houston, Dallas and Denver found themselves with excess office and residential space and unfinished projects. As a result, financial institutions that have large exposure in these areas stand the risk of large losses if the economy were to slow substantially. The problems of the thrift institutions and large international banks are somewhat similar. The thrift institutions have been experiencing problems with asset-liability mismatching since inflation began to accelerate twenty years ago. Their problem originated from the fact that during periods of low inflation, they extended low interest, fixed rate, long-term mortgages which they had to fund by acquiring short-term liabilities at current market rates of interest. Over the past twenty years various actions were taken to aid the thrifts, including deregulation of interest rates, adoption of variable rate mortgages, broadening of authorised lending activities into new fields, and merger of "bankrupt" banks with viable institutions. However, by moving to variable rate mortgages, thrift institutions increased their credit risks while reducing their interest rate risks, especially as the economy moved to a lower inflationary environment, and real estate value flattened out or even declined in some regions. Moreover, as a way to diversify their portfolio and improve their rates of return, some of the larger thrifts went into risky investments that are now experiencing payment problems, such as commercial real estate in the energy-rich states. The risks and problems associated with bank loan exposure to the developing countries – particularly Latin America – are also well known. The large international banks remain therefore highly vulnerable, and the experiences of Penn Square and Continental Illinois illustrate how fragile the situation can be.

*The dollar, inflation and interest rates*

Though a further depreciation of the dollar is necessary and desirable to restore competitiveness and reduce the current account deficit, this would be at the probable expense of upward pressure in the general price level. Econometric estimates indicate that a 10 per cent depreciation of the dollar exchange rate would raise the GNP implicit price deflator by 1 to 1.5 percentage points, with roughly two thirds of the increase due to the direct impact of higher import prices and one third to the indirect effect. Most of the inflation would occur within two years of the change in the exchange rate. However, since these estimates are based on the somewhat limited historical experience of floating exchange rates (i.e. since the early 1970s), there is a question of how valid they remain for the current situation, especially if a substantial fall in the dollar would restore union bargaining power in the manufacturing sector, which could have wide demonstration effects on other sectors as well. On balance, if the dollar were to decline by a further 20-25 per cent over the next year and a half, it would probably add 2-3 percentage points to the inflation rate in the first year. Under such a scenario, the GNP deflator would rise by around 6 per cent in 1986 instead of the projected 3½-4 per cent. In this case, it would probably have some short-term economic cost if the Federal Reserve sought to choke off any inflationary impulse by allowing interest rates to rise. This possibility is discussed more fully in Section IV below.

## IV. DEFICITS, DEBT AND MEDIUM-TERM IMBALANCES

### A. Budget deficits, interest rates and investment

Persistent large budget deficits pose a threat to the longer-term prospects for balanced growth. Three aspects of the situation are discussed in the following paragraphs; they relate to:

- The impact of government debt on interest rates;
- The build-up of interest payments, and its significance for medium-term stability;
- The effect of deficits on private interest-sensitive spending, allowing for the fact that cuts in marginal tax rates, and other factors affecting the cost of capital, may have offset high interest costs.

By running a current external deficit, and financing the domestic saving gap by capital imports, some of the expected adverse effects of the deficit on private spending have been avoided. But via its possible impact on the dollar, foreign interest rates and world saving, the federal deficit may also have had negative implications. In the next Section B the possible medium-term consequences of the current external deficit are discussed, in the context of the sustainability of capital imports and the implications for the exchange rate of the dollar.

*The Federal deficit and interest rates*

It would be a mistake to view high real interest rates in the United States as determined solely by the size of the federal budget deficit. Monetary stance, inflation expectations inherited from past price performance, and the greater after-tax profitability of investment arising from the 1981 tax reforms may all have contributed to higher interest rates[70]. Substantial controversy surrounds the conventional view that large federal deficits raise interest rates. The theoretical arguments that they do not do so are generally related to the proposition that government expenditure, if financed by borrowing, will necessitate higher future taxes to pay for the debt service. Since these will be anticipated by taxpayers, personal savings will rise and interest rates will remain unchanged. This view has not been validated by empirical studies of the consumption function. But it is probably true that a budget deficit will have different effects on demand depending on the type of spending it finances and on the tax structure (i.e. marginal tax rates) with which it is associated. It has been argued, for instance, that the improved savings incentives arising from ERTA, together with the extra wealth generated by greater industrial efficiency and faster economic growth, should have automatically increased funds available to finance the federal deficit, by stimulating personal saving. But the extent of this appears to have been over-estimated. As noted, despite the rapid economic recovery, the household saving ratio has not risen above its historical average and the structural deficiency of U.S. national savings has increased. This has been met by foreign saving.

More importantly, perhaps, the extent to which the deficit raises investment and/or consumption has to be taken into account in assessing its effect on interest rates. Productive investment generates a rate of return in the form of higher growth and tax revenue and should not in principle prompt offsetting "Ricardian" savings responses by consumers. In this respect, two factors are relevant to the U.S. situation. First, a proportion of the federal deficit has gone towards increasing company cash flow. This has probably helped keep companies off credit markets (the government effectively borrowing on behalf of companies). By offering tax depreciation allowances in excess of true economic depreciation (see the "capital consumption adjustment in Diagram 12A) tax cuts have reduced non-financial corporate borrowing needs by up to $30 billion (Annex 2). In 1983 it meant that all investment could be financed from internal sources (see Diagram 12). By raising stock holders' equity, and working capital, this has probably helped offset some of the "crowding out" effects stemming from higher interest rates. Secondly, the deficit has been associated with lower effective marginal corporate tax rates on borrowing. Improved after tax real rates of return have allowed firms to pay higher real interest rates. As more capital projects exceed a "threshold" rate of return, firms bid up interest rates to attract more savings, investment rises and the capital stock grows. Higher interest rates resulting from this mechanism do not have the adverse connotations associated with "crowding out".

Even if allowance is made for the benefits of the deficit to company cash flow, a significant proportion still seems to have been allocated to financing public consumption. However, this relates largely to defence spending (see above), which confers benefits on future as well as present generations. There is therefore little reason to suppose that present tax payers will be induced to save more (rather than to expect future tax payers to bear part of the burden through interest payments). If this is so, the deficit is likely to contribute to greater claims on national savings. However, establishing an empirical link between the federal deficit and interest rates has proved difficult. For instance, the Congressional Budget Office surveyed twenty-four studies on the subject and found that they differed widely in findings, neither outstanding government debt nor the deficit being consistently positive and/or significant in its relationship to interest rates[71]. More recently it has been recognised that it is important to allow for the effects of the business cycle and monetary policy on interest rates. Not doing so can lead to biased results. Private credit demands and government borrowing vary automatically, but inversely, with the cycle, so that budget deficit increases can be correlated with interest rate declines. Adjusting deficits and debt for their structural and cyclical components tends to generate links between fiscal variables and interest rates consistent with conventional views about deficits and pressures on savings[72]. Particularly interesting is the correlation, documented by the Bureau of Economic Analysis, between cyclically-adjusted federal debt and interest rates[73], which the Congressional Budget Office has found to be one of the most robust of research results in the area[74]. Indeed, as a general rule it can be said that studies which adjust for cyclical influences on the budget tend to find significant or quantitatively important effects on interest rates more consistently than those which estimate relationships between interest rates and unadjusted deficits or debt[75]. Even so, quantifying the contribution of the federal deficit to interest rates levels cannot be precise. Among the studies not subject to "simultaneity bias" criticism, the impact of a $100 billion budget deficit averages as much as 300 basis points. If this were the case, it would imply that up to one half of the 9 per cent real interest rate in 1984 could be associated with general government credit demands, but the margin of possible error is, as noted, potentially quite large[76].

If, in fact, U.S. interest rates have been raised by the budget deficit, this has implications for interest rates in the OECD area. The effect of higher U.S. interest rates on exchange rates may have caused other OECD economies to follow tighter monetary policies than they otherwise would have, while higher world demand for credit would have increased long-term interest rates directly[77]. Average long-term rates of interest in Europe have, in general, tracked United States interest rates very closely in nominal terms since 1979 (see Diagram 16 below). However, there is no reason to suppose that the U.S. government debt accumulation has any different effects on world interest rates than government debt accumulation elsewhere[78]. Although European interest rates seem to have moved in tandem with U.S. rates, the government indebtedness-interest rate connection, if it exists, should be valid for all countries, not just the United States. Despite budgetary restraint in Europe and Japan, debt/GDP ratios have risen faster in these countries than in the United States. It is therefore plausible that, in addition to the U.S. deficit, the causes of high (long-term) OECD interest rates are also to be found in domestic budgetary conditions elsewhere[79]. This is not to deny that the U.S. deficit has had an effect on world interest rates[80], but this needs to be seen in the context of budget trends – and government claims on saving – in the OECD at large[81].

### Medium-term debt accumulation, interest payments and inflation

Generally speaking, deficits can affect interest rates through interactions with monetary constraints (via the demand for money function), through competition for credit between government and private sector, and through growing portfolio imbalances as the stock of government bonds increases faster than other financial assets. All of these have real interest rate effects and may have been factors behind high U.S. rates. But government debt accumulation may also raise inflation expectations if it is so rapid as to generate fears that the process will become unstable and add to pressures for monetisation. It is then difficult to tell whether the interest rate response is one due to an excess supply of debt *per se* or to the perceived links between deficits and inflation risk. This risk derives from the level and rate of increase of public debt, the rate of interest paid on that debt (given the instability problems caused by the "roll over" of debt interest payments by new borrowing) and the attitude of the monetary authorities. In this respect the United States situation often seems more favourable than in the OECD as a whole (the existing ratio of government debt to GNP is lower and the credibility of monetary control greater, for instance); in other respects (e.g. the rate of interest paid on its debt relative to the underlying growth rate of the economy) it is no worse than elsewhere. Nevertheless, the prospective medium-term rate of growth of U.S. government debt, together with the possibility that rates of interest will stay above the economic growth rate for some time, may result in a persistent medium-term increase in the debt interest burden relative to GNP. The mechanisms are slow-working, but this latent disequilibrium could eventually lead to a recession or a resurgence of inflation.

The increase of 6 percentage points in the general government gross debt/GNP ratio since 1979 compares with an average increase of 13¼ percentage points in other OECD countries. It leaves the ratio currently at about 46 per cent of GNP, which is still some way below the average of 56 per cent for the rest of the OECD area (53 per cent for OECD Europe and 68 per cent for Japan) (Diagram 13). Federal Government debt held by the public (excluding Federal Reserve Banks) has risen significantly faster – from 22 to 32 per cent of GNP since 1979 (Diagram 14), but in relation to national wealth the comparison with the rest of the OECD remains favourable: in 1984, 9½ per cent of private financial wealth was comprised of government debt, compared with about a quarter in Japan, a third in Italy and as

*Diagram 13.* **General government indebtedness**

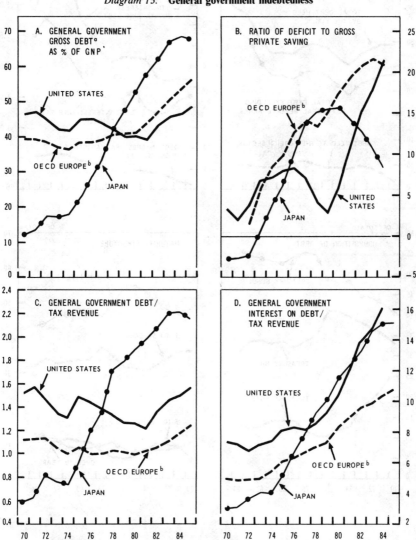

a) Debt outstanding at the end of the financial year.
b) GDP-weighted average of major four European countries.
*Source :* Secretariat estimates.

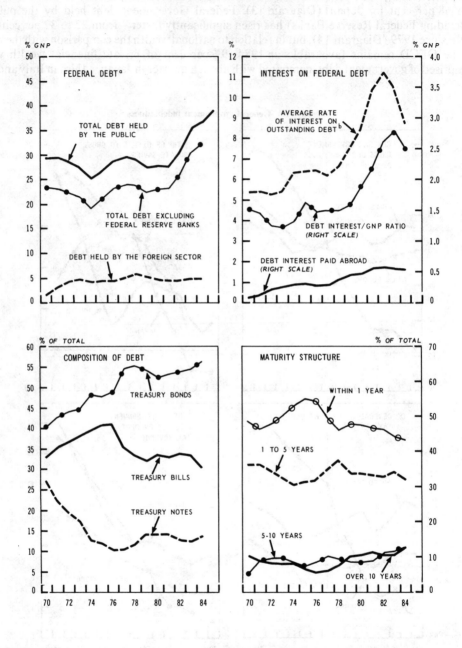

*Diagram 14.* **Federal debt**

**FEDERAL DEBT**[a]

TOTAL DEBT HELD BY THE PUBLIC

TOTAL DEBT EXCLUDING FEDERAL RESERVE BANKS

DEBT HELD BY THE FOREIGN SECTOR

**INTEREST ON FEDERAL DEBT**

AVERAGE RATE OF INTEREST ON OUTSTANDING DEBT[b]

DEBT INTEREST/GNP RATIO *(RIGHT SCALE)*

DEBT INTEREST PAID ABROAD *(RIGHT SCALE)*

**COMPOSITION OF DEBT**

TREASURY BONDS

TREASURY BILLS

TREASURY NOTES

**MATURITY STRUCTURE**

WITHIN 1 YEAR

1 TO 5 YEARS

5-10 YEARS

OVER 10 YEARS

*a)* Debt outstanding at the end of the financial year.
*b)* Interest paid on public debt excluding Federal Reserve holdings; calculated as $DI/[(D+D_{t-1})/2]$, where $DI =$ debt interest paid and $D$ is outstanding debt at the end of the financial year.
*Sources:* Office of Management and Budget ; Treasury and Secretariat estimates.

much as a half in the United Kingdom[82]. However, the general government gross debt interest/GNP ratio is very near to the OECD average (Table 5). And a greater problem emerges if the debt situation is seen in relation to existing tax revenue, or to domestic saving, which is relatively low (Diagram 13B and C), implying increased resort to foreign saving. Indeed, the United States is about to become a net external debtor (see paragraph 68 below). Furthermore, debt/GNP ratios are stabilizing (or falling) in Japan, Germany and the United Kingdom, while in the United States the ratio will continue to rise, perhaps taking interest payments beyond the threshold where compensating tax increases or spending cuts are politically acceptable. The situation is exacerbated by the high rate of interest on government debt (again a feature not confined to the United States), because this creates greater pressure to increase taxes if debt and deficits are not to rise indefinitely (Diagram 15)[83]. There is then a danger that expenditure and tax resistance will eventually lead to mounting pressures to monetise the debt.

The prospect of a persistently expanding debt burden has given budgetary retrenchment greater momentum in the past year, as the Administration and legislators have fought a holding action to prevent a continuing expansion of the federal deficit[84], especially in the face of upward pressure on interest rates through 1984. Higher interest rates can undermine attempts to control debt accumulation by "discretionary" spending cuts (see Section II on the sensitivity of debt to interest rates). However, if the proposed spending cuts are put into effect, the CB0 and the Administration see the debt/GNP ratio stabilizing by 1988, at just over 40 per cent of GNP declining thereafter as the federal deficit is scheduled to fall below 3 per cent of GNP; assuming 8 per cent nominal income growth, a deficit over 3 per cent would continue to raise the ratio[85]. (Under the Administration's "current service" (i.e. existing

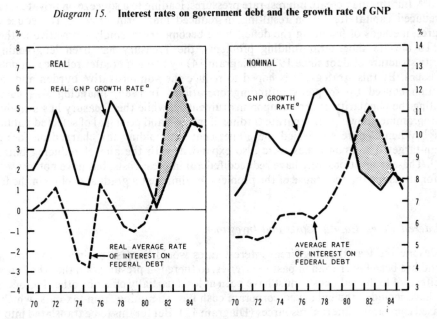

Diagram 15.   Interest rates on government debt and the growth rate of GNP

a)   Three year moving average of growth rate.
Source :   Secretariat estimates.

legislation) projection of 4 per cent deficits in 1990 the ratio would reach 54 per cent of GNP.) More pessimistic growth and interest rate assumptions would lower the target deficit/GNP ratio needed to stabilize the debt GDP burden and raise the eventual debt/GNP ceiling reached with a given deficit. The CBO has projected structural deficits of about 5 per cent of GNP on pre-Budget policies and foresaw the prospect of debt rising to 50 per cent of GNP by 1990 in the absence of deficit cuts (Table 15)[86]. Interest payments would then amount to nearly 4 per cent of GNP, compared with 3 per cent in 1985, and – on the assumptions adopted – would continue to rise for some time. This would imply the need to find a further 1 per cent of GNP in taxes and/or spending cuts in the next half-decade. But since the increase in debt would probably cause upward pressure on interest rates, the eventual debt service problem could be greater and any medium-term scenario based on budgetary inaction and constant interest rates may be unreliable. Substantial deficit reduction is thus essential. This is doubly so because fiscal policy – having been one of the forces behind the recovery up to now – will eventually become a drag on demand growth, because of the "stock" effects of persistent deficits on interest rates, and debt service payments. Persisting high real interest rates are likely to have increasingly detrimental effects on private spending. And even with 5 per cent deficits, the "primary structural deficit" (the deficit excluding rising interest payments) is bound to contract, reflecting slower growth of public services (Table 15).

With the risk that fiscal policy may work to reduce economic growth while sustaining high interest rates, avoiding excess monetary growth could become difficult[87]. Pressures to stabilize or reduce interest rates could grow, as interest costs become more and more of a burden and the temptation to finance government spending by money creation increases. So far, despite the more flexible approach to monetary aggregate control (Section II above), interest rate stability has not become a key central bank objective and in the short term the extent to which federal deficits are associated with monetary expansion will be strictly limited[88]. But this may create interest rate pressures, leading to a squeeze on private spending and reduced capital formation resulting in reduced long-term growth. To reduce these pressures, methods of financing the deficit have become increasingly innovative in the past year. To obviate short-term funding problems, the Treasury has been lengthening the maturity structure of debt since 1976 (Diagram 14) by placing greater reliance on note and bond issues. By this strategy, it is hoped to reduce the administrative burden and market disruption caused by frequent refunding operations. In 1984, financing was eased by exploiting the popularity of zero-coupon instruments[89], while the Treasury has introduced a new programme allowing for separate trading of interest and principal of selected public debt issues[90]. When Congress repealed the 30 per cent withholding tax charged on foreigners, 'foreign-targeted' coupon issues were also expanded, with the aim of reducing borrowing costs[91]. These innovations may have reduced federal interest costs, but have not lessened the need for attacking the root cause of the problem by aiming at a gradual decline in the federal deficit.

### Interest Rates, Capital Costs and Investment

Despite the fear that high real interest rates would depress business investment, the rebound has been faster than in past recoveries, so there is a presumption that the "crowding out" effects of high credit costs must have been at least partially offset by other factors. These could have included the enhanced corporate cash flow stemming from tax cuts, which have increased companies' internal resources (Diagram 12). But for this to be translated into much higher capital investment, marginal rates of return – i.e. the after-tax profitability of new asset purchases – would have had to rise also. This would have occurred if tax legislation had

Table 15. **Federal debt and the primary deficit**

FY 1986 budget

| Fiscal year | Publicly-held federal debt | Primary deficit[1] | Interest payments on debt[2] | Total deficit | Implied tax rate change[3] (cumulative) |
|---|---|---|---|---|---|
| | | % of GNP; Unified budget basis | | | |
| 1979 | 27.3 | 0.2 | 1.5 | 1.7 | — |
| 1980 | 27.8 | 1.3 | 1.6 | 2.9 | — |
| 1981 | 27.5 | 0.8 | 1.9 | 2.7 | — |
| 1982 | 30.5 | 1.9 | 2.3 | 4.2 | — |
| 1983 | 35.4 | 4.2 | 2.3 | 6.5 | — |
| 1984 | 36.7 | 2.5 | 2.7 | 5.2 | — |
| 1985 | 39.6 | 2.6 | 3.0 | 5.6 | 0.2 |

| | Budget[4] resolution | CBO budget baseline[4] | | | |
|---|---|---|---|---|---|
| 1986 | 41.1 | 41.8 | 2.1 | 3.1 | 5.2 | 0.3 |
| 1987 | 41.7 | 44.0 | 1.9 | 3.3 | 5.2 | 0.5 |
| 1988 | 41.6 | 46.0 | 1.7 | 3.5 | 5.1 | 0.6 |
| 1989 | 41.1 | 47.9 | 1.6 | 3.6 | 5.2 | 0.8 |
| 1990 | 40.2 | 49.7 | 1.5 | 3.8 | 5.3 | 0.9 |
| Ceiling[5] | 29.2 | 73.0 | −0.4 | 5.7 | 5.25 | 2.5 |

1. The primary deficit is the total federal deficit (on- and off-Budget) *less* net interest payments, adjusted for Federal Reserve payments to the Treasury.
2. Net interest payments *less* Federal Reserve payments to the Treasury.
3. Cumulative increase in interest payments from 1985 on, net of an assumed tax clawback of 15 per cent. This measures the *net-of tax* increase in interest payments by the government.
4. The Budget resolution and baseline deficit projections are as described in Table 8; they include off-budget outlays proposed to be on-budget.
5. Equilibrium level to which the federal debt/GNP ratio and interest payments would rise (or fall) if the deficit/GNP ratio stabilized at its level in 1990 (5¼ per cent of GNP in the baseline projection, 2.1 percent in the Budget resolution scenario). Nominal GNP growth is projected at 7¼ per cent a year, with a 7¾ per cent cent average rate of interest on debt.
*Source:* Congressional Budget Office, *1985 Annual Report*, p. 91 and *Budget Update*, p. 64; OMB, *FY 1986 Budget*; Secretariat calculations.

lowered the "user cost" (or rental price) of capital (see Annex 2). This measures the marginal cost of investment funds after allowing for credit costs, inflation expectations, depreciation of the buildings and equipment purchased, and the marginal tax rates shown in Diagram 7D. Estimates of the effects of recent tax changes on user costs vary with the the type of asset involved and the interest rate and inflation assumptions used, but according to recent estimates the tax reforms seem to have reduced the cost of investment in structures by nearly 15 per cent and of all assets by just under 5 per cent[92].

Table 16 examines the present value of the depreciation allowances and investment tax credit (per dollar of investment) applying to capital expenditure on equipment, under the pre- and post-tax reform systems. As a point of reference, it may be noted that if the tax system leaves the after-tax return of a dollar of investment equal to the pre-tax return, the tax system can be said to be 'neutral' or non-distortionary; and if real interest costs are deductible, this would be the case if depreciation allowances and other credits exactly offset true "economic" depreciation[93]. Technically, this occurs if the present value of investment allowances is equal to the statutory marginal rate of corporation tax (which would give an effective marginal tax rate of zero). Since in the U.S. case the statutory tax rate is 46 per cent, any value of allowances over 46 cents per dollar of investment thus acts as a subsidy, reducing the cost of capital below what it would be if no corporate tax was imposed. The Table shows that the combined effect of tax legislation and lower inflation has apparently been to move the tax system nearer to neutrality (i.e. towards an average tax allowance of $0.46), and that tax

Table 16. **Investment incentives 1980 and 1984**

Equipment[1]

A. PRESENT VALUE OF DEPRECIATION ALLOWANCES

$ per $ of investment

| Real interest rate | Tax law | Inflation rate | |
| --- | --- | --- | --- |
| | | 4 % | 10 % |
| 1 per cent | PRE-ERTA[2] | 0.495 | 0.436 |
| | ERTA | 0.516 | 0.472 |
| | TEFRA | 0.495 | 0.454 |
| 7 per cent | PRE-ERTA[2] | 0.435 | 0.390 |
| | ERTA | 0.471 | 0.434 |
| | TEFRA | 0.452 | 0.418 |

B. CHANGE IN PRESENT VALUE OF DEPRECIATION ALLOWANCES 1980-1984[3]

| Due to change in inflation | Real rates of interest | Tax law | Total |
| --- | --- | --- | --- |
| + 0.059 | − 0.060 | 0.017 | 0.016 |

1. Five year property.
2. Assumes depreciation over 9.5 years using double declining balance switching to sum of years digits.
3. Taking 4 percent inflation and 7 percent real interest rates as typical of post-TEFRA conditions and 10 percent inflation with 1 percent real interest rates as representing pre-ERTA conditions, the change from an allowance of $ 0.436 to $ 0.452 can be decomposed into three factors:
   a gain of $ 0.495 - $ 0.436 due to the effect of 6 per cent lower inflation (measured under the pre-ERTA regime);
   a loss of $ 0.435 - $ 0.495 due to the effect of 6 per cent higher real interest rates; and
   a gain of $ 0.452 - $ 0.435 due to the impact of tax legislation (measured at a real discount rate of 7 percent and an inflation rate of 4 percent).
   It should be noted that the value of the tax concessions vary significantly with the inflation and interest rate assumptions made.
*Source: Economic Report of the President,* February 1983.

changes *per se* have reduced the cost of capital by the relatively small proportion of 3 per cent, measured at 7 per cent real interest rates and 4 per cent inflation. However, the combined effect of lower inflation and tax reform may have just exceeded the effect of higher real interest rates on the cost of capital since 1980. The effects of improved tax incentives could thus have been enough to offset about half of any potential interest rate crowding out, even in the case where one half of the 6 per cent real interest rate increase were attributable to the budget deficit.

Within the overall picture of falling user costs, however, producer's durable equipment, non-residential structures and owner-occupied housing have fared differently. The user costs for both non-residential structures and owner-occupied housing have broadly followed movements in the interest rate, reaching peak levels by recent historical standards in 1981. Despite some decline since then, they have remained at high levels. By contrast, the user cost for equipment has been affected only slightly by movements in interest rates. It rose very little despite the sharp rise in interest rates in 1978-1981, and has since declined to a relatively low level by historical standards. There are two explanations for these differences.

- The user costs for structures and housing are more sensitive to changes in interest rates than is the case for equipment[94];
- The user cost for equipment has benefited from the slow growth in prices of producers' equipment relative to the prices of structures and prices in general.

58

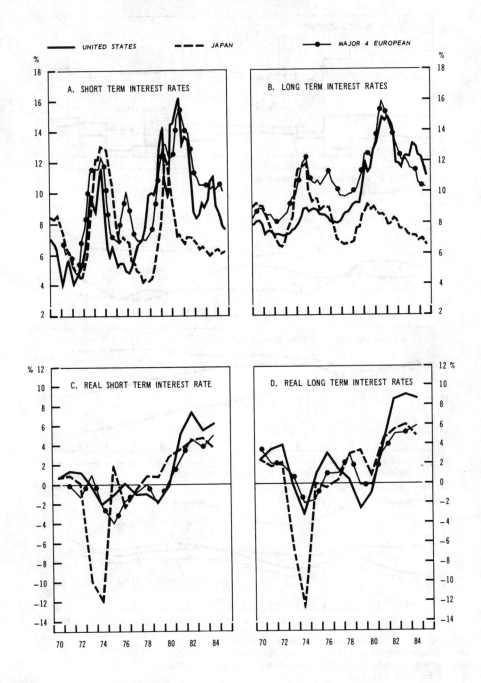

*Diagram 16.* **Interest rates in the OECD area**

UNITED STATES — JAPAN — MAJOR 4 EUROPEAN

A. SHORT TERM INTEREST RATES

B. LONG TERM INTEREST RATES

C. REAL SHORT TERM INTEREST RATE

D. REAL LONG TERM INTEREST RATES

*Source :* Secretariat estimates.

59

*Diagram 17.* **Investment, profits and the relative price of capital goods**

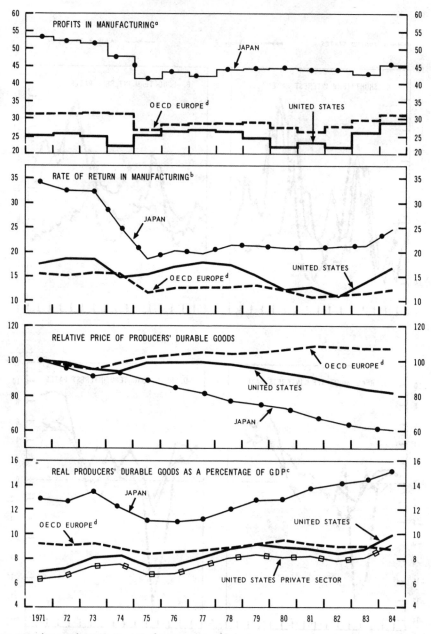

a) Gross operating surplus as a percent of gross value added.
b) Gross operating surplus as a percent of the capital stock.
c) All equipment expenditures, including purchases by the government.
d) Major 4 European countries.

*Sources: OECD Economic Outlook 37,* Secretariat estimates and Department of Commerce (Bureau of Economic Analysis).

60

While the impact of ERTA/TEFRA business tax cuts was proportionally bigger in the case of buildings, the sharp 1981 rise in nominal interest rates had a proportionally larger offsetting impact on the discounted value of higher tax allowances compared to investment in machinery. The personal tax provisions of ERTA/TEFRA also acted to increase the user cost of owner-occupied housing (by reducing the tax value of interest deductions). These differences may help explain why business fixed investment has been strongest in producers' durable equipment. In this sector higher interest rates have been more than neutralized by falling relative prices of capital goods[95], tax changes and lower inflation, while investment in industrial structures has been less strong partly because the relevant user cost has more fully reflected interest rates. Similarly, the rate of growth of housing investment, though relatively strong because of demographic factors, has not been as dynamic as in some past cycles. To the extent that interest rates have been raised by the budget deficit, some investment in structures and in housing may thus have been crowded out (though the main burden of crowding out thus far has fallen on export and import-competing industries). Moreover, if real interest rate were to rise further, non-residential structures and housing may be more likely to be crowded out than equipment because their user costs rise more sharply in response to an increase in interest rates.

The fact that the recovery has been stronger in the United States than in Europe may thus be partially explained by tax factors. Though average nominal long-term rates of interest in Europe have been very similar to those in the United States since 1979, real rates have been lower and the relative strength of the private spending upturn has been weaker (Diagrams 16 and 17). Though many factors (budgetary stance for instance) may have contributed to this difference, high real interest rates seem to have had a more depressing effect on activity in Europe than in the United States. It is difficult to determine the role of the corporate tax system in this. But the fact that rates of return have recently recovered faster in the United States than in Europe, must be related to removal of the former bias against investment (which kept the investment GNP ratio artificially low in the 1970s) (Diagram 17). Moreover, changes in the relative price of capital equipment have been much more favourable in the United States than in Europe (because of the strong dollar). However, the relative impact of high real interest rates also depends on the extent to which individuals can deduct interest payments on debts acquired to finance consumption from their taxable income. Most European countries allow tax deductibility of interest payments on capital spending (including house purchase) but most of the major OECD economies do not allow, as the United States does, interest costs of consumption to be offset against taxes[96]. This means that if capital flows equalise gross interest rates internationally, European consumers (and sometimes house purchasers, where mortgage costs are allowable only up to a ceiling) may have suffered more in terms of net credit costs than those in the United States. This also applies to sovereign borrowers in the third world (as well as such OECD governments which have resorted to overseas borrowing) who have to pay the full rate of interest without possibility of tax offset.

## B. The dollar and the sustainability of the external deficit

As discussed earlier, some of the major imbalances are to be found in the external sector – the unprecedented current account deficit, the massive capital inflows and the high dollar. The question arises whether such an imbalanced situation is sustainable and whether – in addition to the danger of rising protectionism – it involves substantial, potential risks for the domestic economy. While a sharp reversal of the dollar in the near future cannot be excluded with any certainty, it might be better to assess the sustainability of the external deficit and the exchange rate of the dollar in a medium-term context. Some of the relevant mechanisms are slow-working, and given the margin of error attaching to this kind of analysis, the best that can be achieved is to identify forces casting doubts on the stability of the present situation without being able to determine with any confidence when and how a break might take place.

In its simplest formulation, the sustainability issue can be considered in terms of whether projected current account deficits will be matched by roughly equivalent intended *(ex ante)* capital inflows at around the present exchange rate of the dollar. The shift towards net capital inflows has been accompanied by a deterioration of the current account and a strong appreciation of the dollar. This suggests that intended capital inflows – which cannot be measured – have been larger than the current account deficits and the net inflows that have actually taken place. In fact, intended capital flows have been the driving force, causing large variations in real exchange rates and forcing current account positions to adjust. Before this episode, the normal chain of causation – for developed countries, at least – was considered to run from the current account to capital flows and the exchange rate. It is particularly difficult to form a view on whether the new situation will persist or not. The reasons for the strength of the dollar over the last four years are indeed not fully understood. Many observers have associated the strength of the dollar mainly to high U.S. interest rates (nominal and real), themselves seen as being linked to the policy mix – large Federal budget deficits combined with a non-accommodating monetary policy. Others have attributed the strength of the currency to the inherent attractiveness of U.S. and dollar assets, a view supported, in addition to "safe haven" considerations, by the recent good performance of the U.S. economy in respect of real growth and inflation. Even if these factors were not to change substantially, it might be wondered whether this would be sufficient to generate growing intended inflows in line with the projected deterioration of the current external account. Even a continuation of the current account deficit in the range of $150 billion a year involves the question of whether wealth holders around the world would be willing to continue acquiring U.S. assets at that rate without a marked shift in portfolio preference against the dollar.

A disaggregated analysis of the flows which so far have financed the current account deficit provides no convincing answer to these questions (Tables 17 and 18). For various

Table 17. **External debt position**

Billions of dollars

| | U.S. current account balance | Balance of payments statistical discrepancy | Net international assets[1] | U.S. assets abroad | Foreign assets in the United States | | | Net investment income |
|---|---|---|---|---|---|---|---|---|
| | | | | | Total | U.S. government securities (privately held) | Corporate bonds and stocks | |
| 1976 | 4.2 | 10.5 | 83.6 | 347.2 | 263.6 | 7.0 | 54.9 | 16.0 |
| 1977 | − 14.5 | − 2.0 | 72.7 | 379.1 | 306.4 | 17.6 | 51.2 | 18.0 |
| 1978 | − 15.4 | 12.5 | 76.1 | 447.8 | 371.7 | 8.9 | 53.6 | 20.6 |
| 1979 | − 1.0 | 25.4 | 94.5 | 510.6 | 416.1 | 14.2 | 58.6 | 31.2 |
| 1980 | 1.9 | 25.0 | 106.1 | 606.9 | 500.8 | 16.1 | 74.1 | 30.4 |
| 1981 | 6.3 | 22.3 | 143.1 | 719.6 | 576.5 | 18.5 | 75.4 | 34.1 |
| 1982 | − 9.2 | 32.9 | 149.5 | 838.1 | 688.6 | 25.8 | 93.6 | 27.8 |
| 1983 | − 41.6 | 9.3 | 106.0 | 887.5 | 781.5 | 33.9 | 114.6 | 23.5 |
| 1984 | − 101.6 | 30.0 | 4.0 | 908.6 | 904.5 | .. | .. | 18.1 |
| 1985[1] | − 128.0 | 0 | − 124.0 | .. | .. | .. | .. | .. |
| 1986[1] | − 146.0 | 0 | − 270.0 | .. | .. | .. | .. | .. |

1. Data for 1985 through 1986 based on OECD estimates and projections of the current account balance.
*Source:* U.S. Department of Commerce, Bureau of Economic Analysis; OECD estimates.

Table 18. **Capital account of the balance of payments**

$ billion

| | Levels | | | | | Changes | | |
|---|---|---|---|---|---|---|---|---|
| | 1980 | 1981 | 1982 | 1983 | 1984 | 1982 | 1983 | 1984 |
| **Gross flows** | | | | | | | | |
| Gross outflows of U.S. capital[1] ( − ) | −78.0 | −105.8 | −113.9 | −48.3 | −18.0 | −8.1 | 65.6 | 30.4 |
| Long-term | −28.0 | −20.4 | −9.4 | −17.6 | −16.2 | 11.0 | −8.2 | 1.4 |
| Direct investment | −19.2 | −9.6 | 4.8 | −4.9 | −6.0 | 14.4 | −9.7 | −1.1 |
| Others | −8.8 | −10.8 | −14.2 | −12.7 | −10.2 | −3.4 | 1.5 | 2.5 |
| Short-term | −3.2 | −1.2 | 6.6 | −5.3 | 5.6 | 7.8 | −11.9 | 10.9 |
| Banks | −46.8 | −84.2 | −111.1 | −25.4 | −7.3 | −26.9 | 85.7 | 18.1 |
| Gross inflows of foreign capital[2] ( + ) | 44.2 | 77.0 | 92.6 | 75.6 | 88.2 | 15.6 | −17.0 | 12.5 |
| Long-term | 26.2 | 32.5 | 23.0 | 22.5 | 53.4 | −9.5 | −0.5 | 30.9 |
| Direct investment | 16.9 | 23.1 | 14.9 | 11.3 | 21.2 | −8.2 | −3.6 | 9.9 |
| Others | 9.3 | 9.4 | 8.1 | 11.2 | 32.2 | −1.3 | 3.1 | 21.0 |
| Short-term | 7.3 | 2.4 | 3.7 | 4.0 | 7.1 | 1.3 | 0.3 | 3.1 |
| Banks | 10.7 | 42.1 | 65.9 | 49.1 | 27.6 | 23.8 | −16.8 | −21.5 |
| Total recorded capital | −33.8 | −28.8 | −21.3 | 27.3 | 70.2 | 7.5 | 48.6 | 42.9 |
| **Net flows** | | | | | | | | |
| Long-term capital | −1.7 | 12.0 | 13.5 | 4.9 | 37.2 | 1.5 | −8.6 | 32.3 |
| Foreign direct investment | −2.3 | 13.5 | 19.7 | 6.4 | 15.2 | 6.2 | −13.3 | 8.8 |
| Others | 0.6 | −1.5 | −6.1 | −1.5 | 22.0 | −4.6 | 4.6 | 23.5 |
| Short-term capital | 4.1 | 1.2 | 10.3 | −1.3 | 12.7 | 9.1 | −11.6 | 14.0 |
| Errors and omissions | 25.0 | 22.3 | 32.9 | 9.3 | 30.0 | 10.6 | −23.6 | 20.7 |
| Banking flows | −36.1 | −42.0 | −45.1 | 23.7 | 20.3 | −3.1 | 68.8 | −3.4 |
| Total capital | −8.7 | −6.5 | 11.6 | 36.6 | 100.2 | 18.1 | 25.0 | 63.6 |

1. Transactions in U.S. assets abroad, excluding official reserve assets.
2. Transactions in foreign assets in the United States, excluding transactions of monetary authorities.
*Note:* Detail may not add due to rounding.
*Source:* Department of Commerce, Bureau of Economic Analysis.

reasons – including the fungibility of money, the large "errors and omissions" item in U.S. balance-of-payments statistics and the world current account discrepancy – the final use and ultimate source of these funds cannot be determined with any precision, and the interpretation of the data which do exist is fraught with difficulties[97]. Nevertheless, it may be noted that the most important single item accounting for the swing of the U.S. capital account from small deficits in 1980 and 1981 to a surplus of $100 billion in 1984 has been net banking flows. These have essentially reflected the near-cessation of the accumulation of foreign assets by U.S. banks (from an average of some $65 billion to less than $10 billion). Hence, the counterpart of the growing current account deficit so far has been more a drying-up of outflows of U.S. funds than an acceleration of inflows of foreign funds[98]. These developments may be taken as an indication that future improvements in the capital account may have to be accounted for by changes in other flows. While this seems plausible it does not necessarily imply that it will be more difficult to achieve. U.S. banks' own claims on foreigners were some $400 billion at end-1984, about half of which were vis-à-vis Latin American and Caribbean countries. Because of the debt problem, it might be difficult to reduce substantially these outstanding claims. Only $100 billion were vis-à-vis European countries. Under certain conditions some reduction could be envisaged here but the magnitude of these figures suggest that from now on, the bulk of any further increase in net inflows should probably result from stepped-up inflows of foreign funds – through U.S. banks or other channels – rather than from a new slow-down, or actual repatriation, of U.S. funds. The elimination of the U.S. with-holding tax on certain types of interest paid to foreigners in mid-1984 contributed to a doubling of net foreign purchases of U.S. Treasury securities (to $20 billion for the year as a whole): large amounts of foreign funds could continue to be invested in these securities. More important perhaps, the size and sophistication of the Eurodollar and Eurobond markets provide a nearly unlimited pool of funds for U.S. banks and corporations to tap if conditions are right – that is, if the constellation of interest differentials, growth and inflation prospects and confidence in the dollar relative to other currencies justifies such borrowing.

While a disaggregated analysis of past flows is largely inconclusive, the interaction between financial flows and stocks provides a slow-working but powerful destabilizing mechanism. The counterpart of the current account deficits and net inflows of the last few years has been a major deterioration of the international investment position of the United States – from a net creditor position of $150 billion at end-1982, to virtual balance at end-1984. Moreover, the United States is expected to become a net debtor country – for the first time since the first World War – sometime this year and to see its position deteriorate further in coming years[99]. Apart from a possible psychological impact on intended capital movements, the main implication of this change should be for investment income and the current account. As a large net creditor, the United States used to have its current account position strengthened by substantial net income on investment. If the country in fact becomes a large net debtor as projected, income on investment will progressively decline and eventually become negative, adversely affecting the current account position. But a large deficit will accelerate the deterioration of the investment position and the growth of net interest payments to foreigners. Hence, large current account deficits feed on themselves: to be stabilized, their trade and non-factor services components have to improve continuously to offset the progressive deterioration of investment income associated with the worsening international investment position. For example, by 1986, the U.S. current account may have deteriorated by some $25 billion because of changes in net investment income associated with the cumulated current account deficits since 1982. A continuation until say 1990 of the U.S. deficit on its present scale of some 2½ to 3 per cent of GNP would imply a net U.S. debtor position of the order of $700-800 billion or 10-15 per cent of GNP. Assuming an effective interest rate of 8½ per cent this would require a surplus on trade and non-factor services of around 1 per cent of GNP merely to cover interest charges, even if the current account then returned to balance. These simple, hypothetical examples illustrate the danger of allowing the international investment position to move too far into debt. If this were to happen as a result of persisting trade deficits, correction of this flow imbalance may not be sufficient. To prevent the debtor position from getting worse – and possibly to improve it – the trade imbalance may eventually have to be "over-corrected". The longer the adjustment is delayed, the larger the trade surplus that will have to be recorded on a sustained basis.

So far the emphasis has been on the financial side. But in the longer-run, the sustainability question is likely to hinge on developments in the real sector of the economy. In theory, as long as the rate of return on U.S. capital exceeds the real rate of interest paid to foreigners, extra production will more than match interest payments – provided of course that net inflows (and the real resources acquired through the current account deficit) translate into real investment, rather than consumption. However, even if resources were available, exports would not materialise if competitive conditions were not appropriate – and downward pressure on the exchange rate could develop. Hence, the two crucial questions are whether the additional real resources provided by the current account deficit do translate into productive investment, and whether the competitive position is sufficient to allow additional net exports in the future to match interest payments on today's net capital inflows. As noted above, according to one view, the root cause of the U.S. external deficit is the strength of the economy and an increase in the expected rate of return on physical capital which has resulted in an excess of ex-ante investment over savings. This has translated into high real interest rates relative to other OECD countries and, through intended capital flows, has caused the dollar to appreciate and the U.S. current account to move into large deficit. According to this view, the sharp movements in real exchange rates of the last few years away from positions of broad purchasing power parity are the mechanism through which excess savings in countries with relatively low returns on capital are channelled to the United States, thereby assuring an optimum allocation of world savings and welfare maximisation. In this model, sustainability is not a major issue since the United States will produce an additional stream of output at least matching interest payments on the related foreign debt. And the dollar may decline progressively, as real rates of return are equalised across countries. This view may have some validity as an explanation of developments over the last couple of years. But the rise in U.S. interest rates and the appreciation of the dollar started in late 1980, long before the surge in real investment. This is probably why many observers have linked the early strength of the dollar to the change in policy mix. To the extent that high real interest rates have been due to the policy mix, notably the large budget deficit, as well as to other factors, the role played by the exchange rate and the transfer of excess savings to the United States are more likely to have financed additional government spending, private consumption and non-productive investment (housebuilding), rather than productive investment. Moreover, while the current account deficit is expected to widen further, the investment boom may already be tapering off, so that even if the situation was basically sustainable up to now, it might no longer be so in the future[100].

These doubts seem largely confirmed by available figures and projections. Over the four years to 1986, the United States is expected to record a cumulative current account deficit of over $400 billion, compared to a position of rough balance in 1981-1982. Net business fixed investment over this period may be of the same order of magnitude representing an increase of only some $125 billion compared to the extrapolated cumulated level of 1981-82 ($304 billion)[101]. It might of course be claimed that without the deterioration of the current external account, investment would have been even lower than the 1981-1982 average, but the gap

Table 19. **Domestic and foreign saving**

% GNP

| | 1973 | 1974 | 1975 | 1976 | 1977 | 1978 | 1979 | 1980 | 1981 | 1982 | 1983 | 1984 |
|---|---|---|---|---|---|---|---|---|---|---|---|---|
| Domestic saving | | | | | | | | | | | | |
| Net private saving | 5.2 | 4.9 | 6.5 | 4.8 | 4.0 | 4.1 | 3.6 | 3.8 | 4.8 | 4.7 | 4.1 | 5.4 |
| Government saving | 0.6 | −0.3 | −4.1 | −2.1 | −0.9 | 0 | 0.6 | −1.2 | −0.9 | −3.8 | −4.1 | −3.4 |
| Total net saving | 5.8 | 4.6 | 2.4 | 2.7 | 3.1 | 4.1 | 4.2 | 2.6 | 3.9 | 0.9 | 0 | 2.0 |
| Net foreign saving | −0.5 | −0.3 | −1.2 | −0.3 | 0.7 | 0.7 | 0.1 | 0.2 | 0.1 | −0.2 | −1.1 | −2.6 |
| Net domestic non-residential investment | | | | | | | | | | | | |
| Nominal | 5.3 | 4.5 | 1.5 | 2.7 | 3.9 | 4.7 | 4.3 | 2.5 | 3.9 | 1.1 | 1.1 | 4.3 |
| Real | 5.4 | 4.4 | 1.4 | 2.5 | 3.7 | 4.4 | 4.1 | 2.4 | 3.8 | 1.1 | 1.1 | 4.7 |
| *Memorandum item:* | | | | | | | | | | | | |
| Real business fixed investment (gross) | 10.8 | 10.9 | 9.7 | 9.7 | 10.2 | 11.0 | 11.5 | 11.3 | 11.4 | 11.3 | 11.1 | 12.5 |

*Source:* OECD Secretariat calculations.

Table 20. **Imports by general type**

| | Imports 1984 $ billion | % change over 1982 | % share of change |
|---|---|---|---|
| Machinery and transport equipment | 123.1 | 62.6 | 54.9 |
| Manufactured goods | 94.4 | 46.0 | 34.5 |
| Mineral fuels, etc. | 63.3 | −6.4 | −5.1 |
| Food and live animals | 19.4 | 23.5 | 4.3 |
| Chemicals etc. | 14.4 | 45.5 | 5.2 |
| Crude materials, inedible | 11.9 | 27.7 | 3.0 |
| Other | 14.7 | 23.2 | 3.2 |
| Total | 341.2 | 33.9 | 100.0 |

*Source:* Department of Commerce, Bureau of Economic Analysis.

between the cumulated changes in the external position and investment is rather large and may be expected to widen in the future. Looking at actual developments only, flows-of-funds data also show that changes in the current external position have been significantly larger than changes in investment. From 1979 to 1984, net investment remained broadly unchanged at 4¼ per cent of GNP, whereas the current account position deteriorated by around 2½ per cent of GNP. Its counterpart was a decline in domestic savings, as taxes were cut and the budget deficit increased. As for real net investment, at 4½ per cent of GNP, it was somewhat higher in 1984 than in 1979: but a similar ratio at the 1978 and 1974 peaks was associated with a real net export surplus of about 2 per cent of GNP, rather than an external deficit of nearly 1 per cent of GNP as in 1984. Hence, practically all the deterioration of the real current external position from 1978 (or 1974) to 1984 – some 2½ to 3 per cent of GNP – had as a counterpart a decrease in domestic savings. The rather negative implications of these figures must be somewhat qualified in view of the unusual buoyancy of gross fixed investment until very recently. To the extent that it has embodied better technology and has resulted in higher productivity, replaced capital – like import-related additions to the stock of net capital – will generate extra output and possibly reduce the competitive disadvantage of U.S. exports at present levels of the dollar.

If a major correction of the U.S. external position were deemed necessary – because of the above considerations or for other reasons – a sizeable, albeit gradual depreciation of the dollar would logically be called for. This would have a large, permanent impact on the current account only if it were accompanied by appropriate expenditure reducing policies to make room for increased net exports. The counterpart to any external balance improvement has to be an increase in total domestic saving, including reductions in the budget deficit. For the U.S., a risk, given the rate at which foreigners are currently acquiring dollar-denominated claims, is that an abrupt and discontinuous shift in asset preferences might lead to an excessive and too precipitous decline in the dollar, thus creating upward pressure on U.S. prices. If the monetary authority did not accommodate this pressure by permitting a more rapid expansion of the money stock, interest rates could rise, possibly offsetting the expansionary effects of depreciation on domestic output or even causing absolute declines in activity in the short run, both in the United States and abroad. In a more extreme case, the monetary authority could conceivably be confronted with a marked loss of confidence in the dollar, to which it might find it necessary to respond by inducing a sharp increase in interest rates with the attendant risk of significant financial dislocation. Furthermore, with the U.S. becoming a net debtor, changes in capital flows and in exchange market conditions could become more important considerations for the monetary authority. The recent Group of Five agreement, however, has probably significantly reduced the possibility of such a pessimistic scenario resulting from a delayed correction followed by a collapse of the dollar.

The existence of large, potentially destabilizing external imbalances among major industrial countries, together with growing protectionist pressures, was part of the background of the agreement on policy intentions of the Ministers of Finance and Central Bank Governors of the Group of Five countries in late September. The lasting impact of the agreement on the market remains to be seen. Nevertheless, co-ordinated official intervention, in the context of changes in economic performance and policies to promote convergence, could have a useful role to play in assuring an orderly return of the dollar and other major currencies to levels which better reflect fundamental economic conditions.

# V. ECONOMIC DEREGULATION:
## TRANSPORTATION AND COMMUNICATIONS

This chapter of the Survey deals with efficiency issues in several industries that have undergone substantial regulatory decontrol in recent years: air transportation, surface transportation (railroads, trucking, busing) and telecommunications. Following a brief historical Survey of the regulatory environment in the U.S., the motivation and extent of deregulation are examined. Post-deregulation developments are then analysed using the contestable market theory as a broad framework of reference. The concluding paragraphs try to draw together the main lessons from the U.S. experience on deregulation.

## A. The motives and extent of deregulation

In both transportation and communications, the U.S. regulatory institutions were established during the latter quarter of the 19th and first third of the 20th century. The premise was that without regulatory control of entry, destructive competition in these industries would ensue. The limiting of entry, however, conferred monopoly pricing power, which was controlled by regulating price as well. Initially, the railroads accepted regulation to ensure stability and orderly growth, while the agricultural interests actively sought regulation to protect them from monopolistic exploitation by the railroads. However, technological change lowered the costs of some services and brought new modes into being, thereby complicating the task of regulation. In transportation, the regulatory net spread from railroads into structurally competitive sectors such as trucking. In communications, cross-subsidy became the rule as political (rather than economic) forces distributed the benefits of technological change. Over the past twenty-five years or so, economic studies began to reveal inefficiencies imposed by regulation and to undermine the natural monopoly argument for regulation; and the government eventually became convinced that its own intervention had contributed to inflation and inefficiency. It also began to be recognised that the regulatory agency was an inadequate forum in which to decide if there was a market for new technology, especially as new firms began to clamour for permission to enter when technological change made such entry feasible. In addition, it was evident that regulation had reduced the motivation for companies to keep costs under control or to be responsive to consumer demands. Reforms began in communications as early as the 1950s and gradually spread to the transportation sector, reaching a peak in the late 1970s and early 1980s. In the communications sector, reform took the form of government intervention through divestiture – the break-up of American Telephone and Telegraph (AT&T) – as well as deregulation. In contrast, in air transportation, economic deregulation meant virtual elimination of government intervention, through removal of governmental control of routes and fares. In transportation, Congress and the Commissions played the major reforming roles; in communications, it was the Justice Department, the Courts, and the Commission that undertook the significant deregulatory steps.

This section begins by reviewing the regulatory policies of the Civil Aeronautics Board (CAB), the growing evidence for reform, and the nature and extent of deregulation in the airlines. CAB entry policies established boundaries between types of carriers: trunk airlines served major markets; local carriers provided subsidized service within regions and gathered feeder traffic for the trunk lines; commuter airlines with small aircraft served the thinnest markets without rate or route regulation; supplemental carriers provided charter services; and a few carriers provided jet services wholly within state boundaries. The rates and routes of the intra-state airlines were not subject to CAB regulation, whereas the fares for CAB-regulated trunk and local service carriers were determined according to a set formula. The early impetus for deregulation was provided by studies comparing costs and fares in the regulated trunk lines with those in the unregulated intra-state carriers. Analyses by economists showed that fares were nearly fifty per cent lower in these non-regulated state services than in the regulated trunk lines and, moreover, that these large intra-state carriers were generally profitable even with the lower fares[102]. Other studies[103] argued that lack of CAB jurisdiction over investment in aircraft and frequency of flight, along with a regulatory price formula in which the excess of prices above costs tended to be greater the longer the haul, had produced uneconomically low load factors (percentage of seats filled) on long haul flights. Still other analyses[104] found that scale economies did not exist to a significant degree in the airline industry. Thus, when administrative deregulation at the CAB began in 1976, and when Congress passed the Airline Deregulation Act in 1978, a scheme of total deregulation was adopted. Route authority was to be phased out on 31st December 1981, and fare regulation one year later. The remaining tasks, involving international negotiations and small community service, shifted to the Department of Transportation on 1st January 1985, at which time the CAB ceased operations.

Deregulatory measures in surface transportation have not been as pervasive as those in the airlines. The jurisdiction of the Interstate Commerce Commission (ICC) over railroads began in the last quarter of the 19th century, and that over trucks and buses began with the Motor Carrier Act of 1935. Regulatory control of trucking took the form of certificates describing the commodities permitted to be hauled and the specific routes along which each commodity could be carried. Unlike those in aviation, these ICC-granted certificates could be bought and sold. Railroad rates were strictly controlled, and fares for manufactured goods were set high relative to those for bulk and agricultural commodities. Yet, costs of delivering manufactured goods were not much different for rail than for truck, which allowed trucks to draw this profitable business away from the railroads (see Table 21)[105]. Thus, over time, the high-rate, high-margin traffic of the railroads eroded; and the low-margin traffic remained. Return on rail investment averaged a mere 2.42 per cent between 1962 and 1978, contributing to low investment, inadequate maintenance and deteriorating service. Bankruptcy of the Penn Central focused interest on the plight of railroads[106], and in 1976 the Railroad Revitalisation and Regulatory Reform Act (the 4R Act) was passed. In 1980, Congress passed the Staggers Act for railroads and the Motor Carrier Act for trucking. The two pieces of railroad legislation codified the view that competitive spheres (where railroads and trucks could compete effectively) and market-dominated spheres (where railroad had a clear advantage over trucks,

Table 21. **Comparative transportation cost estimates**

### A. URBAN PASSENGER[1]

| | Passengers/hour | | |
| --- | --- | --- | --- |
| | 1 000 | 10 000 | 30 000 |
| Cost per passenger (1972 dollars) | | | |
| Auto | $ 4.15 | $ 4.15 | $ 4.15 |
| Rail BART | $ 26.85 | $ 5.63 | $ 3.73 |
| Bus | $ 4.46 | $ 2.98 | $ 2.50 |

### B. SURFACE FREIGHT[2]

| | Manufactured commodities | | Bulk commodities | |
| --- | --- | --- | --- | --- |
| | Official region | Southwest region | Official region | Southwest region |
| Marginal cost (1972 cents/ton-mile) | | | | |
| Rail | 4.892 | 2.925 | 1.931 | 0.981 |
| Motor carrier | 4.922 | 4.602 | 4.169 | 3.972 |

### C. INTERCITY PASSENGER[3]

| | Boston-New York | Chicago-Los Angeles |
| --- | --- | --- |
| City pair costs (1968 dollars) | | |
| Rail | $ 6.90 - $ 9.50 | $ 44.00 - $ 110.00 |
| Bus | $ 8.40 | $ 54.60 |
| Auto | $ 13.60 | $ 132.00 |
| Plane | $ 15.00 | $ 60.00 |

1. Estimates are full costs (including value of time) for six-mile line-haul work trip, assuming 12 per cent discount rate, $ 3.00/hr. value of time, and optimizing service quality.
2. Estimates are marginal costs for each commodity-shipping region pair evaluated at actual 1972 output levels of motor carriers of specialised commodities and Class I railroads. Costs for official region comprise New England, the Mid-Atlantic States, and the East-Central States.
3. Rail, bus, and plane costs are based on cost per passenger mile, auto costs are based on cost per vehicle mile. Rail costs vary due to different assumptions regarding seating plans.
*Source:* See Winston (1985) *op. cit.* p. 66.

such as in coal transportation) coexisted. Rate regulation and price intervention was to be maintained only in those captive markets where effective competition was missing, such as coal transport. Pressures to deregulate trucking also stemmed in part from studies which indicated that decontrol policies would result in efficiency gains and lower prices[107]. The U.S. trucking reform liberalised entry policies by shifting the burden of proof to opponents to show that entry of new firms would be harmful to consumers. The Act did not eliminate antitrust immunity for collective rate-making, although it did grant a zone of rate freedom. Reform of the interstate bus industry, passed in the Bus Regulatory Reform Act of 1982, paralleled that of trucking deregulation and reform[108]. Thus, the surface transportation legislation was permissive, but it was not nearly as deregulatory as the legislation that had been passed for the air transport industry in 1978.

The purpose of regulating telecommunications was to make high quality service available to everyone in the country at reasonable prices. Regulation of AT&T's long-distance services by the Federal Communications Commission (FCC) began in 1934, but state regulation of intra-state services continued. With interstate services connecting through the local exchanges, and with new technology greatly reducing long-distance costs, state regulators sought to allocate more of the local phone costs to long-distance calls[109]. The resulting cross-subsidy is suggested in Diagram 18. Subsequently, new technical possibilities in telecommunications, such as microwave and satellite, lessened the natural monopoly aspect of long-distance lines[110]. Bit by bit the FCC moved in the direction of permitting new entry, and the courts went even further. For example, beginning in 1959 with its "Above 890" decision, the FCC gave firms the right to use microwave transmissions for private lines, i.e., telephone services not involving any connection with the local Bell exchange. In 1969 it allowed Microwave Communications, Inc. (MCI) to build limited microwave facilities connecting Chicago, St. Louis, and nine intermediate points. The D.C. Circuit Court, in the 1977-1978 "Execunet Rulings", went beyond the FCC decisions, by extending freedom of entry and allowing direct competition with AT&T on long-distance service[111]. However, the most important deregulatory move in telecommunications came with the antitrust suit against AT&T by the U.S. Department of Justice which was filed in 1974 and settled in early 1982. As part of the settlement, AT&T agreed to divest itself of the local portions of its twenty-two Bell operating companies, which were restructured into seven separate regulated monopolies. These seven new operating firms were permitted to buy terminal equipment from any source

Diagram 18. Cross-subsidy issue in telecommunications: local and long distance

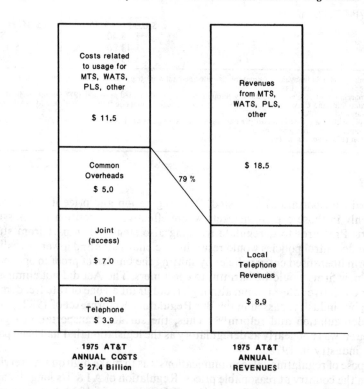

*Source:* Breyer (1982) taken from an AT&T. Embedded Direct Cost Study.

70

they chose (not just AT&T), and (after a modification of the decree) they were allowed to market (but not manufacture) the equipment as well. AT&T can continue to provide long-distance service and to manufacture terminal equipment, but customers can choose any long-distance carrier they wish. This choice is enhanced by the equal access provisions of the decree, which require that all long-distance companies get (by 1986) the same connection to local networks as that afforded to AT&T. In return, the government has removed the restrictions limiting AT&T to provision of common carrier services, and has permitted AT&T to enter the information systems area.

The philosophy of deregulation offers the view that the government should seek policies that promote contests for markets. According to the contestable market theory[112], neither large size nor few number of firms necessarily means that markets will function poorly. Impediments to entry and exit rather than degree of concentration or scale of operations may be the primary source of interference with market efficiency (in the sense of promoting cost-minimising industry structures). While neither transportation nor communication markets are likely to be perfectly contestable, the contestability benchmark provides a useful framework for evaluating deregulatory policies and outcomes in these sectors. For example, regulatory policies tend to support cross-subsidisation; deregulation should, if the industries have elements of contestability, lead to a dramatic lessening of the cross-subsidy. Similarly, regulatory policies tend to encourage a high price/high service product; deregulation should, if lower price/lower service options are viable, lead to the creation of a larger selection of products at different prices. Regulatory policies draw artificial boundaries that interfere with the scope of a firm's operations and lack incentives for firms to operate efficiently; deregulation should, if the industries display the properties of contestability, provide enormous pressure to improve productivity.

## B. Consequences of deregulation

Significant technological, productivity and cost developments have occurred in the transportation and communication industries since deregulation. However, these cannot be entirely attributed to the decontrol movement. The transportation sector has had to adjust to rapid increases in cost (most notably from fuel prices), the firing of the air traffic controllers, and a prolonged recession. Precise quantitative measures attributing differences to one cause or another are nearly impossible to provide. Therefore, much of the analysis focuses on qualitative issues, such as whether the industry's performance displays an increase in efficiency and competition and whether changes are consistent with the contestability benchmark. The communications sector is even more difficult to assess, since divestiture occurred only a little over one year ago. However, the qualitative issues can be touched upon and some insight offered on productivity and efficiency issues. For both sectors, four sets of issues are considered: productivity improvements in labour and delivery systems; increases in the diversity of price-service options; adjustment of prices toward incremental costs; and transitions in market structure and profitability.

### Delivery system productivity

Generally, all modes of transportation are characterized by economies of vehicle size (see Annex 3). These economies derive from the more efficient use of labour and fuel associated with larger vehicles. Although buses and trucks display significant vehicle size economies, because of particular labour practices and vehicle dynamics increasing returns to scale are greater for aircraft and trains. In aviation, economies of aircraft size have meant that only in the most dense markets can more than two carriers provide competitive city-pair services economically. A significant productivity gain from airline deregulation has resulted from a move away from linear railroad-like routes and toward sunbursts of routes emanating from various hubs. By combining passengers with different origins and destinations, a carrier can increase the average number of passengers per flight and thereby reduce costs by allowing the airline to take advantage of the aircrafts' economies of scale. In 1978 none of the regulated airlines had 20 per cent of their domestic departures out of their lead city; by 1983, most of them had achieved this level of concentration.

In trucking a significant hub-and-spoke type of route structure has also evolved after the elimination of vehicle routing restrictions. Less-than-truckload (LTL) shipments from several originating points are consolidated at major terminal hubs, reshuffled among trucks, and sent out to their various destinations. In addition, there are strong economies to be gained by developing joint distribution networks and by centralizing repair, administrative and other services. Firms benefitting from these economies cannot raise prices much above their costs without losing business to enterprises on nearby routes that can fairly readily extend their operations.

The railroad industry, like the aviation industry, was subject to corporate balkanization[113] under regulation. There was no railroad with an integrated national route structure, and hubs such as Chicago were often congested. Moreover, a basic linearity was inherent in rail transport because of the fixed railroad tracks. It has been argued that coordination with other types of transport might serve the same purpose in rail that hubbing had served in aviation, and the ICC has begun to encourage such activities by easing restrictions on intermodal ownership[114].

The effects of divestiture on communications are just beginning to emerge. Unlike transportation, which had been prevented by regulatory fiat from achieving efficient delivery systems, the telephone system had been able to coordinate operations through an integrated network[115]. For example, AT&T commonly routed calls during busy periods through distant switching centers if nearer ones were operating at full capacity. Not surprisingly, there has been some transitional upheaval in the delivery systems since divestiture. As part of the break-up agreement, the local operating companies are required to provide equal connection convenience, i.e. "equal access", to all carriers[116]. The FCC is trying to equalise the competition between AT&T and the smaller long-distance carriers by playing handicapper during the transitional period. Because AT&T has better access, it must pay the local telephone exchange a premium, which means that in February 1985, AT&T's access cost was nearly double that paid by the smaller carriers. A second transitional problem arises because of continued efforts by the FCC to charge access fees on a usage sensitive basis (per minute) rather than on a non-usage sensitive basis, which has resulted in large users moving to supply their own services, "bypassing" the local exchanges in order to internalize the benefits of their lower costs (See Annex 3). In this case, the issue is whether the effort to bypass is economic or uneconomic; that is, whether the half-regulated, half-free regime is encouraging bypass that is more costly in terms of real resources, yet in which a company pays less than it would under the regulatory regime of cross-subsidy.

### Labour costs and employment

In addition to route flexibility, adjustments in labour costs and work rules have played a major role in improving productivity in the post-reform era. There is evidence that regulation allowed workers, particularly Teamster union members, to earn from 30 to 45 per cent more than employees in unregulated trucking[117]. Truck owners also benefitted significantly from regulation. Thus, both the Teamsters and the American Trucking Association were outspoken

Table 22. **Indexes of real freight rates and average compensation**

| Sample | Size | 1975 | 1976 | 1977 | 1978 | 1979 | 1980 | 1981 | 1982 |
|---|---|---|---|---|---|---|---|---|---|
| | | | | Rates paid by shippers | | | | | |
| TL | 35 | 100 | 100 | 100 | 99 | 95 | 88 | 81 | 75 |
| LTL | 30 | 100 | 103 | 105 | 104 | 101 | 98 | 91 | 89 |
| Rail | 23 | 100 | 102 | 96 | 102 | 101 | 100 | 90 | 93 |
| | | | | Average compensation | | | | | |
| All employees | | 100 | 94 | 103 | 96 | 94 | 93 | 87 | 89 |
| Drivers and helpers | | | | | | | | | |
| Mileage basis | | 100 | 117 | 124 | 109 | 105 | 105 | 106 | 100 |
| Hourly basis | | 100 | 88 | 114 | 92 | 92 | 92 | 92 | 90 |

*Source:* Moore (1985), *op. cit.*

against reform, and it was only after successful deregulation in the aviation industry that the pressures to reduce surface freight regulation proved successful. Indeed, reform efforts in both 1962 and 1971 in trucking were blocked because of Teamster union opposition. A recent analysis of the effect of deregulation indicates labour costs have fallen about 14 per cent for all workers since 1977 (Table 22)[118]. Despite the price pressures, employment in trucking has remained fairly constant since deregulation (with 473 073 employed in 1977 and 475 700 in 1983).

In contrast, the number of railroad employees reached a peak of 501 390 in 1977 and then declined steadily to 317 119 in 1983, a drop of 37 per cent[119]. Yet, burdensome protective provisions and work rules still plague the rail industry. Two recent examples dramatise the issue. A few years ago, backers of Europe's Orient Express considered running a luxury train through the scenic mountains between Denver and San Francisco, but were deterred by union work rules requiring trains to stop every 150 miles to change crews. The second example involves Amtrak's passenger rail service which costs roughly $35 per passenger in federal subsidy, for a total of some $716 million in 1984[120]. In order to reduce the need for federal assistance, Amtrak recently considered dropping all service except that in the heavily travelled Northeast Corridor. Amtrak estimated that such a move would reduce its subsidy needs from $650 million in 1985 to $250 million, but its labour protection costs for workers laid off outside the Corridor would run about $400 million during the first year alone, leaving its total shortfall unchanged[121].

Similar findings about inflated costs under regulation have recently been documented for aviation[122]. Table 23 compares the cost of serving a 200-mile market with a B-737 aircraft for United (a trunk), Piedmont (a local service carrier) and Southwest (a former intra-state carrier). United's average cost per passenger of $58 is more than double Southwest's at $24. Some of Southwest's cost advantage lies in passenger-specific items, such as its simplified reservation and ticketing system. It does not issue composite tickets for interconnecting flights and it limits the number of fares so it can use preprinted tickets; it also uses cash register receipts as boarding passes and it does not provide food service. However, part of Southwest's cost advantage derives from the higher productivity of its employees. Differences in work rules, for example, are substantial[123].

As was the case with trucking, wages in the airline industry appear to be substantially higher than elsewhere in the economy, even for jobs where no special industry-related skills

Table 23. **Comparison of airline costs for serving 200-mile markets**[1]

In dollars

| Cost category | Southwest | Piedmont | | United | |
|---|---|---|---|---|---|
| | | Actual | Adjusted | Actual | Adjusted |
| Flight crew | 130 | 251 | 251 | 460 | 307 |
| Aircraft fuel, loading fees and aircraft servicing | 1 215 | 1 469 | 1 374 | 1 683 | 1 359 |
| Cabin crew | 70 | 86 | 72 | 149 | 124 |
| Passenger specific costs | 349 | 927 | 1 122 | 989 | 1 171 |
| Overhead (excluding aircraft) | 136 | 134 | 144 | 332 | 338 |
| Fully allocated costs | 1 900 | 2 867 | 2 963 | 3 613 | 3 298 |
| Seats per aircraft | 118 | 110 | 118 | 103 | 118 |
| Load factor (%) | 67 | 56 | 67 | 60 | 67 |
| Fully allocated costs per passenger | 24 | 47 | 37 | 58 | 42 |

1. Adjusted costs assume crew complements, landing fees, load factors, and seats are the same for United and Piedmont as are observed for Southwest. Data are for twelve months ending June 30, 1981 and for a B-737 aircraft.
*Source:* CAB, "Domestic Fare Structure Costing Programme, Version 6, update".

are required[124]. While the regulated airlines benefitted from enormous productivity gains relative to most other industries, they also experienced very large relative increases in wage rates. This rise in relative wages is not fully explained by differences in skills in airlines relative to other industries, but at least in part it seems to reflect the airline workers' success in the pre-deregulation era of capturing a share of the industry's productivity gains[125].

In the post-deregulation environment the major airlines have sought to renegotiate their labour contracts in response to the competitive pressures resulting from the rapid growth of low-cost carriers, such as People Express and Southwest, and from the greater competition in general among all airlines. Recent agreements include the easing of restrictive work rules, the ability to hire part-time workers, the institution of two-tier wage structures (under which the newly employed workers are paid substantially less than those hired before the contract), and in some cases the granting of equity positions to labour[126]. Overall, employee productivity in airlines has risen dramatically since the end of 1981, from about 175 available ton miles per full-time employee in mid-1979 to 210 by mid-1984. Yet, average employee productivity for Southwest and People Express is still more than three times greater than for the major carriers. This suggests that a substantial disparity in labour costs between the formerly regulated carriers and the new entrants will persist for some time. While employment at the large airlines dropped 10 per cent since the peak in 1980, growth in the smaller carriers has been sufficiently strong to offset most of the decline so that employment in the industry as a whole decreased only slightly from 334 216 in 1979 to 313 777 in 1984.

Just as in transportation, the wave of competition in communications following divestiture and deregulation has led to a hard look at labour costs, productivity, and employment levels. This was especially true for AT&T. Table 24 shows that AT&T reduced its labour force by roughly 6 per cent in the two years after divestiture was announced. The regional operating companies also cut their work force by 25 per cent, with many of the workers moving to the competitive sector[127]. Management was not the only group affected; so were the Communications Workers of America (CWA), the labour union which traditionally represented most communications workers. Before deregulation, it was easier for AT&T to pass along higher labour costs to consumers, much as was done in the regulated transportation sector. But the deregulated environment has provided strong incentives to introduce efficient

Table 24. **Employment reductions after AT&T divestiture**

| January 1982 breakup announced | Number of employees | January 1984 breakup takes effect | Number of employees |
|---|---|---|---|
| AT&T corporate headquarters | 13 302 | AT&T corporate headquarters | 2 000 |
| Long Lines (interstate long distance) | 42 834 | AT&T Communications (interstate | |
| AT&T International | 530 | and some intrastate long distance) | 120 000 |
| Bell Labs | 24 000 | AT&T International | 900 |
| Western Electric | 159 862 | Bell Labs | 19 000 |
| 22 operating companies | 798 000 | Western Electric[1] | 135 000 |
| | | 7 independant regional | 580 000 |
| | | Central Services Organisation | |
| | | (research and systems engineering | |
| | | group owned by the 7 regionals) | 8 800 |
| | | AT&T Information Systems | |
| | | (unregulated subsidiary formed | |
| | | January 1, 1983 with 28 000 people) | 110 000 |
| Total | 1 038 528 | Total | 975 700 |

1. Western Electric is now called AT&T Technologies.
*Source:* AT&T estimates, as reported in Business Week, September 26, 1983.

pay scales and work rules. According to certain estimates, the labour cost for installation and maintenance of products and equipment, including salary, benefits and overhead, was $61 per hour for AT&T in early 1984. For other regulated entities such as General Telephone and Electronics and Western Union the rate was $53 and $49, respectively. For non-regulated competitor IBM, it was $33, almost 50 per cent lower than for AT&T; and for new competitor MCI, it was only $28[128]. These pay differences are similar in magnitude to those discussed in aviation. Clearly AT&T is far from competitive in this labour dimension. The lessons on labour productivity are thus clear. First, labour was a major beneficiary of regulation. Second, non-union labour gained employment and gradually replaced union labour as new entrants appeared in the post-deregulation period. Third, the adjustment process of labour contract renegotiation for the regulated-era companies has been slow and fraught with difficulty, but competitive pressures are ensuring that it takes place.

### Diversity in price-service options and cost-based pricing

A third cluster of issues that are important in the post-deregulation period centers around pricing and service. In trucking, the first signs of the effectiveness of entry decontrol were the loss in value of operating authorities (ICC-granted transport certificates which could be bought and sold) and the growth in the number of carriers[129]. Not only has the number of new carriers risen but the existing firms have been granted increased authority, adding substantially to competitive price pressure. Price data displayed in the top half of Table 22 indicate that freight charges paid by shippers declined significantly in the post-reform period. Real rates for truck-load (TL) shipments decreased steadily from an index of 100 in 1975 to one of 75 in 1982. Less-than-truck-load (LTL) charges went from an index of 100 in 1975, to 105 in 1977, down to 89 in 1982. Thus, the increased entry into the TL business, relative to that into LTLs, meant that real rates for TLs have decreased more dramatically than LTLs. Significantly, these price declines (25 per cent for TL and 11 per cent for LTL) occurred during a period when fuel costs for the industry more than doubled.

In comparison, rail rates did not start to decline until 1979 and have fallen only 7 per cent, far less than in trucking. Nevertheless, railroads did reduce charges in many cases and

Table 25. **Index of rail carloadings**

| Traffic | 1978 = 100 | | | | | | |
|---|---|---|---|---|---|---|---|
| | 1978 | 1979 | 1980 | 1981 | 1982 | 1983 | 1984 |
| Fruit | 100 | 104 | 136 | 196 | 232 | 260 | — |
| Vegetables | 100 | 92 | 140 | 203 | 232 | 192 | — |
| Coal | 100 | 119 | 129 | 130 | 127 | 118 | 134 |
| Grain | 100 | 107 | 117 | 101 | 94 | 103 | 106 |
| TOFC[1] | 100 | 101 | 90 | 95 | 105 | 127 | 146 |

1. Trailer on flat car.
*Source:* Moore (1985), *op. cit.*

increased traffic as well. Perhaps more significantly, railroads substantially increased their transportation of non-bulk commodities, where they previously had a cost disadvantage because of regulated fares. Table 25 displays indices of rail carloadings for various types of traffic in the post-reform period. Rail more than doubled its shipment of fruit and vegetables after May 1979, when it was allowed to offer rates based on costs (rather than rates aimed at cross-subsidy). Similarly, its carriage of trailer-on-flat-car went up by one-half, whereas, its haulage of grain remained fairly constant. Thus, the relative cost advantages of the different modes of transportation began to exert themselves in the post-reform period. Where rail had a cost advantage that was not permitted to be reflected in pre-deregulation prices, rail service went up. Where the cost advantage was adequately reflected in pre-reform rates, such as in the carriage of bulk commodities, it maintained its traffic.

The Staggers Act set a new precedent by authorising railroads to negotiate prices with shippers rather than charging fixed, regulated rates. At the end of 1983, some 13 000 negotiated contracts had been filed with the ICC, covering practically every commodity[130]. Many are for bulk commodities, such as chemicals and minerals, on which the shippers now pay reduced rates. Negotiated contracts are also used to attract traffic from other modes[131] and they now account for more than 25 per cent of the operating revenues of the major railroads. In trucking a significant trend toward use of negotiated rates is also evident, stemming in part from the elimination of the tariff-filing requirement for contract carriage. According to recent surveys, shippers report that carriers are much more willing to negotiate rates and services than before deregulation. Moreover, various innovative price and service options are arising. For example, in the household goods moving industry, several carriers are now offering binding-estimates and guaranteed service dates, and shippers are being given more insurance options than were offered before the Motor Carrier Act became law[132].

Busing has also exhibited innovative pricing and servicing practices since deregulation. For nearly two decades before passage of the 1982 Act, bus fares pretty much followed inflation and fuel prices but there was little flexibility to reflect shifting demand or changing costs for different types of services. Perhaps, the Act's largest effect on tariff setting will result from a provision that enables the ICC to override state commission rulings on intra-state fares. Unrealistically low state-regulated rates, which have been a problem in bus as in air cargo and telecommunications, may now be set aside by the ICC. While deregulation is leading to some service cutbacks and some price increases, it is also enabling bus companies to respond to consumer demands for new services. For example, some bus firms offer convenient connections to airports where low-fare carriers operate. Peak and offpeak fare differentials have emerged in Florida and Arizona, where intra-state service was deregulated two years before the Bus Reform Act was passed. Similar pricing patterns are beginning to evolve in interstate service as well[133].

In aviation, fares began to be deregulated in 1977. The supersaver fare which was introduced on an experimental basis between New York and the West Coast in April 1977 marked the beginning of discount pricing. The supersaver fares featured deep discounts to travellers willing to purchase tickets well in advance. This two-tier pricing allowed airlines to improve efficiency by shifting discretionary travellers to off-peak hours through the use of a capacity-control feature that makes more seats available on such flights. Also, the low fares stimulated traffic and thereby increased the average load factor and aircraft size that could efficiently serve a market. The trunk carriers preferred this option to that of offering separate flights for the two markets: i.e. scheduled service at regular coach fares and charter service at substantially reduced prices. When used intelligently, the discount fare lowers the cost of providing service to the full-fare as well as discount-fare passengers. The use of discount fares were extended to most major routes as it soon became apparent that they could not be limited to a few flights, because passengers became adept at backhauling to the cities that offered the more attractive price options.

Airlines are increasingly using fare flexibility to provide quality-price options that match market demands. Under regulation, load factors not only were too low but they also varied inversely with distance (see Diagram 19). One piece of evidence indicating that service is now more in line with the efficient deployment of airline equipment is that, after deregulation, average load factors tended to be higher and to increase with distance, as predicted by theory. Indeed, post-reform load factors have improved by nearly 30 percentage points on the longer hauls[134]. It is interesting that while efficiency has thereby risen, service has also improved by greater frequency of flight after deregulation. This is a surprise since increased frequency reduces average load factors, ceteris paribus. According to certain estimates[135] there has been a route-weighted average rise in frequencies of 9.2 per cent from 1977 to 1983. This is largely accounted for by the greater number of convenient connecting flights resulting from the increased use of the hub-and-spoke delivery system.

Diagram 19.  **Airline productivity: load factor versus distance**

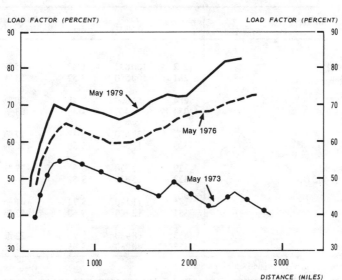

Table 26. **Index of airline fares**

As a per cent of CAB formula fare 1983 Q2

| Market distance (miles) | Market size (passengers per day) | | | |
|---|---|---|---|---|
| | 10-50 | 51-200 | 201-500 | 501-1 000 |
| 1- 400 | 114 | 112 | 95 | 71 |
| 401-1 500 | 110 | 97 | 87 | 80 |
| 1 500 + | [1] | 75 | 65 | 60 |

1. Too few markets to provide reliable comparison.
*Source:* Kaplan (1985), *op. cit.* CAB Origin-Destination Survey.

Air fares were actually lower, on average, in 1983 than implied by regulatory fare formulas, despite the full fare flexibility available to air carriers (Table 26). The reduction in ticket prices was evident in all but the shortest, least-dense markets; and it was particularly apparent in the long distance market where fares were 40 per cent lower in real terms than their pre-deregulation levels. Indeed, competitive prices have now corrected a formula which was known to undervalue short-haul and overvalue long-haul costs. The emerging competition of low-cost airlines is also proving important. Typical examples of comparative price performance are shown in Table 27. For markets of similar density and distance, it is clear that ticket prices are substantially lower and service significantly higher in markets served by the low-cost airlines. The older incumbents often offer service that is viable in these markets

Table 27. **Comparative price performance**

Airline markets entered by People Express** or Southwest*
versus otherwise similiar markets

1st Quarter 1980 and 1984
Dollars of the day

| Market | Distance | 1980 passengers | 1980 fare | Percentage change in fare | Percentage change in passengers |
|---|---|---|---|---|---|
| New York-Buffalo** | 282 | 100 832 | $ 48 | − 25 % | 179 % |
| Boston-Philadelphia | 281 | 100 590 | $ 52 | 53 % | 2 % |
| New York-Norfolk** | 284 | 51 800 | $ 48 | − 30 % | 264 % |
| Chicago-Columbus | 284 | 50 460 | $ 48 | 103 % | 12 % |
| Dallas-Little Rock* | 303 | 23 650 | $ 59 | − 17 % | 123 % |
| Atlanta-Mobile | 303 | 17 340 | $ 56 | 56 % | − 8 % |
| Albuquerque-Phoenix* | 329 | 23 550 | $ 61 | − 27 % | 160 % |
| Columbus-Washington, D.C. | 322 | 25 420 | $ 53 | 96 % | − 18 % |
| El Paso-Phoenix* | 246 | 11 110 | $ 74 | − 41 % | 178 % |
| St. Louis-Tulsa | 351 | 12 100 | $ 60 | 83 % | − 20 % |
| Houston-Tulsa* | 453 | 38 930 | $ 74 | − 23 % | 83 % |
| Philadelphia-Detroit | 453 | 40 880 | $ 65 | 53 % | − 7 % |

*Source:* Kaplan (1985), *op. cit.* CAB Origin-Destination Survey.

because of a name-recognition and service advantage that enable them either to charge higher prices or to achieve higher load factors at the same prices. A number of studies[136] reveal that air travel markets are competitive but not perfectly contestable. Fares in markets with more than one carrier are about 10 per cent lower than in similar monopoly markets; fares in markets with new entrants are about 20 per cent lower. However, it still takes a large number of potential entrants (four or more) to reduce fares substantially. Nevertheless, such residual market power is limited by the ease with which carriers are managing to enter and exit markets.

Airline fare policies are still emerging as carriers experiment with various price-service combinations. Since deregulation, carriers have used capacity-control features to ration the availability of discount seats on peak flights, so that full-fare passengers are assured a high probability of access to these more popular flights, while increasing the availability of discount seats on off-peak flights. Indeed, the number of discount passengers has risen substantially from well below 20 per cent in the deregulation period, to over 60 per cent in recent years. The introduction of reduced connecting fares has also accounted for some of this rise. These fares have been used to induce passengers to travel one-stop to destinations which have non-stop service offered by a rival airline. Since connecting service takes longer than non-stop service, passengers prefer it only at a lower price. A carrier is willing to offer such discounts in order to fill otherwise empty seats on its flights and, thus, make its hub-and-spoke operations more economical. Another innovative pricing practice is the frequent flyer programme, a form of volume discounting. Usually, a corporation pays the fare, but the traveller chooses which airline to fly on. By being loyal to one airline, the flyer can obtain a bonus for himself in the form of first-class seats or extra travel allowance. Gains to pleasure travellers are accruing mainly through lower fares, especially over long distances. As is consistent with findings in Table 26, passengers in the longer routes have benefitted significantly more than those in the shorter ones. Recent evidence suggests that the benefits from airline deregulation have accrued not just to leisure but also to business travellers as a result of the carrier's change to hub-and-spoke operations and the greater ease of obtaining discount fares[137]. Safety in U.S. commercial aircraft has not deteriorated after deregulation. Indeed, there were fewer fatalities in four of the last five years of deregulation than in any year since 1962, except 1970. However, the reduction in accident rates is attributed more to technical advances in air traffic control than to the particular regulatory regime in force[138].

As in transportation, it was felt that competition in telecommunications would reduce overall prices while increasing output. It was apparent that total deregulation would result in higher prices for local services but lower prices for long-distance calls. An estimate of the likely effects of basing prices closer to incremental costs appears in Table 28[139]. Current prices for access to the local network, assuming flat rates for local service, would nearly double from their current level of $11.73 per month to $21.73 per month. However, prices for long distance calls would be lowered by over 60 per cent, from $.25 per minute to $.09 per minute. For individuals who use as much toll as local service, the net bill would exhibit a saving; however, for those whose telephone usage is predominantly local, the total bill would increase. From the economists' viewpoint, there is a welfare gain from the price increases as well as from the price reductions. For, pricing below costs encourages society to purchase too much local usage, just as surely as pricing above incremental costs means foregoing the value of desirable long-distance service.

Since deregulation, competition has been fierce in the growing market for telephone switching systems. In 1983 AT&T's market share of PBXs was 29.1 per cent in contrast to 17.9 per cent for Northern Telecom and 16.7 per cent for Rolm. In 1984 equipment prices were as much as 50 per cent below their usual level, with telephone lines selling for as little as

Table 28.  **Residential communications costs and prices 1985 Q1**

| | Cost | Current price | Price with all common cost on access | Ramsey pricing |
|---|---|---|---|---|
| Residence | | | | |
| Flat access ($/month) | 21.73 | 11.73 | 22.80 | 19.98 |
| Measured access ($/month) | 21.73 | 6.03 | 22.80 | 19.98 |
| Local peak (cents/minute) | 2.00 | 0.11 | 2.07 | 2.35 |
| Local off-peak (cents/minute) | 0.70 | 0.07 | 0.72 | 0.98 |
| Toll usage | | | | |
| Intra LATA (cents/minute) | 6.70 | 17.82 | 6.70 | 7.18 |
| Inter LATA (cents/minute) | 8.00 | 22.85 | 8.00 | 9.50 |
| Interstate (cents/minute) | 9.00 | 25.28 | 9.00 | 9.81 |

*Note:*  Local prices are average revenue per minute, including minutes of customers taking flat service for which there is no charge. The demand elasticity for measured access is about 0.04, for local usage is about 0.2, while that for toll usage is in the range of 0.6-0.8.
*Source:*  Perl (1985) *op. cit.*

$550 each. While AT&T was prohibited from offering its old PBXs at giveaway prices, it has been providing discounts on large orders and commitments for new products. PBXs are being affected by technical change as well as by deregulation; manufacturers are striving to make them compatible with all types of automated office equipment so they can be the "hubs" of the automated office of the future. The post-divestiture world has also been characterised by joint ventures, a phenomenon that was not fully anticipated[140].

*Market structure and profitability*

Diagram 20 displays the post-deregulation market shares and growth rates for the various segments of the U.S. aviation industry. The small airlines have been able to expand overall because of the cost advantages enjoyed by the new entrants and the ability of local airlines to add spokes to their regional hubs. Moreover, the economic shocks that occurred over the past five years of deregulation have affected the smaller carriers relatively less than the large ones. The local airlines and new entrants had the right fleet (two-engine jets) for a period of high fuel prices and low travel demand, dampened by recession and inflation. Thus, the market shares for local and new carriers rose from about 12 per cent of total revenue passenger miles (RPMs) in 1976 to 21 per cent in 1982. Although overall demand grew, largely because of the availability of more discount fare options, the trunk RPMs remained at about the same level (1982) as before deregulation (1976). Among the trunk lines the two largest national carriers, American and United, maintained their market shares while the smaller trunk lines lost shares to the more efficient local and new carriers.

The different experiences of the various airlines are reflected in their earnings as well. Profit margins for the trunk carriers were negative during the first four years of deregulation before recovering in 1984. In 1979 finances were adversely affected by a strike at United and the grounding of the nation's DC-10 fleet for a substantial portion of the peak summer period, and in 1981 margins were reduced by the controllers' strike and the recession. The trunks' difficulties were epitomized by the bankruptcy of Braniff Airways in May 1982[141]. However, even with the Braniff bankruptcy, the values of the trunk airline stocks as a group were about the same in 1983 as in 1976, whereas the New York Stock Exchange index as a whole for this period was down 3 per cent (Table 29)[142]. Certain carriers gained, American Airlines being

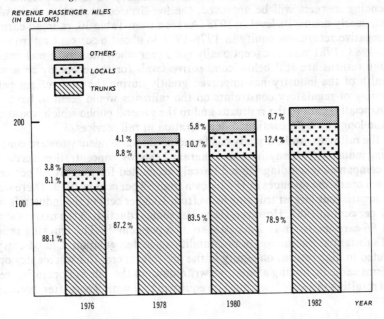

Diagram 20.  Post-deregulation airline market share and growth

REVENUE PASSENGER MILES
(IN BILLIONS)

one clear winner, while other trunk carriers did less well. The local service carriers as a group were clearly the largest winners.

Market shares and growth patterns in the railroad industry differ sharply from those in aviation, in that concentration has risen sharply, and promises to rise further. The five largest railroads (which included Conrail, Burlington-Northern, Southern Pacific, Union Pacific and the Atchison, Topeka & Santa Fe) accounted for 43.9 per cent of the industry's operating

Table 29.  Stock values of trunk airlines[1]

Millions of 1983 dollars

|  | 1976 | 1983 |
|---|---|---|
| American | 635 | 1 819 |
| Braniff | 348 | n.a. |
| Continental | 168 | 89 |
| Delta | 1 233 | 1 655 |
| Eastern | 302 | 202 |
| Northwest | 1 148 | 1 031 |
| Pan Am and National | 1 527 | 840 |
| TWA | 274 | 38 |
| United | 1 092 | 1 202 |
| Western | 218 | 69 |
| Truck total | 6 944 | 6 945 |
| Local total | 479 | 2 803 |
| All NY stock exchange: down 3 % | | |

1. Price times number of outstanding shares.
*Source:*  Moore (1984), *op. cit.*.

revenues in 1978, but 67.8 per cent in 1984 (Diagram 21)[143]. If it is assumed that two currently pending mergers will be approved, the five-firm concentration ratio will rise to 84.7 per cent, nearly double its level in 1978. As seen from Table 30, railroad earnings have risen from negative returns-on-equity in 1976-1977 to about 6 per cent return on average during 1979-1983 (1981 was an exceptionally good year when the return was nearly 12 per cent). Though returns are still below competitive levels for the economy as a whole, the financial health of the industry has improved greatly during the post-reform period. The partial loosening of regulatory constraints on the railroads would seem to have been very beneficial financially, both to the railroads and to the general public which would have been harmed in the long run by a continued deterioration in rail services.

Unlike the railroads, an ICC study has found no similar tendency toward concentration in the trucking industry[144]. If anything, as Diagram 22 shows, concentration has declined: the largest 100 companies (excluding United Parcel) accounted for roughly 49 per cent of the industry's total operating revenues in 1982; down from 57 per cent in 1979. There was a small increase among the four largest trucking firms from 10.5 per cent of the industry's revenue in 1978 to 13.1 per cent in 1983. However, there was some reduction in the market share of the next largest 96 carriers, from 41.2 per cent to 35.5 per cent[145]. The trucking industry has experienced substantial fluctuation in profitability since deregulation. Closed-entry policies had contributed to high returns on equity in the pre-reform era. But when entry opened up, many new firms came in, forcing a one-time write-down of the value of operating certificates in 1980, and resulting in a very low return on equity in that year. Thereafter, profitability has

Diagram 21. **Post-reform railroad market share and growth**

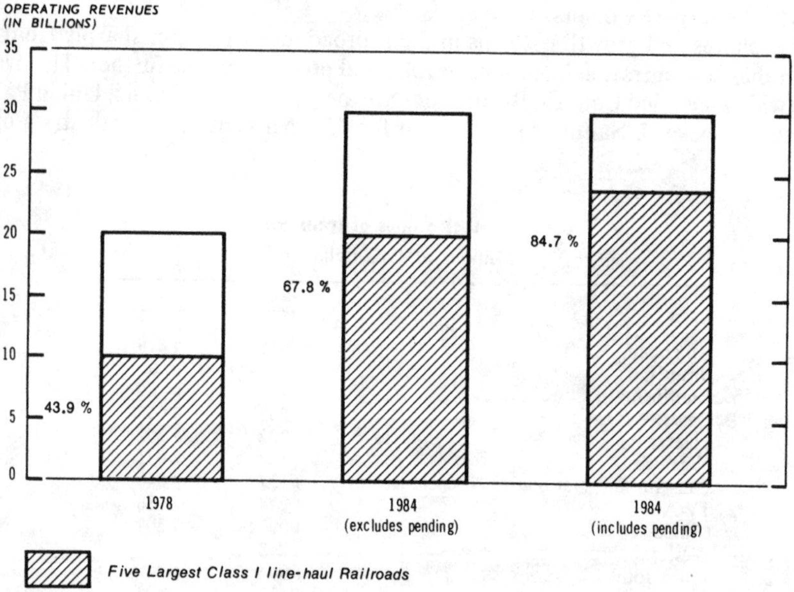

OPERATING REVENUES
(IN BILLIONS)

Five Largest Class I line-haul Railroads

1978 :   Conrail, Burlington-Northern, Southern Pacific, Union Pacific, Atchison, Topeka & Sante Fe

1984 :   (excludes pending) : CSX Corp. (1979), Conrail, Norfolk-Southern (1982), Union Pacific Group (1982), Burlington-Northern

1984 :   (including pending) : Norfolk-Southern with Conrail (pending) Southern Pacific group (pending)

Table 30.  **Return on equity for surface transportation**

Net income basis per cent

|  | Class I<br>Linehaul<br>railroads | Class I<br>Intercity motor<br>carriers<br>of property | Class I<br>Intercity motor<br>carriers<br>of passengers |
|---|---|---|---|
| 1976 | − 0.34 | 23.67 | 9.01 |
| 1977 | − 1.34 | 16.37 | 8.56 |
| 1978 | 1.55 | 17.21 | 8.25 |
| 1979 | 5.44 | 11.72 | 9.96 |
| 1980 | 6.00 | 1.16 | 14.46 |
| 1981 | 11.76 | 17.26 | 9.82 |
| 1982 | 7.19 | 7.29 | 5.14 |
| 1983 | 6.95 | 16.97 | 5.87 |

*Source:*   *ICC Annual Report;* data for railways (1981-3) have been restated based upon
rateable depreciation accounting for track structures.

followed a more normal cyclical pattern. The increase in bankruptcies in recent years suggests that regulation might have protected inefficient carriers that could not survive the influx of greater competition.

Continuing a trend which began in 1981, the bus industry has reported declines in revenues, profits and bus ridership in recent years. The industry remains highly concentrated with the Greyhound Lines and the Trailways System continuing to account for approximately

*Diagram 22.*  **Post-reform trucking market share and growth**

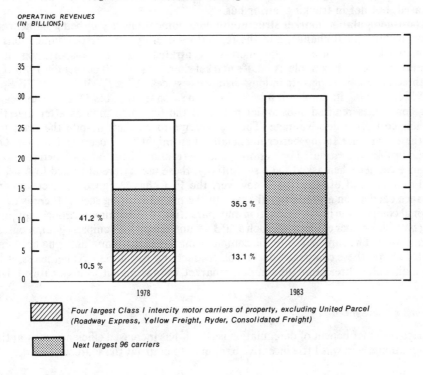

OPERATING REVENUES
(IN BILLIONS)

Four largest Class I intercity motor carriers of property, excluding United Parcel
(Roadway Express, Yellow Freight, Ryder, Consolidated Freight)

Next largest 96 carriers

83

Table 31.  **Profit for bell operating companies**
First nine months of 1984

|  | Level of profit (dollars) | Net income as a percentage of forecast for all of 1984 |
|---|---|---|
| Ameritech | 788 | 85 |
| Bell Atlantic | 732 | 77 |
| Bell South | 894 | 75 |
| NYNEX | 724 | 77 |
| Pacific Telesis | 660 | 80 |
| Southwestern Bell | 660 | 76 |
| U.S. West | 634 | 72 |

*Source: Business Week,* December 3, 1984.

60 per cent and 20 per cent, respectively, of the industry's total operating revenues. The industry's ridership decline is generally attributed to discounted airline fares and to increased automobile usage – owing to relatively stable gasoline prices and an improved economy over the past two years. A strike at Greyhound Lines during the final two months of 1983 also adversely affected the industry. However, according to the 1984 annual report of the ICC, the effects of the recession in the early 1980s, and the continuing decline in bus ridership during the current recovery, would have been more severe had there been no industry reform. In sum, reform policy has not contributed to a worsening of financial conditions in the transportation sector; instead, truck, bus and airline firms appear to be about as well off as they would have been without deregulation and the railroads are much better off. Market concentration in rail has increased, but not in trucking, air or bus.

The post-deregulation market structure in communications is still being influenced by divestiture, technological change, and the regulatory overlay. In telecommunications, the pre-reform market structure was far more concentrated than in transportation; in the long-distance market, for example, AT&T's market share was still 80 per cent in 1980. There are now three oligopolistic players in long-distance services: AT&T, MCI and GTE Sprint, with AT&T continuing its dominant role[146]. As can be seen from Table 31, the seven regional operating companies realised substantial profits in the first nine months after divestiture despite their cost-price disadvantage. The view seems to be that, despite the transitional turmoil, these firms are faring better financially than might have been anticipated. Other transitional problems continue. For example, a large fraction of customers failed to choose a long-distance carrier when asked to do so. Initially, these users were allocated to AT&T by default. From the end of May 1985, however, the FCC has assigned such customers to long-distance carriers on a proportional basis. In the manufacturing sector, there is healthy international competition in the production and marketing of telecommunications equipment, including both subscriber equipment, such as PBXs, and telephone company equipment, such as cable and wire. The same holds in the computer market. Like manufacturing firms in the unregulated sector, these companies depend on productivity for success. Nonetheless, AT&T is finding it difficult to break into the computer market, even though it seems a natural rival to IBM.

## C.  Lessons of deregulation

Perhaps the chief benefit of deregulation is that it has increased efficiency substantially. Under regulation, there was little incentive to plan or to pinpoint the sources of markets that were successful and those that were failures, nor to keep costs under control and be responsive to consumer demands. In contrast, deregulation would seem to be leading to a substantially more efficient industry, one in which cross-subsidy is absent, a diversity of price/service options is present, and cost-minimizing behaviour is prevalent, both in delivery systems and in other operating costs. These developments reflect fundamental changes in the way firms are conducting business. Companies are finding that they must be driven by market opportunities and financial needs, not by regulatory considerations. They must calculate their costs on a market-by-market basis, and must learn to base their prices on costs, competitors prices and market strategy. Regulatory principles such as rate averaging, value-of-service pricing, and so on, cannot survive in a competitive environment. Corporations are seeking to develop products and to market them strategically and to find niches which confer some economic rent. Companies are seeking integrated routes structures, suited to moving people or freight through the system efficiently. All in all, a more competitive, and innovative spirit emerges from deregulation. Useful lessons may be learnt from the U.S. experience. It may be argued in particular that a move towards a more liberalised system in other Member countries could have beneficial effects, although not necessarily to the same degree as in the United States. Regulatory reform could make a significant contribution to price and wage moderation in the transportation and communications sectors, leading to more diverse consumer options, with the prices of different services reflecting their costs.

From a macroeconomic point of view, deregulation has essentially meant lower inflation and higher productivity, although the overall impact is difficult to quantify precisely. With regard to wage and price formation, there is no doubt that the economy as a whole has benefitted. Wage costs in deregulated industries have been kept down and a two-tier wage system has tended to emerge. There have also been real welfare gains through lower costs of services and increased productivity in deregulated industries, and a significant demonstration effect has also been exerted on other industries. Moreover, deregulation has added a new element in industrial dynamics, by providing greater inter-relations between the various modes of transportation and by cross-fertilization in computers and telecommunication technology. In sum, there have been, so far, obvious benefits from deregulation. It is not clear, however, whether competitive forces that have been unleashed will not ultimately be blurred by excessive concentration in the industries concerned, though free entry should reduce this risk. Finally it should be noted that this chapter has taken only a selective, though detailed, look at the impact of deregulation. Other important aspects of the liberalisation process include the partial dismantling of restrictions on commercial banking (a legacy of the Great Depression) and the impact of Federal Administrative deregulation. The latter is discussed briefly in Annex 4. Tighter control over new "social" regulations has been an important element in containing the spread of compliance costs and improving the framework for evaluating costs and benefits in the public sector.

## CONCLUSIONS

When the last Survey of the United States was published in 1983, the economy had recently emerged from its worst recession in post-war history. Activity was picking up rapidly while unemployment and inflation were coming down. The recovery was then expected to continue in 1984, albeit at a relatively moderate pace by past cyclical standards. Accordingly, profits, investment and employment levels were projected to be quite disappointing. Only a modest reacceleration of inflation was predicted. However, the rising domestic and external imbalances, notably prospects for continuing large budget deficits, high real interest rates and widening current external deficit were seen as casting doubts on the medium-term sustainability of the recovery.

As expected at the time, some of the underlying imbalances have worsened but in many respects the performance of the economy has been more favourable than anticipated. The first two years of the recovery have indeed displayed the most impressive combination of rapid expansion of activity, strong employment growth and slow inflation seen in recent decades. In the two years to the end of 1984, real GNP increased by more than 12 per cent, spurred *inter alia* by a strong expansion in non-residential investment. By all measures, inflation has remained subdued, hovering around 3-4 per cent. Unemployment has fallen by nearly 4 percentage points to some 7 per cent, a situation accompanied by the creation of 8 million new jobs and standing in marked contrast to developments in Europe. Also, the benefits bestowed on the rest of the world, in 1983 and 1984, by more buoyant domestic demand growth in the United States and the strength of the dollar have on balance probably greatly outweighed the adverse influences emanating from high real interest rates and inflationary pressures associated with exchange rate developments.

The recovery is now well into its third year but its pace has tended to become distinctly slower and more hesitant. On the whole, in spite of considerable uncertainty, forces making for continuing, albeit moderate, growth are still expected to prevail over the next eighteen months or so. OECD Secretariat projections point to real GNP growth in the order of 2½-3 per cent, with continued low inflation and unemployment rising little from its present level. Risks that the current recovery may be jeopardised in the near future by domestic inflation and supply constraints are clearly less important than in similar phases of past cycles. But other risks and tensions, notably those associated with rising imbalances, should not be underestimated. These are both of a short and medium-term nature, and they raise complex and problematic issues in the sense that there is no general agreement on the workings of some of the important mechanisms involved. In view of the inter-dependance of the world economy, they pose serious challenges for policy both in the United States and abroad.

Risks that can be more directly associated to the short-term outlook relate essentially to:

- *The balance sheet position of the private sector.* In spite of the rapid build up of debt, the household sector may not be overburdened as yet. But enterprises, in view of the deteriorating structure of corporate balance sheets and return of profits to more normal levels, may overreact to temporary demand weakness by sharply curtailing their investment plans;
- *The sectoral imbalances associated with weak external competitiveness.* The decline in agricultural income and weak or stagnating output growth in other export and import-competing industries while services and non-tradeable sectors expand rapidly is a potential source of instability. It also tends to fuel protectionist sentiment. Related financial problems in certain other sectors (the savings and loans associations in some states, energy production and commercial real estate), could compound the destabilizing influences stemming from an eventual marked weakening of the economy;
- *Possible strong downward pressures on the exchange rate.* A markedly lower dollar could lead to substantial upward pressure on the general price level. Conversely, a policy response by the monetary authorities to avoid rekindling inflation expectations and a loss of confidence could entail higher interest rates.

Some of these risks are not very important *per se* and/or are mutually exclusive. But many of them are interrelated. Should one of them materialise, the probability of the others taking their toll would be significantly enhanced. A sequence of events could therefore be set in train leading to a cumulatively destabilising movement.

More complex and controversial issues relate to the medium/long-term sustainability of the U.S. current account imbalance, that of the Federal budget deficit and the precise nature of any possible relationship between the two. Views on the sustainability of the U.S. current account deficit and the forces behind the strength of the dollar differ. Some observers argue that capital inflows and the strong dollar mirror the good performance of the U.S. economy and its attractiveness as an investment outlet because of the tax cutting and supply side policies. Others attribute capital inflows to higher interest rates resulting from rising claims on world savings caused by domestic dissaving in the United States. According to such views, the large current account deficit would be, at least partly, the counterpart of the large and expanding structural budget deficit. While different policy implications may be drawn from these different assessments, it is uncertain how long market participants may be willing to continue acquiring U.S. assets at the rate of perhaps $150 billion a year before losing confidence in the dollar. Moreover, the interaction between financial flows and stocks provides a slow-working but powerful destabilizing mechanism:

- The large current account deficit will tend to feed on itself because of the deteriorating international investment position and the associated unfavourable evolution of net investment income;
- With the United States expected to become a net debtor country sometime this year – for the first time since World War I – correcting the initial trade imbalance might not be sufficient. Adjustment over the medium term might well involve a sustained period of trade surpluses. The longer the adjustment is delayed, the larger the eventual trade surplus that will have to be achieved and sustained.

When assessing the sustainability issue from the point of view of the real economy, there is also considerable uncertainty as to whether net capital inflows (i.e. the counterpart of the current account deficit) are financing real productive investment which would permit higher net foreign indebtedness to be serviced without either depressing future consumption or investment. Analysis in the Survey suggests that this has been, at best, only partially the case. But even if capital inflows were enhancing the supply potential of the economy, competitiveness would have to be appropriate for the transfer of real resources abroad to materialise. Since the marked deterioration of the current external balance over the last few years can be largely ascribed to different growth rates of domestic demand in the United States and other countries as well as to the strength of the dollar, any correction – whether desirable or inevitable – is likely to be associated with changes in both relative demand pressures and the world configuration of exchange rates. A gradual – rather than a sharp – depreciation of the dollar would clearly be desirable from the point of view of minimising inflationary risks, maintaining confidence and avoiding the need for a tightening of monetary policy. The correction of the external imbalance would obviously take longer, involving certain risks. But on balance, these would appear to be smaller than those implied by a sharp fall of the exchange rate. In this context, the recent agreement on policy intentions of the Ministers of Finance and Central Bank Governors of the Group of Five countries is to be welcomed. Co-ordinated official interventions in exchange markets in the context of policy initiatives to promote a convergence of economic performance should contribute to the orderly achievement of a configuration of exchange rates which would better reflect fundamental economic conditions. It should also help to defuse protectionist pressures.

While views differ on the sustainability of the external position, there would seem to be more consensus on the unsustainability or at least the undesirability of persistent large U.S. budget deficits.

- As noted, the causes of high real interest rates are a matter of controversy. Nevertheless, it is the OECD Secretariat's view that the Federal budget deficit has probably increased long-term interest rates – at least to some degree. Even if tax cuts have also enhanced the supply side potential, the federal deficit can therefore partly be seen as having increased net claims on world savings;

- Although the general government debt interest/GNP ratio is comparable to the OECD average, the rise of the public debt in the United States appears more worrisome when assessed in relation to existing tax revenue or internal savings. If not corrected, the fiscal imbalance would risk taking interest payments beyond the threshold where spending cuts and/or necessary tax increases are politically acceptable. Expenditure and tax resistance would then accentuate the burden on monetary policy. And if, as a result, the Federal Reserve were to allow faster monetary growth to prevent a rise in, or reduce, interest rates, this could adversely affect confidence in future inflation performance and the dollar, thus causing an abrupt drying up of capital inflows.

Overall, decisive, credible action to reduce the Federal budget deficit over the medium-term should be a key objective of policy. This would lower public sector's demand on the private savings, reduce or eliminate whatever "budget deficit premium" may be embodied in long-term rates, while easing the potential conflict between the stance of fiscal policy and the anti-inflationary orientation of monetary policy. To the extent there is – as suggested by the OECD Secretariat's analysis – a relationship between the budget deficit and the current account imbalance, external adjustment would also be promoted. It is to be hoped that the spending cuts agreed by Congress in August will be implemented as announced. However, given the relatively optimistic economic growth assumptions on which official budget projections are based, and the possibility of some programmes exceeding estimates, additional measures, such as those discussed in the context of the proposed "balanced budget" amendment, appear to be necessary. It is also essential that the overhauling of the tax system proposed by the Administration remains at least revenue neutral. Given the importance of the issues at stake, it would be regrettable if, as a result of the Congressional process, the tax bill were to result in a substantial tax cut in the out-years that would undermine the deficit-reducing effect of the proposed spending reductions.

Failure to correct the fiscal position would risk putting undue – and potentially conflicting – pressure on monetary policy. The earlier more rigid attachment to narrow money targeting has been modified in recent years in favour of a more pragmatic approach, placing more emphasis on real growth, credit market conditions and the dollar as well as on inflation. This has allowed greater flexibility in responding to short-term disturbances in the economy. In view of conditions prevailing in the economy, the more accommodating stance pursued since last autumn appears appropriate. It is to be hoped that it will help the economy to overcome its present weakness. But there are limits to what can be expected from monetary policy. Even if the important objective of keeping inflation under control were to be abandoned – obviously not a desirable course – there is not much monetary policy can do to resolve the imbalance between domestic savings and investment. Greater monetary expansion cannot substitute for higher national saving, nor is it well suited to relieving sectoral strains in the economy.

Increasing competition through deregulation is one of the pillars of the Administration's recovery programme. The Survey has attempted to assess the microeconomic effects of deregulation in two areas: transport and telecommunications. Deregulation has tended to eliminate cross-subsidy, to diversify price/service options and to enhance cost-minimising behaviour, both in delivery systems and in other operating costs. Overall, the chief benefit of deregulation is that it has increased efficiency. In the airline industry for instance, companies have had to adopt corporate strategies which exploit the airline's particular strengths and which rely on coherent route structures to achieve economies. The travelling public has benefitted through lower airline fares and a greater variety of services. Experience with deregulation and divestiture in the telecommunications sector has also been beneficial in the main, but it remains partial. Competition has been enhanced, especially in the long-distance sector; this has allowed the exploitation of technological advances (microwave and satellite technology etc.), through the entry of new companies. Prices have fallen on long-distance calls, as cross-subsidisation of local calls has been reduced. But the costs and benefits have not necessarily been attributed equally and it is too early to evaluate their net effect. More generally, although there have been clear benefits from deregulation, it is not clear whether competitive forces that have been unleashed will not ultimately be blurred by excessive concentration in the industries concerned. So far, with the exception of railroads, there is no evidence that such a trend is emerging. From a macroeconomic point of view, the overall effect of deregulation has also been beneficial, but to an extent which is difficult to quantify. Wage costs in deregulated industries have been kept down and productivity has dramatically increased. Besides its direct positive impact on the wage formation process in the industries concerned, deregulation has probably had a non-negligible demonstration effect on other industries. There may be useful lessons to be drawn by other countries from U.S. deregulation. But the nature of national markets and other considerations could influence the benefits that may accrue.

All Member countries have a responsibility to pursue domestic policies that will promote sustained non-inflationary growth in the OECD area and strengthen the open multilateral trade system. Given its weight in the world economy, that of the United States is even greater. For both domestic and international considerations, correcting the large imbalances that have built up in recent years is an urgent priority. On the other hand, it is not sure whether the reduction of the external stimulus stemming from the U.S. would be offset by an endogenous growth of domestic demand in the rest of the world. The international configuration of exchange rates may also change. Action in the U.S. would have a better chance of succeeding if other countries were to further contribute to an international configuration of policy settings conducive to a sustainable and satisfactory performance of the world economy.

# NOTES AND REFERENCES

1. In the first year of the recovery, federal non-defence purchases declined in absolute terms but in the second year this was offset by a sizeable increase in defence expenditures.

2. See OECD *Economic Outlook,* June 1985.

3. These are "first round" effects, before taking account of the impact of the lower exports and higher imports on domestic incomes (which would reduce imports, thus offsetting the relative price effect to some degree). See R. A. Feldman, "The Impact of the Recent Strength of the Dollar on the U.S. Merchandise Trade Balance", *Journal of Policy Modelling,* 6 (1), 1984.

4. This coincides broadly with the observed average growth rate of total domestic demand in the OECD area excluding the United States.

5. Statement of the Hon. D.C. Mulford before the Committee of Foreign Affairs, Sub-Committee on International Economic Policy and Trade, March 5 1985.

6. For the private non-farm business sector compensation per hour declined from a peak range of 10-12 per cent in 1980 and early 1981 to 3¾ per cent in mid-1984.

7. Profits and prices have also been favourably influenced by the weakening in commodity prices and the effects of the dollar strength on input costs. Since 1981, US prices of non-petroleum imports have been essentially flat – or even declined slightly – which has exerted pressures on American manufacturers to maintain price competitiveness by keeping production costs down. However, as indicated above, moderation has not been confined to export- and import-competing sectors but has been a feature of the non-farm business sector as a whole.

8. See OECD *Economic Outlook,* June 1985.

9. See, for example, Ann and James Orr, "Job Cuts Are Only One Means Firms Use to Counter Imports", *Monthly Labor Review,* June 1984 (Conference Papers).

10. See OECD *Economic Outlook,* June 1985, pp. 30-31.

11. See *ibid.* p. 30 for a chart setting out such a cross-section correlation between short-run real wage rigidity and the rise in unemployment between 1975 and 1982.

12. See George Gilder, "The Real Economy"; Thomas K. Plewes, "The US Economy: Incubators of Jobs" and Dorothy Chansy "The Rise of Women Entrepreneurs" in *Economic Impact,* 1985-2.

13. The ratio of individual income tax receipts to taxable personal income (personal income less other labour income and transfers, plus personal contributions to social insurance) fell from 13.7 per cent in 1980 to 12.2 per cent in 1984. Because of shifts in the composition and distribution of income, this should not be entirely attributed to tax policy changes.

14. Between 1980 and 1984 the revenues of the general government sector (which includes state and local sectors as well as social security) fell from 32 to 31 per cent in the United States, while rising in the rest of the OECD; U.S. general government spending rose from 33 per cent to 34½ per cent.

15. In general, the Administration has favoured cuts in non-defence outlays, while Congress has favoured higher taxes and lower defence spending, with a reluctance to prune non-defence spending.

16. This estimate refers to the mid-cycle trend level of GNP, rather than to the more conventional peak-to-peak trend. Since the BEA estimates of potential GNP do not attempt to measure the non-accelerating inflation rate of unemployment (NAIRU), the use of the term "structural" to describe the cyclically adjusted estimates in Table 5 may not be fully appropriate.

17. Non-defence discretionary spending plus entitlements and other mandatory spending, excluding debt interest.

18. Interest on debt held by the public *excluding* the Federal Reserve Banks. Gross interest payments including those to the Federal Reserve System rose from 8.1 to 12.8 per cent of federal outlays between 1977 and 1984.

19. Net interest paid to the public includes payments to Federal Reserve Banks, less deposits of earnings by the Federal Reserve System.

20. The average interest rate paid on government debt issued to the public (excluding Federal Reserve Banks) was about 6 per cent in 1977 and 8½ per cent in 1984 (see Diagram 15 below).

21. The increase would be $18-$22 billion, rising to $30 billion if the interest payments were added to debt, rather than offset by cuts in other spending. See *Budget of the United States Government FY 1985,* pp. 2-23 and CBO, *Federal Debt and Interest Costs,* September 1984.

22. The House proposal was for a 3½ per cent real defence growth, compared with a 6.8 per cent real growth endorsed by the Senate and agreed to by the President.

23. Part of the increase was due to the inclusion of $12 billion of borrowings which had previously been defined as "off budget". The estimate for 1985 was reduced to $211 billion in the *Mid-session Review.*

24. This was to be achieved by: *i)* a selective one-year freeze in funding certain programmes; *ii)* a wide range of programme terminations, reforms and cuts; *iii)* a 10 per cent cut in administrative expenses for many programmes; and *iv)* a 6 per cent pay cut for federal civilian employees.

25. The Administration's defence baseline continued to be the "Rose Garden" agreement included in the *Mid-session Review,* rather than the Senate-House defence agreement. Scheduled increases for procurement and research (especially in relation to strategic nuclear programmes) amount to 19 per cent and 22 per cent in 1986.

26. The estimated saving was put at $39 billion in relation to the lower baseline used by the CBO (which incorporated the Congressional agreement on defence cuts noted above). Agreement on lower defence spending seems to have been made easier because of reports of defence underspending – including that due to previous overestimates of inflation in defence goods – coupled with instances of laxness in monitoring prices and profits in certain defence equipment sectors.

27. In the past five fiscal years Congress has surpassed its own budget resolutions by an average of $28 billion a year.

28. The Balanced Budget and Emergency Deficit Control Bill, proposed as an amendment to the annual Debt Ceiling Bill, was passed by the Senate on October 9th with substantial bipartisan support. It would require the enactment of Budgets which adhere to a steady decline in the deficit, from $180 billion in FY 1986 to zero in FY 1991. If the projected deficit should threaten to overshoot, the President would be authorised to make across-the-board cuts in "controllable" government spending.

29. See *Economic Report of the President,* February 1985, p. 79.

30. See CBO, "Revising the Individual Income Tax", July 1983, p. 5.

31. Although less than half of personal income is currently subject to income taxation, this is not particularly low by post-World War II standards. The methods by which income is sheltered from taxation have changed markedly, however, over this period. In 1947, personal exemptions and standard deductions accounted for roughly half of all income not subject to tax. Between 1947 and the present, the relative value of personal exemptions was sharply eroded, and the number and use

of special exclusions, itemised deductions, and credits increased dramatically. One of the most significant changes in the individual income tax during the postwar period was the growth of these special tax preferences. *(Ibid.* pp. 10-12.)

32. The literature suggests that tax rate (increases) decreases do (reduce) increase the number of hours worked. Moreover, the second member of a family to enter the labour force often faces particularly high tax rates (the first dollar earned by the second worker being taxed at the same rate as the last dollar of the first). Empirical studies (e.g. J.A. Hausman, "The Effect of Taxes on Labour Supply.", in H. Aaron and J. Pechman, *How Taxes Affect Economic Behaviour,* Washington D.C. 1981), show that the elasticity of labour supply with respect to after-tax wages for mean-income earners is small for husbands (about 0.2) but large for wives (in the order of 1.4). Account being taken of the income effect, the total elasticity is nil for the husbands and 0.9 for the wives. It is however, worth emphasising that even if the total effect on labour supply is small, the distortions and welfare costs derive from the marginal (substitution) effect alone. (See the discussion in "The Role of the Public Sector", OECD *Economic Studies,* No. 4, Spring 1985, pp. 162 *et seq.)*

33. See B. P. Bosworth, "Taxes and the Investment Recovery", *Brookings Papers on Economic Activity; 1:1985,* pp. 13-16.

34. An assessment of the effects of fiscal policy on activity necessitates a model of income and wealth determination. There is much disagreement over which model is appropriate. The Administration for instance, has perceived fiscal policy in classical price theory terms and not Keynesian terms. Tax cuts – and the resultant deficit – do not add to total demand because government borrowing is seen as crowding out private borrowing dollar-for-dollar, as tax payers are assumed to raise their saving in anticipation of future taxes (see below Section IV). However, irrespective of the long-run properties they attribute to fiscal deficits, most models identify positive short-run effects in activity. These are analysed here in a "reduced form" framework.

35. Since the state and local financial balance incorporates the surplus on government employee retirement funds, which are included in household saving in the standardised national accounts, it is probably inadviseable to make too much of the fact that the U.S. general government ratio is larger than the OECD average.

36. "Recent Trends in State-local Finances and the Long-term Outook for the Sector", Office of State and Local Finance, U.S. Department of the Treasury, Working Paper, 28th November 1984.

37. This difference can be traced further back to the evolution of the deficit after the first oil crisis. Uniquely at a time when other OECD economies were experiencing an increase in budget deficits, the U.S. general government financial balance returned to equilibrium (see OECD *Economic Studies,* no. 3, Autumn 1984, p.35).

38. The "inflation-adjustment" here refers to the incorporation into the deficit/surplus of the inflation-induced loss in the purchasing power of outstanding government debt held by the public, which may be looked on as an "inflation tax" and treated as a receipt. As inflation varies, so does this "tax".

39. See "Structural Budget Indicators and the Interpretation of Fiscal Stance in OECD Economies", OECD *Economic Studies,* No. 3, Autumn 1984, p. 61. The role of monetary policy in the recovery is discussed below.

40. S.H. Axilrod "U.S. Monetary Policy in Recent Years: An Overview", *Federal Reserve Bulletin,* January 1985.

41. Interest bearing accounts against which checks could be written ("Negotiable Order of Withdrawal" [NOW] accounts) began to be introduced on a nationwide basis from 1981. Money Market Deposit Accounts (MMDA's) were introduced in December 1982 and included in M2 and M3. Super-NOW accounts, introduced in January 1983, are included in all the aggregates.

42. Research into this problem has focused on the construction of "Divisia aggregates", assigning different weights to the components according to their liquidity. However, this type of aggregate

has not outperformed conventional M1 in money demand simulations, so the Federal Reserve has not formally used such a construct in monetary targeting. (See A. Broaddus, "Financial Innovation in the United States – Background, Current Status and Prospects", Federal Reserve Bank of Richmond, *Economic Review,* January/February 1985, pp. 17-18.)

43. "Monetary Policy and Open Market Operations in 1984", Federal Reserve Bank of New York, *Quarterly Review;* Spring 1985, pp. 36 *et seq.*

44. Axilrod, *op. cit.* Debt of domestic non-financial sectors consists of outstanding credit market debt of the general government and private non-financial sectors. Private debt consists of corporate bonds, mortgages, consumer credit (including bank loans), other bank loans, commercial paper, bankers acceptances and other debt instruments. It excludes equities.

45. Growth of the broader aggregate is influenced by capital inflows and the balance of payments deficit, which restrains measured money growth in relation to credit expansion.

46. Under the former system deviations of money from its specified growth path, were allowed to show through automatically in changed levels of banks' borrowings at the discount window. This tended to lead to changes in the federal-funds rate and hence to other market rates, as banks sought to reduce their borrowings.

47. This has entailed the introduction of new operating procedures designed to adjust the non-borrowed reserve path, as necessary, in inter-meeting periods. At the FOMC meetings an intended borrowing level is set as a policy decision. This level of borrowing is deducted from the total of required reserves in order to derive an initial path of non-borrowed reserves. During inter-meeting periods as money and reserve demands deviate from the paths set at the FOMC meeting, the intended borrowing level is achieved through appropriate adjustments to the initial non-borrowed reserves path. In contrast, from October 1979 to autumn 1982 discount window borrowing was allowed to change automatically, consistent with the attainment of a non-borrowed reserves path targeted for the entire inter-meeting period. Previously, therefore, borrowed reserves would react endogenously to changing monetary conditions, whereas they diverge now only through discretionary action on the part of the System.

48. The relation of the borrowing level to the Federal Funds rate is relatively loose. Since a chosen level of borrowing is consistent with any of a range of values of the Federal Funds rate, current operating procedures cannot be regarded as a form of rate-pegging. (During the 1970s the prevailing tendency to overshoot monetary growth targets was associated with the Federal Reserve's policy of maintaining the Federal Funds rate – the rate on interbank borrowings – within a narrow range. This led to a failure to adjust interest rates rapidly enough in the face of upward pressure in the monetary system).

49. Continental's borrowing was initially deducted from the non-borrowed reserve target. Provision of funds through the discount window has the effect of expanding total bank reserves, and unless otherwise offset, the lending to the bank would have had the effect of expanding the money supply well beyond targeted ranges. To maintain consistency of the reserve provision with FOMC intentions, equivalent amounts of reserves were absorbed by open market operations. While the large borrowings necessarily involved some added technical difficulties and uncertainties in the conduct of open market operations, the Committee was able to achieve its reserve objectives. During the summer many other banks became reluctant to use the discount window as it might be interpreted as a sign of weakness.

50. At its October meeting, the Committee endorsed the need for a "lesser degree of reserve restraint" in the light of significantly slower growth in the aggregates, evaluated in relation to the strength of the business expansion and inflationary pressures, conditions in domestic and international financial markets and the rate of credit growth.

51. M1 was expected to be relatively strong in the early part of the year, easing later. However, at its meeting of 12th and 13th February the F.O.M.C. agreed that modest increases in reserve-restraint would be sought if growth of M1 appeared to be exceeding a rate of about 8 per cent and growth of M2 and M3 was running above 10-11 per cent from December to March. This caution (reflected in

rising interest rates) gave way, in the 26th March meeting, to greater tolerance towards growth in the aggregates.

52. Record of Policy Actions of the Federal Open Market Committee, 26th March 1985.

53. See *Economic Report of the President,* February 1985, p. 33. Price expectations (as measured by the GNP deflator) are based on NBER/American Statistical Association *Economic Outlook Survey.*

54. *Economic Report of the President,* February 1985, pp. 49-51.

55. T. D. Simpson, "Changes in the Financial System: Implications for Monetary Policy", *Brookings Papers on Economic Activity,* 1:1984, pp. 251-253.

56. Analysis of production, sales and inventory figures over the past two and a half years of recovery also suggests that firms have been quicker than normal to adjust output to orders and sales. In mid-1984 and again in early 1985 when sales fell off, businesses quickly ran down inventories and production schedules. Anecdotal reports also indicate that firms are more willing to tolerate a back-log in orders rather than an accumulation of undesired stocks. Such information is naturally difficult to assess, but to the extent that it is valid, the chance of an economic downturn due to an inventory correction is reduced.

57. The target ranges for 1986 were provisionally set at 6-9 per cent for M2 and M3 – virtually the same as 1985 – and 8-11 per cent for domestic non-financial sector debt increases. The latter embodied a reduction over 1985 of 1 percentage point.

58. Tax brackets have been indexed since 1st January 1985.

59. Multifamily housing appears vulnerable given apparent overbuilding in some parts of the country. Construction of single family housing, though rising, may be affected by lenders and insurers imposing stricter credit standards after experiencing losses.

60. "The Growth of Consumer Debt", *Federal Reserve Bulletin,* May 1985.

61. The use of credit cards for transactions rather than borrowing is approximated by the proportion of card users who pay in full within the billing period, estimated at about 50 per cent by the Federal Reserve Board.

62. An increase in the life of the loan implies slower repayment and a higher equilibrium debt ratio, but this need not imply a greater burden.

63. State usury laws kept rates on loans from rising as much as free market rates.

64. *Ibid;* p. 396.

65. The valuation (or "Q") ratio in Diagram 12B measures the ratio of the actual value to the replacement value of the capital stock. A declining ratio thus signifies falling stock values and profitability. Since 1982, because of tax reform and low inflation in capital goods markets, there has been a recovery in the ratio, but it remains far below its early 1970s value.

66. Capital income is defined as economic profits plus net interest paid, so that the gap between the two represents net interest payments.

67. A substitution of longer-term debt and equity for shorter-term debt has typically occurred in the earlier stages of a recession and early part of the recovery. See "Recent Financing Activities of Non-financial Corporations", *Federal Reserve Bulletin,* May 1984.

68. The ratio of liquid assets to short term liabilities is still above its 1981 trough, however, and since part of the decline may be related to the greater access to immediate lines of credit, the fall in the ratio should probably be interpreted with caution.

69. Up to 1½ percentage points of the 13 per cent growth of private debt in 1984 can be attributed to mergers, leveraged buyouts and stock repurchases, which all have the final effect of substituting debt for equity. Despite some sizeable sales of new stock, non-financial corporations retired equity at an annual rate of $77½ billion in 1984 and the first half of 1985.

70. For a statement of the view that tax reforms have dominated see *Economic Report of the President,* February 1985, p.35.

71. Congressional Budget Office, "Deficits and Interest Rates: Empirical Findings and Selected Bibliography", Appendix A, *The Economic Outlook,* February 1984.

72. This is the conclusion of a recent CBO study. See J. R. Barth, G. Iden and F. S. Russek, "Do Federal Deficits Really Matter?" *Contemporary Policy Issues,* Vol. III, Fall 1984-85. Budget deficits may affect interest rates in three interelated ways: via the impact on money demand, through increased pressures on domestic savings, and through the impact of government debt accumulation on portfolio balance.

73. F. de Leeuw and T. M. Holloway, "The Measurement and Significance of the Cyclically-Adjusted Federal Budget and Debt", *J. M. C. B.,* Vol. 17, No. 2 May 1985.

74. Barth *et. al., op. cit,* p. 85.

75. Though research in the United States has regularly concluded that a positive connection between deficits and interest rates is not supported by the facts (e.g. P. Evans, "Do Deficits Produce High Interest Rates?", *American Economic Review,* Vol. 75, No. 1, 1985.), most of the recent studies that fail to find significant effect on interest rates may be suspect on the basis that they do not adequately allow for the effects of the cycle in lowering interest rates and raising deficits.

76. De Leeuw and Holloway identify a long-run effect of 250; some other studies show a somewhat higher impact.

77. Though monetary growth in major European economies has shown little tendency to undershoot targets, decisions as to monetary target ranges, whether to aim for the top or the bottom of the range, or whether to allow overshooting may have been influenced by the behaviour of the exchange rate and interest rate differentials.

78. It is sometimes argued – to the contrary – that because of its prominence the effect of the U.S. deficit on financial market expectations may be more marked than an equivalent deficit change in other countries, but these arguments are difficult to substantiate by empirical evidence.

79. Cross-section evidence seems to corroborate the link between deficits, debt and interest rates on an area-wide basis. (See P. Muller and R. Price, "Public Sector Indebtedness and Long-term Interest Rates", World Bank/Brookings Institution Seminar on the International Consequences of Budget Deficits and the Monetary Fiscal Mix in the OECD, Washington, September 1984.) For the OECD excluding the United States up to 2 per cent of the 2¾ per cent increase in real long-term rates since 1979 may be attributable to budget deficits and debt in the OECD at large. About a quarter of this 2 per cent can be traced to the U.S. deficit.

80. The United States long-term interest rate does seem to be a statistically significant determinant of long-term interest rates in other OECD countries, but, other things equal, there appears to be only a relatively modest feed-through (about one-fifth) from the United States bond rate to rates in other countries. *Ibid.*

81. Because the structural budget balance for the OECD area has not moved significantly since 1979 (restraint in the rest of the OECD area offsetting fiscal expansion in the United States), it is often argued that budget deficits, looked at collectively, can have had no net impact on OECD interest rates (see OECD *Economic Outlook* 37). However, an alternative indicator of credit market pressures would seem to be a weighted average of both present and future deficits relative to private savings (See Diagram 13). This indicator increased significantly between 1979 to 1984.

82. *Budget of the United States Government, FY 1986,* p. 3-19. International comparisons are difficult, so these figures need to be interpreted with caution. See "Medium-term Financial Strategy; the Co-ordination of Monetary and Fiscal Policies", OECD *Working Paper* No. 9, 1983.

83. The equilibrium debt/GDP condition depends on the relationship of the budget deficit/GDP ratio (b) to the nominal long-term annual growth rate of GDP (g), so that if b and g are fixed the debt ratio reaches a ceiling of $b/((1+g)/g)$ (or $b/g$ if expressed in continuous time). Assuming interest rates are constant, the sole criterion relevant to the issue of whether the debt/GNP ratio (and interest/GDP ratio) will expand indefinitely is thus the stability of the deficit/GNP ratio. If this is fixed, the debt and debt interest ratios will eventually stabilize, as the economy grows. (The rate of increase in debt diminishes automatically in this case and at some point it will equal the

growth rate of GNP.) However, pressures to increase taxes and/or cut public spending in order to stabilize the deficit will be greater to the extent that interest rates are higher than the growth rate of the economy.

84. Cf. the testimony of the Hon. D. T. Regan, Secretary of the Treasury, before the Joint Economic Committee, 8th August 1984. The *Mid-term Review* emphasised the stability of the debt/GDP ratio as a medium-term policy goal.

85. Since nominal GNP growth is assumed by the Administration to be 8 per cent, a deficit of 3 per cent eventually raises the debt/GNP ratio to .03 (1.08/.08) = 40.5 per cent, which is the ratio reached in 1988.

86. CBO, "The Economic and Budget Outlook: Fiscal Years 1986-1990", *Report to the Senate and House Committees on the Budget,* February 1985. The Administration's "current service" projection is for 4 per cent deficits in 1990.

87. This argument (as set out by Sargent and Wallace) depends on the cumulative interaction between expanding interest costs, sluggish growth and increasing interest rates, which will ultimately mean that debt expands indefinitely. It is based on the presumption that the fiscal authorities cannot act effectively enough to increase taxes or cut non-interest spending.

88. See CBO, *op. cit.,* p. 100 for a discussion of this issue. If the 1985-1990 federal deficits (as projected by the CBO) were to be accompanied by monetary expansion at the same rate as in 1984, M1 would expand by 9 per cent per annum. (The increase in outstanding debt of almost $1.5 trillion would contribute to about $130 billion to the monetary base and raise M1 by a cumulative $364 billion – an average annual growth rate of 9 per cent.) This is 2 per cent more than the upper bound of the current M1 target of 4 to 7 per cent, fixed by the Federal Reserve in anticipation of lower deficits than those projected by the CBO.

89. The estimated volume of Treasury securities used to create zero-coupon issues nearly tripled to about $45 billion in 1984. The essence of the zeros is to "strip" a 20-year bond, for example, into its 41 component parts – 40 twice-yearly interest payments and the principal repayment at maturity. A custodian holds the components, and securities backed by principal and interest are sold separately.

90. The new STRIPS (separate trading of registered interest and principal on securities) programme, announced in October 1984 and detailed in January 1985 is designed to take advantage of the demand for zero coupon issues by providing a direct Treasury liability for splitting interest and principal.

91. The foreign-targeted issues are sold through foreign institutions and foreign offices of U.S. financial institutions which certify that the investors are not U.S. citizens or residents, but do not disclose the identity of the buyer to the Treasury. The first offering of $1.0 billion was sold in October at a yield about 32 basis points below that on a companion domestic offering with the same maturity. A month later, the second foreign-targeted issue yielded only seven basis points below a companion domestic issue. Subsequently, yields on these special issues moved in line with, or slightly above, those on the comparable domestic issues.

92. See Bosworth, *op. cit.,* p. 8 *et seq.* The overall user cost varies with the assumption made about inflation expectations and type of financing, which determines the real (opportunity) cost of borrowing. This can be negative if inflation exceeds the rate of interest on debt (giving real holding gains to the borrower) and this will act as an offset to the impact of inflation in eroding the real value of depreciation provisions fixed in terms of historic cost.

93. In the case of a bond-financed investment real interest payments only need to be deducted to achieve neutrality; offsetting the inflation component of interest rates acts as a subsidy. For equity-financed investments neutrality depends upon the opportunity cost of alternative forms of investment.

94. The user cost of equipment is less sensitive to interest rates because interest is a smaller fraction of its total. Real depreciation, the percentage by which the asset wears out in a year's time, accounts for much of the remaining cost, and depreciation rates are much higher for equipment. Thus a

given increase in interest costs represents a smaller percentage change in the overall user cost of equipment.

95. The falling relative price of capital goods reduced the user costs of acquiring equipment by 11 per cent between 1980 and 1984 according to some estimates (see Bosworth, *op. cit.*, p. 8). However, on a fixed weight basis PDE prices have not fallen as much as is shown in Diagram 17. The steep decline reflects a shift in the mix of investment spending toward high tech equipment, which has a low deflator.

96. All interest payments are deductible from taxable income, without any ceiling, in Denmark, Italy, Luxembourg, Netherlands, Norway, Portugal and Switzerland. They are generally deductible up to a ceiling in Belgium, Finland and Ireland. They are *not* generally deductible in Austria, France, Germany, Spain and the United Kingdom, but are usually allowable in the case of house purchase.

97. First, if in a floating exchange rate regime there are large variations in exchange rates, ex-post capital flows may be considerably different from *ex ante* flows. They cannot therefore provide an accurate picture of the international financial transactions responsible for pressure in exchange markets. Second, owing to recent financial innovations and new intermediation techniques the proper attribution of international capital movements to specific economic agents or types of transactions has become blurred.

98. The force of these considerations is somewhat reduced when allowance is made for the impact of certain structural factors and changes which have affected capital flows over this period. These relate notably, to borrowing abroad by U.S. corporations through Eurobonds issued by their Netherlands Antilles finance affiliates and to the establishment of International Banking Facilities in the United States in December 1981 and early 1982.

99. The swing of the net international investment position of the United States from credit to debit could have already taken place. The United States seems to have received a substantial amount of unrecorded capital inflows over the last 20 years or so: according to many estimates these flows have accounted for the bulk of the typically positive and large "errors and omissions" item in the U.S. balance-of-payments statistics. For the 1979-1984 period, cumulated "errors and ommissions" amounted to $130 billion. If they are assumed to represent only unrecorded capital inflows (and no underrecording of current account transactions), they must be added to cumulated recorded flows to gain a better estimate of the true stock position. This approach indicates that by end-1983 the United States might already have been a net debtor (by some $15 billion).

100. In the above analysis, the capability of servicing the external debt is related to business fixed investment. If it were related to a wider concept of capital such as net reproducible tangible wealth – which amounts to some $10 trillion – capital inflows of $150-200 billion per year could be serviced out of additional output with only a relatively small annual increase in the marginal product of capital.

101. The evolution of the current account and productive investment was as follows:

| | Average 1981-82 | $ billion cumulated flows 1983-86 | Cumulated changes from 1981-82 average[1] |
|---|---|---|---|
| Current account | –1½ | –420 | –415 |
| Net business fixed investment | 76 | 430 | 125 |

1. These figures are the difference between the cumulated flows for the 1983-1986 period – $– 420 billion and $430 billion, respectively – and what these cumulated flows would have been had the average levels for 1981-1982 continued in 1983-1986 – $– 6 billion and $304 billion, respectively.

102. M. Levine, "Is Regulation Necessary? California Air Transportation and National Regulatory Policy?" *Yale Law Journal*, Vol. 74, July 1965, pp.1 416-1 447. See also W.A. Jordan, *Airline Regulation in America: Effects and Imperfections*, Baltimore and London: The John Hopkins Press, 1970.

103. G. Douglas and J. Miller, *Economic Regulation of Domestic Air Transport: Theory and Policy.* Washington, D.C.: The Brookings Institution, 1974.

104. R. Caves, *Air Transport and its Regulators: An Industry Study.* Cambridge, Mass.: Harvard University Press, 1962.

105. C. Winston, "Conceptual Developments in the Economics of Transportation: An Interpretive Survey," *Journal of Economic Literature,* March 1985, pp.57-94.

106. See T. Keeler, *Railroads, Freight and Public Policy.* Washington D.C.: The Brookings Institution, 1983.

107. See, for example, T.G. Moore, *Trucking Regulation.* American Enterprise Institute – Hoover Policy Study, 1976.

108. E.A. Pinkston, "The Rise and Fall of Bus Regulation", *Regulation,* Sept./Dec. 1984, pp.45-52.

109. See R.G. Noll, "Let Them Make Toll Calls: A State Regulator's Lament," *American Economic Review,* May 1985, pp. 52-56.

110. See S. Breyer, *Regulation and its Reform,* Cambridge, Mass.: Harvard University Press, 1982.

111. For a history, see, M.A. Sirbu, "A Review of Common Carrier Deregulation in the United States", *M.I.T. Paper Research Programme on Communications Policy,* February 1982, and R.G. Noll, "The Future of Telecommunications Regulation" in E. Noam, Ed., *Telecommunications Today and Tomorrow,* San Diego, California: Harcourt Brace Jovanovich, 1983, pp. 41-77.

112. For a non-technical overview of contestable market theory and its usefulness in evaluating the consequences of deregulation, see E.E. Bailey and W.J. Baumol, "Deregulation and the Theory of Contestable Markets", *Yale Journal on Regulation,* Vol. 1, 1984, pp. 111-137. For a technical description of the theory see W.J. Baumol, J.C. Panzar and R.D. Willig, *Contestable Markets and the Theory of Industry Structure,* San Diego, California: Harcourt Brace Jovanovich, 1982.

113. The term "balkanization" was popularised by the productivity report, *Improving Railroad Productivity,* National Commission of Productivity and Council of Economic Advisors, Washington, D.C., U.S. Government Printing Office, 1973. This report argued that the "balkanized structure has been a primary factor in preventing the industry from developing and implementing an industry-wide strategy for responding to changes in the freight market" (p. 231).

114. The merger between the railroad, CSX Corporation, and the barge company, American Commercial Line Inc., in 1984 has created the nation's first fully integrated shipping company to provide "one-stop" transportation "shopping" through its coordinated, multi-mode shipment offerings. The ICC is currently considering another intermodal consolidation, that between the Norfolk Southern Railroad and North American Van Lines.

115. D.S. Evans and J.J. Heckman, in "A Test for Sub-additivity of the Cost Function with an Application to the Bell System," *American Economic Review,* Vol. 74, September 1984, pp. 615-623, argue that when all factors are taken into account (including input costs as well as network integration), there is no evidence that the Bell System exhibits economies of scale and/or scope. In contrast, A. Charnes, W.W. Cooper and T. Sveyoski, in "A Goal Programming/Constrained Regression Review of the Bell System Break-up," manuscript 1985, used the same data but with improved techniques, to find substantial economies of scale and scope.

116. By 1986 users will be able to choose any long-distance company and access it through the local system by dialing just one extra digit. This means that carriers such as MCI and GTE Sprint will be able to compete fully with AT&T. However, in the interim, customers choosing MCI or GTE Sprint may have to dial thirteen to fifteen digits for access.

117. T.G. Moore, "The Beneficiaries of Trucking Regulation", *Journal of Law and Economics,* Vol. XXI, October 1978, pp. 327-343.

118. Drivers and helpers, who were paid on the basis of hours (rather than distance) lost even more, 21 per cent. (Drivers and helpers are the core of Teamster membership in trucking). Thus, the Teamsters' opposition to deregulation proved to be justified; deregulation has indeed lowered their earnings sharply. Recently, the Teamsters signed a 3-year contract, that limited annual pay raises for 1985-87 to about 3.6 per cent; these were the first wage increases in three years. Concessions included the virtual elimination of the annual cost-of-living provision, a 30 per cent lower starting salary for newly hired workers, and an 8.3 per cent pay cut for temporary, or "casual" workers. Even then, a number of the smaller trucking firms said they could not afford the package. T.G. Moore, "Trucking and Rail Deregulation: The Creation and Redemption of Surface Freight Transportation", Manuscript, 19th March 1985.

119. *ICC Annual Reports.*

120. Reported in *The Wall Street Journal,* 8th May 1985 and *Business Week,* 6th May 1985. However, at least one railroad, the Florida East Coast Railroad, provides an example of a road in the U.S. which has managed to lower its costs and improve its service as a result of getting out of union wages and work rules (see Harris and Keeler (1983) *op. cit.).*

121. Similarly, Amtrak could save as much as $60 million by renegotiating contracts with freight railroad employees who run passenger trains over certain tracks for Amtrak. Unlike Amtrak's own crewman on the company's Northeast Corridor, they are still paid on the basis of mileage instead of hours. And even though the trains rarely travel faster than 80 miles an hour, the work rules require two crewmen in the locomotive, compared with one on the Corridor trains. Closing Amtrak altogether would trigger severance payments estimated to be more than two billion dollars.

122. See Bailey, Graham and Kaplan (1985), *op. cit.*

123. In the case of the flight crew, Southwest's pilots flew 73 hours per month, United's 43 hours, and Piedmont's 49 hours. In addition, United's labour agreement (which was later revised) required that it operate its B-737s with a three-man crew, while most other carriers, including Piedmont and Southwest, used two-man crews. Just on work rules alone, then, Southwest's pilots were more than twice as productive as United's. Southwest's base pay for its pilots was also less, but this is hard to sort out since Southwest has a profit-sharing plan with its employees.

124. For example, in 1980, keypunch operators who worked for airlines earned 31 per cent more than the average for all keypunch operators. Aircraft mechanics were paid about 28 per cent more than motor vehicle mechanics. Aircraft inspectors received about 48 per cent more than the average for blue collar supervisors. Aircraft cleaners earned about 82 per cent more than janitors.

125. For a study of total productivity improvement under deregulation, see D. Caves, L. Christensen and M. Thetheway "Airline Productivity under Deregulation", *Regulation,* Nov./Dec. 1982, pp. 25-28.

126. To cite two examples: captains of American Airlines 727-200s employed before 1st November 1983 receive a maximum salary of $9 057 per month, whereas those hired after that date are paid one half as much; employees of Eastern Airlines were granted nearly 25 per cent of the outstanding shares of the company in the Fall of 1983 in return for concessions in wages and work rules. See D.P. Kaplan, "The Changing Airline Industry", Manuscript, 1985.

127. As early as November 1983, AT&T offered early retirement to 13 000 people as a way to streamline its work force. By June 1984, a 20 per cent cost reduction programme was announced. One month later, for the first time in its history, AT&T introduced a freeze on the salary structure of all of its managers – a move that affected 114 000 employees; and one month after that, AT&T eliminated 11 000 positions in the technologies sector. A study by Eastern Management Group, a New Jersey consulting firm, found four workers for each AT&T manager, compared with a 9-to-1 ratio at major competitors. See W.B. Tunstall, *Disconnecting Parties,* New York: McGraw-Hill 1985, and *Business Week,* 13th May 1985.

128. As reported in *The New York Times,* 5th August 1984.

129. Starting in 1979, the number of purchased route authorities declined sharply (to nearly zero by 1982); but, even more significant, the value of the authorities fell by more than 80 per cent, from over $350 000 per transaction in the pre-reform years to about $55 000 by 1979. As the ICC began to grant more certificates, the number of licensed carriers grew from about 17 083 in 1979 to 25 722 by 1982. See Moore (1985), *op. cit.*

130. According to *Traffic World,* 26th March 1984.

131. Many suggest that freedom to contract and hence to match financial committments and risk should be encouraged. See e.g., J.R. Meyer and W.B. Tye, "The Regulatory Transition", *American Economic Review,* May 1985, pp. 46-51.

132. *ICC Annual Report* 1984.

133. *The Inter-City Bus Industry,* ICC Report, January 1984. See also Pinkston (1984) *op. cit.*

134. These increases are in line with the economic model of efficient delivery systems developed by Douglas and Miller, *op. cit.*

135. See Morrison and Winston, *op. cit.*

136. See, for example, D. Graham, D. P. Kaplan and D. Sibley, "Efficiency and Competition in the Airline Industry," *Bell Journal of Economics,* Spring 1983, pp.118-138; and S.A. Morrison and C. Winston, "An Empirical Test of the Contestability Hypothesis", Manuscript, April 1985.

137. See S.A. Morrison and C. Winston, "The Welfare Effects of Airline Deregulation", Manuscript, April 1985.

138. As reported in the *New York Times,* 28th April 1985.

139. These estimates appear in L.J. Perl, "Social Welfare and Distribution Consequences of Cost-Based Telephone Pricing", NERA, Manuscript, 23rd April 1985.

140. Some of these have an international flavour. For example, in August 1983, AT&T and Philips (Netherlands) entered into an agreement to market switching and transmission equipment in Europe and in December 1983, AT&T bought a 25 per cent stake in Olivetti to make it easier for the two parties to distribute and manufacture each other's products. Some of the ventures are entirely U.S. affairs. For example, in November 1983 AT&T established links to Wang and Hewlett-Packard to produce compatible computer equipment for the first time. In March 1984, AT&T Information Systems joined Rockwell International, Honeywell and Data General to find ways for computers to swap data with telephone switching equipment. In June 1985, IBM, which had already acquired Rolm in order to become a major force in telephone equipment manufacturing, announced that it had agreed to buy as much as 30 per cent of MCI, in an effort to obtain a substantial presence in the long-distance communication market as well.

141. Braniff, which had been the nation's tenth largest airline, expanded aggressively under the Deregulation Act. Its expansion was far greater than that of any other carrier (especially when its new services to the Far East and Europe are taken into account). It proved overly ambitious as fuel prices increased, the economy declined, and the new routes proved far thinner than expected, and by mid-1980, operating losses began to mount. A new management was brought in which tried, but failed, to stem the flow of red ink. The South American routes were sold to Eastern (much as Pan American is now trying to sell its Pacific routes to United) and much of the Braniff fleet was sold to People Express (other planes were used to restart Braniff in 1984).

142. This evidence was drawn together in T.G. Moore, "U.S. Airline Deregulation: Its Impact on Consumers, Capital and Labour", Manuscript, 1984.

143. The merger of the Chessie System and Seaboard Coast Line Industries into CSX Corporation represented the fifth largest corporate merger in U.S. history up to that time. In 1982, the consolidation of Norfolk Western and Southern railroads was approved by ICC, with the new company being called the Norfolk-Southern. By the last quarter of 1982, the ICC had issued its approval of the fourth major rail consolidation of that year – the merger of the Union Pacific,

Missouri Pacific and Western Pacific railroads. Two further mega-mergers are pending in 1984-85: one is between the Southern Pacific, the Atchison, Topeka & Santa Fe and the St. Louis-South-western railroads; the other is between Norfolk-Southern and Conrail.

144. The number of new entry applications rose from less than 7 000 in 1976 (of which 70 per cent were granted in full or in part) to more than 22 000 in 1980 (of which 97 per cent were awarded). About 8 per cent of the entry approvals in recent years have gone to new firms.

145. These data are drawn from the *ICC Earnings Data* of the 100 largest Class I motor carriers and from the *ICC Annual Reports.*

146. The Fortune 500 (29th April 1985) ranked AT&T as the eighth largest corporation in terms of sales (fifth largest in terms of assets); its net income for the 12-month period ending 31st December 1984 was $1.4 billion, which made it twelfth in this category.

*Annexes*

# CONTENTS

# LABOUR MARKET FLEXIBILITY[1]

## A. Introduction

A striking feature of U.S. economic performance over the past fifteen years or so has been the strong growth of employment. Since 1970, employment in the United States has grown by nearly 30 million jobs, whereas in Western Europe there has been little if any increase. Labour market flexibility is a common argument used to explain this disparity. It has various dimensions, but can loosely be divided into two components:

*Labour cost flexibility*, which includes real wage flexibility relative to productivity changes; flexible wage differentials across skill levels, occupations and industries; ease of hiring and firing; the extent of payroll taxes, job security taxes and other non-wage elements of labour costs; and interference of government in labour markets;

*Manpower flexibility*, which includes such features as occupational and geographical mobility, adaptability to changing skill requirements, ease of entry and exit of firms, flexibility of working time and availability of part-time work, transferability of pension benefits and demographic characteristics of the labour force.

Because many of the adjustments occur at the micro level, and can only be captured through industry analyses and household surveys, most of the effects are difficult to quantify. However, the main issues are discussed below, following a description of trends in the U.S. labour market.

## B. Labour market trends

During the current recovery alone, the U.S. economy has added over 7 million jobs, and since 1970 non-agricultural payroll jobs[2] have risen by roughly 25 million (Table A-1). Despite robust labour force growth, employment expansion has been sufficiently strong to allow some decline in the unemployment rate since 1975, in contrast to Europe, where the unemployment rate in the major countries rose by 4½ to 7 percentage points, even with the much slower labour force expansion (Table A-2). Thus, whereas the European countries generally had much lower rates of unemployment than the U.S. in the mid-1970s, the situation had been reversed by 1984. Furthermore, while the male labour participation rate has changed little in the United States, it has fallen roughly 4 to 8 percentage points in the major European countries since 1975.

The overall participation rate (including women) rose nearly 5 percentage points between 1975 and 1984, while it declined roughly 2 to 4 percentage points in France and Germany. There has been a much sharper rise in women entering the U.S. labour force than most European countries, with the exception of some of the Nordic countries. The female participation rate rose nearly 10 percentage points between 1975 and 1984 compared with an increase of only 3½ to 6 percentage points in France, Italy and the U.K., and a slight decline in Germany. Consequently, by 1984 nearly two-thirds of American women were in the work force compared with about one-half in France and Germany. This reflects a significant shift in the attitude of married American women towards work. Whereas single and divorced women have always had a high participation rate, for obvious economic reasons, only 20 per cent of American married women with pre-school children worked in 1960; an estimated half of such women now hold jobs[3].

## Table A.1. Distribution of employment growth by industry

Millions

| Year or month | Total civilian (household survey) | Total non-agricultural (payroll survey) | Manufacturing | Mining and construction | Transportation and public utilities | Wholesale and retail trade | Finance insurance and real estate | Other services | Federal government | State and local government |
|---|---|---|---|---|---|---|---|---|---|---|
| 1950 | 58.9 | 45.2 | 15.2 | 3.3 | 4.0 | 9.4 | 1.9 | 5.4 | 1.9 | 4.1 |
| 1960 | 65.8 | 54.2 | 16.8 | 3.8 | 4.0 | 11.4 | 2.6 | 7.4 | 2.3 | 6.1 |
| 1970 | 78.7 | 70.9 | 19.4 | 4.2 | 4.5 | 14.0 | 3.6 | 11.5 | 2.7 | 9.8 |
| 1980 | 99.3 | 90.4 | 20.3 | 5.4 | 5.1 | 20.3 | 5.2 | 17.9 | 2.9 | 13.4 |
| December 1982 | 99.1 | 88.7 | 18.2 | 4.9 | 5.0 | 20.3 | 5.4 | 19.2 | 2.7 | 13.0 |
| December 1984 | 106.3 | 95.7 | 19.8 | 5.5 | 5.2 | 22.3 | 5.7 | 21.1 | 2.8 | 13.3 |
| Change: | | | | | | | | | | |
| Year 1970-Dec. 1984 | 27.6 | 24.8 | 0.4 | 1.3 | 0.7 | 8.3 | 2.1 | 9.6 | 0.1 | 3.5 |
| Dec. 1982-Dec. 1984 | 7.0 | 7.0 | 1.6 | 0.6 | 0.2 | 2.0 | 0.3 | 1.9 | 0.1 | 0.3 |

*Source:* Bureau of Labor Statistics.

## Table A.2. Labour market indicators in major OECD countries

Per cent

| | Employment growth[1] | | | Labour force growth[1] | | | Unemployment rate | | | Youth unemployment rate[3] | | Labour force participation rates | | | | | |
| | | | | | | | | | | | | Total | | Males | | Females | |
| | 1975-1979 | 1979-1982 | 1982-1984[2] | 1975-1979 | 1979-1982 | 1982-1984[2] | 1975 | 1980 | 1984 | 1980 | 1984 | 1975 | 1984 | 1975 | 1984 | 1975 | 1984 |
|---|---|---|---|---|---|---|---|---|---|---|---|---|---|---|---|---|---|
| United States | 3.5 | 0.3 | 2.1 | 2.8 | 1.6 | 1.5 | 8.3 | 7.0 | 7.5 | 13.3 | 13.0 | 68.7 | 73.4 | 84.7 | 84.3 | 53.2 | 62.8 |
| Japan | 0.9 | 0.5 | 1.2 | 1.3 | 1.0 | 1.4 | 1.9 | 2.0 | 2.7 | 3.6 | 4.8 | 70.4 | 72.7 | 89.7 | 88.3 | 51.7 | 57.2 |
| Germany | 0.2 | −0.5 | −0.9 | 0.0 | 0.7 | −0.2 | 3.6 | 3.0 | 8.3 | 3.9 | 10.5 | 67.9 | 64.1 | 87.0 | 79.3 | 49.6 | 49.4 |
| France | 0.5 | −0.2 | −0.9 | 0.9 | 0.5 | 0.0 | 4.1 | 6.3 | 9.3 | 15.0 | 26.1 | 67.3 | 65.7 | 84.4 | 78.3[4] | 49.9 | 53.5[4] |
| United Kingdom | 0.3 | −2.1 | 0.4 | 0.7 | 0.0 | 0.0 | 4.6 | 6.9 | 11.7 | 13.9 | 21.8 | 58.9 | 60.9 | 84.2 | 80.4[4] | 34.6 | 40.6[4] |
| Italy | 0.9 | 0.5 | 0.4 | 1.3 | 1.0 | 1.6 | 5.8 | 7.5 | 10.4 | 25.2 | 33.5 | 73.5 | 73.3 | 92.1 | 87.6 | 55.1 | 59.0 |
| Canada | 2.8 | 0.8 | 1.6 | 3.0 | 2.1 | 1.8 | 6.9 | 7.5 | 11.3 | 13.2 | 17.9 | 68.1 | 72.8 | 86.2 | 84.5 | 50.0 | 61.2 |

1. At annual rates.
2. Average of 1983 and 1984 yearly growth rates.
3. As per cent of total youth labour force.
4. For 1983.
Source: OECD, Employment Outlook, September 1984 and 1985.

Youth unemployment is another area of difference between the United States and Europe. While the rate of youth unemployment in 1984 (13.0 per cent) declined some from its 1975 level of 15.2 per cent in the United States, it rose to 22 to 33 per cent in France, Italy and the United Kingdom (Table A-2). This partly reflects different timing in the maturing of the post-war baby boom. In the late 1970s the teenage population began to decline in the U.S., as the baby-boom generation moved into the older age group, exerting downward pressure on the youth unemployment rate. In Europe the peak in the birth rate occurred later, so that there has been upward pressure on youth unemployment rates there. High youth unemployment does exist in certain U.S. ethnic groups, but even there unemployment rates tend to drop dramatically for young adults over the age of twenty-four.

The service sector (including transportation, utilities, trade, finance and government) accounted for 23 million jobs or 92 per cent of the increase between 1970 and 1984 (Diagram 4 and Table A-1). Manufacturing employment accounted for less than 0.5 million jobs and construction for an additional 1.3 million. The service sector was relatively immune from overall job losses during the last recession, in contrast to the manufacturing and construction industries. As seen from Table A-1 the goods producing

Table A.3. **Peak-to-peak employment gains and losses by industry**
**The top ten**
1973-1984

| Industry | Employment gains (losses) 1973:4-1984:3 (in thousands) | Share of total gains (losses)[2] (in per cent) | Sub-period employment change[1] | |
|---|---|---|---|---|
| | | | 1973:4-1979:4 (in thousands) | 1979:4-1984:3 (in thousands) |
| **I. The top ten gainers** | | | | |
| Health services** | 2 361.1 | 14.1 | 1 358.9 | 1 002.2 |
| Retail eating and drinking** | 2 265.7 | 13.6 | 1 457.5 | 808.3 |
| Business services** | 2 104.7 | 12.6 | 1 058.1 | 1 046.6 |
| State and local government | 1 147.0 | 6.9 | 2 075.0 | − 928.0 |
| Wholesale trade, durables* | 802.0 | 4.8 | 633.0 | 169.0 |
| Retail food stores** | 753.1 | 4.5 | 461.9 | 291.2 |
| Hotels and lodging** | 533.9 | 3.2 | 198.0 | 335.9 |
| Banking** | 494.9 | 3.0 | 320.9 | 174.0 |
| Miscellaneous services* | 450.5 | 2.7 | 261.1 | 189.3 |
| Special trade contractors* | 434.7 | 2.6 | 207.4 | 227.2 |
| Total of above | 11 347.6 | 67.8 | 8 031.8 | 3 315.7 |
| Total of all rising industries | 16 706.8 | 100.0 | — | — |
| **II. The top ten losers** | | | | |
| Primary metal* | − 411.9 | 20.0 | − 59.0 | − 352.8 |
| Textile mill products** | − 260.0 | 12.6 | − 128.5 | − 131.9 |
| Apparel and other textile** | − 255.7 | 12.5 | − 160.3 | − 95.4 |
| Railroad transportation* | − 205.1 | 10.0 | − 23.0 | − 182.1 |
| Fabricated metals* | − 185.4 | 9.0 | 41.4 | − 226.8 |
| Retail general merchandise** | − 163.0 | 7.9 | 15.6 | − 178.6 |
| Stone, clay and glass* | − 107.8 | 5.2 | − 22.4 | − 85.5 |
| Leather and leather products** | − 84.5 | 4.1 | − 41.1 | − 43.4 |
| Miscellaneous manufactures** | − 77.1 | 3.7 | − 18.2 | − 58.9 |
| Local transit** | − 53.3 | 2.6 | − 14.6 | − 38.6 |
| Total of above | − 1 803.8 | 87.6 | − 410.1 | − 1 394.0 |
| Total of all declining industries | − 2 059.0 | 100.0 | — | — |

1. The fourth quarters of 1973 and 1979 are when the U.S. business cycle peaked, according to the National Bureau of Economic Research.
2. The percent is computed by dividing the increase (decrease) in the number of jobs in the industry by the gross increase (decrease) in the total number of jobs for rising (declining) industries.
*Note:* The asterisks refer to the relation of that industries' average hourly wage to the mean for the private sector in 1984, third quarter, which was $ 8.35. A single asterisk (*) indicates the wage was above the mean, a double asterisk (**) indicates it was below.
*Source:* Bureau of Labor Statistics.

sector (manufacturing, mining, and construction) registered a 10.1 per cent decline in jobs between 1980 and the December 1982 employment trough, while the service sector showed a 0.6 per cent increase. Transportation (partly because of deregulation) and government employment registered slight declines between 1980 and end-1982, while "other services" – which includes business services, professional services, hotels, personal services, and several others – rose 7.3 per cent. Even these aggregate figures do not fully reflect the disparity of growth between service sub-sectors (Table A-3). Among the rapidly growing industries, employment in business and repair services was up nearly 20 per cent between 1980 and 1982; finance was up 15 per cent; eating and drinking establishments up 12 per cent; and health services also up 12 per cent. In contrast, employment in real estate fell nearly 6 per cent, reflecting the slowdown in housing sales, while education, religion and welfare was essentially unchanged. Other service industries with slow or declining employment included railroad transportation, public utilities, motion picture production and distribution, and barber and beauty shops[4].

Various reasons have been cited for the rapid growth of services in the United States: the high income elasticity of demand for services (e.g. health care); the rapid growth of information and other computer technology – much of which falls under services; the greater tendency for manufacturing firms to farm out accounting, advertising, data processing and other services, in order to minimise fixed costs and maximise flexibility; the predominance of small firms, encouraged by easy entry and exit; and relatively low labour costs associated with less unionisation in the service sector. Another factor may have been deregulation. The major deregulatory achievements have been in services, especially banking, insurance, telecommunications, airlines and trucking. For the most part, these have been high growth areas. Moreover, some of the related industries – such as hotels, eating places, tourism and travel-related activities – have been among the fastest growing industries. The reduction in air fares, for example, may

Table A.4.  **Industries with large cyclical losses and gains in employment, November 1982 through January 1985**

| Industry[1] | Per cent loss in recession | Per cent gain in recovery | Ratio of jobs gained to jobs lost |
|---|---|---|---|
| Net job losses | | | |
| Oil and gas extraction | −12.4 | −1.9 | [1] |
| Stone, clay and glass | −13.1 | 4.1 | 0.27 |
| Primary metals | −27.6 | 5.4 | 0.14 |
|   Blast furnace and basic steel | −33.1 | −4.7 | [1] |
| Fabricated metals | −16.3 | 7.7 | 0.40 |
| Machinery except electrical | −18.6 | 6.4 | 0.28 |
| Textile mill products | −13.1 | −1.1 | [1] |
| Leather and leather products | −15.0 | −11.1 | [1] |
| Construction | −8.5 | 3.1 | 0.33 |
|   General building contractors | −12.0 | 11.2 | 0.82 |
| Lumber and wood products | −12.2 | 10.6 | 0.76 |
| General merchandise stores | −4.2 | 3.8 | 0.87 |
| Net job gains | | | |
| Furniture and fixtures | −10.4 | 12.7 | 1.09 |
| Electrical and electronic equipment | −7.2 | 15.2 | 1.96 |
| Transportation equipment | −14.4 | 20.0 | 1.19 |
|   Motor vehicles and equipment | −20.3 | 37.2 | 1.46 |
| Rubber and miscellaneous plastics | −9.4 | 17.4 | 1.68 |
| Business services | 0.8 | 23.7 | [2] |
| Wholesale trade (non-durable) | −0.6 | 5.6 | 9.28 |
| Auto dealers and service stations | −1.6 | 8.2 | 5.04 |
| Real estate | −2.8 | 5.1 | 1.77 |

1. Industry showed no employment gain following the recession.
2. Industry incurred no employment loss during the recession.
*Source:* Bureau of Labor Statistics.

have prompted households and businesses to spend more on lodging, entertainment, restaurants and related activities, while staying within the same travel budget (though this is difficult to quantify).

While the manufacturing sector as a whole experienced little employment growth over the last fifteen years, this masks variations of growth and adjustment patterns among industries within manufacturing (Tables A-3 and A-4). Employment declines in old, large-scale industries – such as auto, steel, textiles – have been offset by rapid employment growth in some of the new, high-tech industries. For example, from a peak employment of just over 1 million payroll jobs in early 1979, employment in the automobile industry fell steeply, to 600 000 during the 1982 recession, before recovering to less than 900 000 currently. This is still 10 per cent below its early 1979 peak. The employment decline in the steel industry has been worse. The industry has regained less than 15 per cent of the jobs lost during the 1981-1982 recession, which came on top of earlier substantial declines in the late 1970s. Among the industries that suffered the heaviest employment losses in the recession, automobiles have recovered strongly, whereas primary metals, non-electrical machinery and textiles have regained only 50 per cent or less of their pre-recession employment levels. On the other hand, lumber, furniture and construction have proved somewhat more resilient, reflecting the surge in residential construction during the early part of the recovery. Besides autos and rubber, electrical and electronic equipment and business services have experienced the most rapid advance during the current recovery[5].

## C. Labour cost flexibility

The contrast between U.S. and European employment performance cannot be explained by differences in output growth. In both cases real GNP has grown by roughly 30 to 35 per cent since the early 1970s[6]. Consequently, productivity growth has been higher in OECD-Europe, resulting in a significant narrowing of the gap in output per employee between the two regions. What has differed in the United States' favour is the correlation between real wage changes and productivity. In contrast to the United States, a "real wage gap" appeared in European countries after the first oil shock, since real wages were not reduced in the face of a downward shift in (the terms-of-trade adjusted) productivity. There are several mechanisms by which such a gap can be closed:

    *i)*   Labour displacement due to substitution of capital for labour;
    *ii)*  Labour shedding due to cuts in unprofitable output;
    *iii)* Eventual downward pressure on real wages in the face of weakening demand for labour.

In conditions of prolonged "real wage rigidity", the real wage gap may disappear because of cost-induced productivity gains (the consequence of the first two mechanisms) rather than real wage moderation. In this situation, the demand for labour shrinks, pushing up "structural" unemployment (particularly if the labour force keeps growing) and creating mismatches between the employment-capacity of the profitable capital stock and total labour supply. Thus European countries[7] adjusted through labour displacement and labour shedding, until the gap narrowed and disappeared through an increase in the capital-labour ratio. Consequently there has been little employment growth in Europe. In contrast, both real labour costs and productivity showed an initial fall in the United States after the first oil shock, but rose in parallel thereafter, preventing the emergence of a real labour cost gap and helping employment to expand strongly long before the 1983-1984 upswing.

A possible assessment of employment developments is thus that real wages have been relatively "flexible" in the United States and "rigid" in Europe: characteristics substantiated by wage equations showing a relatively low response of nominal wages to inflation. However, it should be noted that the substitution of capital for labour has continued in Europe despite the fact that European real labour costs have grown at an average rate of just under 1 per cent – very close to the U.S. growth rate – since 1982. While real wage flexibility may be a pre-requisite for sustained high employment, it does not appear to be a sufficient condition.

Similarly, flexible relative wages between sectors and occupations may be beneficial (in providing the correct incentives for workers to leave declining industries), but not enough in themselves to achieve employment goals. Analysis of industry wage structures in manufacturing shows that the United States and Japan have the most dispersed wage structures, while wage dispersion is typically lower in Europe. The U.S. wage structure, in contrast to other OECD economies, has also widened over the past two decades. However, the implications of this trend are ambiguous, since there is no simple relationship between changes in relative wages across sectors and employment. The 1985 OECD *Employment Outlook* cites the example of divergences between Canada and the United States. Whereas the U.S. experienced lower nominal wage growth and a substantial widening of the manufacturing wage structure, Canada experienced a compression of the wage structure. But despite this greater flexibility, manufacturing employment has increased less rapidly in the United States than in Canada since 1970.

What does seem to matter is the level of youth wages relative to the average, youth unemployment being one of the most marked areas of disparity between the United States and Europe. The United

Table A.5. **Indicators of employment mobility in major OECD countries**

### I. CYCLICAL VARIATION OF EMPLOYMENT AND RELATED VARIABLES[1]

|  | Real GDP | Civilian employment | Unemployment | Manufacturing production | Manufacturing employment |
|---|---|---|---|---|---|
| United States | 8.0 | 5.0 | 56 | 18.9 | 12.9 |
| Japan | 5.6 | 1.9 | 32 | 17.0 | 2.5 |
| France | 3.9 | 1.9 | 28 | 13.5 | 2.5 |
| Germany | 7.0 | 3.2 | 73 | 13.5 | 6.5 |
| Italy | 8.5 | 3.0 | 23 | 19.6 | 5.1 |
| United Kingdom | 7.1 | 3.2 | 51 | 13.0 | 7.2 |
| Canada | 6.9 | 4.4 | 39 | 16.5 | 10.3 |

### II. LONG-TERM UNEMPLOYMENT
As a per cent of total persons unemployed

|  | 1979 | | 1983 | |
|---|---|---|---|---|
|  | 6-months and over | 12-months and over | 6-months and over | 12-months and over |
| United States | 8.8 | 4.2 | 23.9 | 13.3 |
| Japan | 36.7 | 16.5 | 33.8 | 15.5 |
| France | 55.1 | 30.3 | 67.0 | 42.2 |
| Germany | 39.9 | 19.9 | 54.1 | 28.5 |
| Italy | — | — | — | — |
| United Kingdom | 40.0 | 24.8 | 58.1 | 36.5 |
| Canada | 15.6 | 3.5 | 28.0 | 9.5 |

### III. EMPLOYMENT TURNOVER

|  | Current job tenure (per cent distribution) | | | | | Average job tenure (in years) | | |
|---|---|---|---|---|---|---|---|---|
|  | Total | Under 1 year | Under 2 years | Under 5 years | 5 to 10 years | Over 10 years | All persons | Males | Females |
| United States | 100 | 27 | 38 | 54 | 19 | 27 | 7.2 | 8.4 | 5.6 |
| Japan | 100 | 10 | 21 | 33 | 19 | 48 | 11.7 | 13.5 | 8.8 |
| France | 100 | — | 18 | 38 | 28 | 35 | 8.8 | 9.7 | 7.2 |
| Germany | 100 | — | 25 | 49 | 18 | 34 | 8.5 | 8.9 | 5.7 |
| Italy | 100 | — | 20 | 50 | 22 | 28 | 7.1 | 7.4 | 6.6 |
| United Kingdom | 100 | 14 | 24 | 48 | 22 | 30 | 8.6 | 9.6 | 6.4 |
| Canada | 100 | 23 | 33 | 55 | 19 | 26 | 7.5 | 8.6 | 5.8 |

1. Average cyclical amplitude for three major recessions, 1969-1983. Measured as percentage above trend at peak *plus* percentage below trend at trough.
*Source: OECD Employment Outlook,* September 1984.

States (and Japan) experienced an improvement in youth wages (i.e. a reduction in their earnings relative to that for competing groups) in the 1970s, contrary to the trend in the major European economies. This may explain the improvement of youth employment in the United States relative to that in most Western European countries[8].

It is also noteworthy that the United States has a lower unemployment benefit/earnings ratio (the "replacement ratio") than in most European economies, reflecting both lower levels of benefit and shorter periods of eligibility. However, since the replacement ratio has been falling in many European countries (as structural unemployment has risen) while remaining stable in the United States, any direct correlation between "reservation wages" and unemployment is difficult to confirm empirically. In some cases, however, employers' willingness to lay off workers appears to increase with higher benefits, which would make for greater short-term flexibility, but also higher structural unemployment. At the same time, temporary and seasonal lay-offs in the U.S. may be encouraged by the fact that the unemployment insurance scheme in the U.S. is not fully experience-rated (i.e. the unemployment insurance taxes paid by firms do not fully reflect their past lay-off rates)[9].

Other aspects which may favour the addition of labour rather than capital in the United States relate to the relatively large scope for firms to vary their labour costs, if needed. Compared to most European countries the United States appears to have relatively few legal, regulatory or financial restrictions on hiring and firing. Thus there are much greater cyclical swings in employment – particularly in the manufacturing sector – in the United States relative to Western Europe. In the U.S. manufacturing employment fluctuated by nearly 13 per cent on average between peak and trough of the last three major business cycles, compared with only 2.5 per cent in France and 5.1 to 7.2 per cent in Germany, Italy and the U.K. (Table A-5). This implies that U.S. firms have greater ability to adjust their labour requirements to current needs than their European counterparts. (Though there is some evidence that, in adjusting to cyclical fluctuation in demand, European firms tend to rely relatively more than their American counterparts on varying length of workweek than on number of employees)[10]. Small firms in particular may benefit from this. They generally pay lower wages and benefits than large firms, and have a higher death rate. However, the surviving firms as a group have substantially higher job creation and resiliency than the large companies, especially during economic downturns[11]. This may imply a greater flexibility of response in terms of wages and benefits with a corresponding willingness to recruit during upturns. One can point to various factors contributing to this. Generally, employers have the right to hire and fire at will, except where it is against the public interest (meaning, for example, where an employee refuses to commit an illegal action) and where there is a contract[12]. Moreover, where larger firms are restrained by labour agreements they may contract out services. A substantial part of service sector employment growth is (as already noted) attributable to manufacturing firms farming out processes rather than doing them in-house. This is especially true in those areas characterised by high technology, special skills and rapid change – such as in accounting, legal services, advertising, data processing, research etc. This also allows firms to increase flexibility, reduce overhead costs, and shift risks to outside firms that are in a better position to assess and spread the costs and risks. This is one of the fastest growing area of service; during the last two years it grew by 12 per cent annually and accounted for nearly one-fifth of the new jobs in the service sector.

## D. Labour market flexibility

### Duration of unemployment

The strong employment performance in the U.S. is often attributed to its mobile labour force and flexible employment practices. Although it is not possible to provide a comprehensive survey here, it is useful to note some highlights. One feature of note is that in 1983 only 13 per cent of the jobless had been unemployed for twelve months or longer in the United States, compared to 28 to 42 per cent in France, Germany and the U.K. (Table A-5). (In 1979 the corresponding percentages were 4 per cent for the U.S. and 20 to 30 per cent for the three European countries). Viewed from a different perspective, in an average month there are roughly 8 to 12 million people unemployed in the U.S. (assuming an unemployment rate between 7 and 10.5 per cent and a labour force of around 115 million); however, the total number of people actually experiencing spells of unemployment during the year is about two and a half times this number – or 20 to 30 million. In normal times, only about one-half of the people unemployed in any one month would still be unemployed one month later; one quarter would have found jobs and the remaining quarter would have left the job market. Joblessness is thus, to a degree, a reflection of employment mobility in the U.S. whereas it reflects longer-term structural unemployment in Europe[13]. Correspondingly, the rate of employment turnover is much higher in the United States, especially among female, young and new employees. In 1983, 38 per cent of employees had been in their current jobs for less than two years (27 per cent for less than one year), compared with only 18 to 25 per cent for the major European countries and 21 per cent in Japan (Table A-5).

### Youth and female employment

The flexibility of the U.S. labour force is characterised by the large proportion of young people, singles and women in the labour force. Young people between the ages of 20 and 29 account for nearly 30 per cent of the labour force while women comprise 44 per cent. Young and single people are considerably more flexible than prime age, married males, in terms of geographical mobility, skill acquisition and "job hopping". Although married women are less mobile geographically, they are generally more flexible in terms of job-type, employer, and hours. Moreover, since young people and women are relatively new labour force entrants, they are more likely to be employed in the non-unionised service industries which is more mobile by nature than in high-paying unionised manufacturing. The extent to which occupational mobility is an accepted part of American life is illustrated by recent surveys conducted by the Bureau of Labor Statistics[14]. According to one survey of young people between the ages 18 to 24 years, roughly 20 to 30 per cent had been employed in different occupations during the previous year. The percentages for people aged 25 to 34 years and 35 to 44 years were about 12 per cent and 7 per cent, respectively. Moreover, mobility appears to be rather common across occupations as well as among employers. Only 25 to 30 per cent of men in sales and clerical jobs who changed jobs stayed in the same occupation; roughly 30 per cent of them went into precision production, repair services or administrative positions in their next job. Even among managerial and professional people, over half went into other occupations on changing employer. The high participation rate among women and the large number of households with multiple earners also probably enhances labour mobility by providing a more secure income base for experimentation. The Bureau of Labor Statistics has estimated that 75 per cent of the unemployed come from households where another member is employed. In other words, in only 25 per cent of the cases is the unemployed person the sole support of the household[15].

### Geographical mobility

An important indicator of labour mobility is the regional variation in employment and unemployment. As illustrated in Table A-6 there has been wide disparity in unemployment among regions and rates of unemployment have changed rapidly over short periods. In 1975, New England had the highest unemployment rate at 10.2 per cent, reflecting the shift of labour-intensive non-durable manufacturing, (textile, apparel, and shoes) to the South and overseas during the post war period[16]. By 1984, however, New England's unemployment rate was only 4.9 per cent, far below the national average, largely because of the boom in "high-tech" manufacturing and the growth of service industries. Similarly, New York and New Jersey moved from among the highest unemployment rates in the country in the mid-1970s to the lowest in the early 1980s, as they shifted away from the older manufacturing sectors to the fast-growing financial, business and related service industries. They also experienced relatively little increase in unemployment during the 1981-1982 recession as employment in these service industries remained comparatively immune from the downturn. In contrast, the heavily industrialized East North Central and East South Central regions – which have the heaviest concentration of auto, steel, heavy machinery and other older, goods-producing industries – moved from having rather average to the highest unemployment rates between 1975 and 1984. These two areas experienced a doubling of their unemployment rates between 1979 and 1982, before benefitting from the 1983-1984 recovery. One factor since 1979-1980 has been the appreciation of the dollar which has served to squeeze tradeable-goods industries (mainly manufacturing) and shift resources into non tradeables, i.e services.

Table A.6.  **Changing regional disparity in unemployment rates**

Per cent

|  | 1975 | 1979 | 1982 | 1984 |
|---|---|---|---|---|
| United States | 8.5 | 5.8 | 9.7 | 7.5 |
| New England | 10.2 | 5.4 | 7.8 | 4.9 |
| Mid-Atlantic | 9.3 | 7.0 | 9.4 | 7.6 |
| East North Central | 8.9 | 6.1 | 12.5 | 9.4 |
| West North Central | 5.2 | 4.0 | 7.8 | 6.2 |
| South Atlantic | 8.5 | 5.5 | 8.7 | 6.5 |
| East South Central | 7.9 | 6.1 | 12.1 | 9.8 |
| West South Central | 6.4 | 4.7 | 7.5 | 7.0 |
| Mountain | 7.5 | 5.0 | 8.7 | 6.2 |
| Pacific | 9.8 | 6.4 | 10.2 | 8.1 |

*Source:* Bureau of Labor Statistics.

*Employment practices, unionisation and adjustment to high labour costs*

Many "old" manufacturing industries have successfully adjusted to price pressures by reducing real wages through regional relocation rather than by shedding excess labour through labour-saving investment. From studies published by the Bureau of Labor Statistics, it appears that many light manufacturing firms (textiles, apparel, leather, etc.) have been relatively successful in reducing the impact of unionisation on real labour and other costs by shifting regionally (generally to the South). In some cases, they have been able to retain or even increase their previous employment and output levels[17]. Because of their heavy plant investments and geographic requirements, it has been more difficult for heavy manufacturing (particularly auto, steel and heavy machinery) to escape union pressures and other cost disadvantages through regional relocation. Consequently, they have followed more the European model of "shedding" labour by making large labour-saving investments and closing down unprofitable plants and operations.

A consequence of these trends has been the steady decline in the importance of labour unions and collective bargaining agreements over the past two decades. As shown in Table A-7, union members accounted for 15.8 per cent of the private work-force in 1982 compared with 25 per cent in 1966. In fact, the level as well as the share of union membership in the private sector has declined in recent years. This

Table A.7.  **Trends in unionization and collective bargaining**

Millions of workers

|  | Union membership | | | | Collective bargaining |
|---|---|---|---|---|---|
|  | Total workers | Government workers | Private workers | Per cent of labour force[1] | Total workers |
| 1958 | 17.0 | 1.0 | 16.0 | 26.7 | 8.0 |
| 1962 | 16.6 | 1.2 | 15.4 | 24.9 | 8.0 |
| 1966 | 17.9 | 1.7 | 16.2 | 25.0 | 10.0 |
| 1970 | 19.4 | 2.3 | 17.1 | 24.3 | 10.8 |
| 1974 | 20.2 | 2.9 | 17.3 | 22.2 | 10.2 |
| 1978 | 20.2 | 3.6 | 16.6 | 19.2 | 9.6 |
| 1982 | 18.6 | 3.7 | 14.9 | 15.8 | 9.0 |

1. For private sector only.
*Source:* Marvin H. Kosters "Disinflation in the Labor Market", in American Enterprise Institute, *Essays in Contemporary Economic Problems: Disinflation*, 1983-1984 edition.

## Table A.8. Characteristics of wage and benefit concessions 1979-1982

|  | Thousands of workers affected | Number of situations |
|---|---|---|
| Total concessions | 2 533.4 | 139 |
| **Wage concessions** | | |
| Deferral of wage increase | 626.6 | 9 |
| Wage freeze or cutback in increase | 1 295.2 | 53 |
| Wage cut | 239.9 | 43 |
| Wage cut of 5 per cent or more | 201.6 | 34 |
| **Other concessions** | | |
| Changes in work rules | 455.9 | 18 |
| COLA reduction, deferral or limitation | 845.3 | 20 |
| COLA frozen or discontinued | 300.9 | 30 |
| COLA diversion | 888.0 | 13 |
| Offsets to wage or benefit concessions | 230.4 | 14 |
| Contract renegotiated before expiration | 1 225.1 | 51 |
| Plant closing or business failure threat | 305.8 | 25 |
| **Union status** | | |
| Union | 2 174.9 | 123 |
| Non-union | 358.6 | 18 |
| **Applicability of decision** | | |
| Single firm | 2 041.3 | 114 |
| Multiple firm | 492.2 | 26 |
| Single plant | 34.6 | 31 |
| Multiple plant | 2 498.9 | 109 |
| **Duration** | | |
| Current: less than one year (or indefinite) | 428.8 | 45 |
| Long term: more than one year | 2 104.7 | 95 |
| **Industry** | | |
| Construction | 24.8 | 15 |
| Steel | 61.5 | 6 |
| Metal fabrication | 18.7 | 9 |
| Automobiles | 949.8 | 12 |
| Rubber | 87.6 | 10 |
| Equipment manufacturing | 156.5 | 30 |
| Meat packing | 56.6 | 7 |
| Airlines | 74.5 | 13 |
| Trucking | 251.7 | 6 |
| Other transportation | 209.7 | 8 |
| State and local employees | 472.4 | 11 |
| Other | 169.6 | 12 |
| Year: 1979 | 106.4 | 8 |
| 1980 | 212.9 | 14 |
| 1981 | 487.6 | 33 |
| 1982 | 1 726.5 | 84 |

*Source:* Marvin H. Kosters, "Disinflation in the Labor Markets", in American Enterprise Institute: *Essays in Contemporary Economic Problems: Disinflation,* 1983-1984 edition.

has been partly offset by an increase in unionisation of government employees, especially during the 1960s and early 1970s. The number of workers covered by major collective bargaining agreements has also diminished since the early 1970s; currently, such workers total about 9 million members or 8 per cent of the total U.S. civilian labour force. The decline in union membership and collective bargaining probably reflects the decline of the older, heavy manufacturing – which tended to be heavily unionised. The shift of light manufacturing to the South and the growth of services also played a role.

Union membership and collective bargaining agreements have not protected workers from layoffs or wage reductions[18]. It is estimated that over one quarter of the 9 million workers covered by collective bargaining agreements have been affected by wage and benefit concessions over the 1979-1982 period. These concessions took various forms, including renegotiation of existing contracts, deferral of scheduled pay increases, wage and benefit givebacks, pay freezes, modification of escalator formulae, changes in work rules, etc. (Table A-8). These concessions were concentrated in auto, steel and equipment manufacturing. However, over one-half million workers in airlines, trucking, and other transportation were also affected between 1979 and 1982, reflecting among other things the effect of deregulation. Moreover, the wages and benefits of non-unionised workers are frequently tied closely to those of the union members, so that there are often "ripple" effects on related industries. For example, reduction in airline fares exerted downward pressure on inter-city bus fares which, in turn, restricted wage increases for inter-city bus company employees (see Section V of the Survey). These may, in turn, have had some demonstration effects on wage expectations for local bus and truck drivers, other local transportation workers and possibly other city employees. These effects, of course, are hard to quantify.

*The service sector and small firms*[19]

The service sector has accounted for the bulk of new job entrants in recent years, particularly of young people and women. The sector is an important entry point and training ground for the workforce as a whole. An industrial analysis of new job entrants has indicated that nearly all new employees in the goods-producing sector had been employed previously in services, whereas the reverse did not hold. The larger share of employment accounted for by the U.S. service sector (in 1983 it accounted for roughly 69 per cent of total employment in the U.S. and Canada compared to 52 to 56 per cent for the major European countries) also contributes to a higher rate of employment turnover than in Europe, since service jobs tend to have lower job tenure on average. Part-time employment among men also appears to be more prevalent in the U.S. than in the major Western European countries. The importance of services in job creation reflects a number of factors, including the fact that average wages are normally lower in services than in manufacturing. This contributes to making certain services labour-intensive[20]. But this is not a general rule. While the service-producing sector as a whole has lower productivity growth and less capital intensity than manufacturing, industries within the service sector vary widely in terms of their capital intensity, technology and productivity. Table A-9 shows that, of some 145 industries surveyed, services comprise important industries falling in the two most capital-intensive deciles – with petroleum pipelines, transportation, utilities, and broadcasting standing out – while few service industries fell into the four least capital intensive deciles, except for wholesale and retail trade.

That the growth of service employment is not just related to labour-intensity is confirmed by an analysis of small firms. A disproportionately large share of the employment growth comes from small companies – especially new start-up firms. A recent study by the U.S. Small Business Administration claimed that all net new employment in the 1980 to 1982 period came from small firms (100 employees or less). A study of the Californian economy concluded similarly that 80 per cent of its net employment growth during the 1976 to 1979 period occurred in small enterprises (less than 100 employees) and 56 per cent in very small establishments (less than 20 employees). Studies at MIT and the Brookings Institution have attributed smaller, although still very significant, importance to small firms. They estimated that small enterprises (with 100 or fewer employees) accounted for 42 to 70 per cent of new jobs. The large disparity in these estimates results largely from assumptions relating to missing and deficient data. Other studies generally confirm that nearly all net new job creation in recent years has occurred in new start-up rather than existing firms and in the service rather than the manufacturing sector.

Table A.9. **Service industries: some characteristics of capital and labour intensity**

| Service industries ranked in descending order of capital intensity, 1973 | | Service industries ranked by labour intensity, 1981 | |
|---|---|---|---|
| Rank | Capital stock per worker hour | Rank | Labour hours per unit of output |
| First decile (most capital intensive) | Pipeline transportation<br>Railroad transportation<br>Radio and TV broadcasting<br>Electric utilities<br>Gas utilities<br>Water and sanitary service<br>Real estate<br>Advertising | First decile (most labour intensive) | Local government passenger transit<br>Transportation services<br>Hotels and lodging places<br>Educational services<br>Medical services, except hospitals<br>Non-profit organizations<br>Hospitals<br>Post office<br>Agricultural, forestry and fishery services<br>Barber and beauty shops<br>Retail trade, except eating and drinking places |
| Second decile | Water transportation<br>Air transportation<br>Miscellaneous consumer services<br>Automobile repair<br>Amusements | | |
| Third decile | Truck transportation<br>Transportation services<br>Miscellaneous<br>Professional services<br>Medical, education and non-profit | Second decile | Eating and drinking places<br>State and local government enterprises, n.e.c.<br>Other federal enterprises, n.e.c.<br>Personal and repair services<br>Wholesale trade<br>Business services, n.e.c. |
| Fourth decile | Financial institutions<br>Miscellaneous business services | Third decile | Banking<br>Local transit and intercity buses<br>Amusement and recreation services<br>Professional services, n.e.c.<br>Radio and broadcasting |
| Fifth decile | Local transportation and buses | | |
| Sixth decile | — | | |
| Seventh decile (least capital intensive) | Wholesale trade<br>Retail trade | Fourth decile | Truck transportation<br>Credit agencies and financial brokers<br>Railroad transportation |
| | | Fifth decile | Advertising<br>Insurance |
| | | Sixth decile | Doctors' and dentists' services |
| | | Seventh decile | Air transportation |
| | | Eight decile | — |
| | | Ninth decile | Automobile repair<br>Electric utilities, public and private |
| | | Tenth decile (least labour intensive) | Pipeline transportation<br>Gas utilities, excluding public<br>Real estate |

*Note:* The data base for the labour intensity measure does not have the same industry configuration as that for the capital intensity measure. Thus, some slight variation in industries can be noted between exhibit 1 and exhibit 2.
n.e.c. = not elsewhere classified.
*Source:* Reprinted from Ronald & Kutscher and Jerome A. Mark, "The Service-Producing Sector: Some Common Perceptions Reviewed", *Monthly Labor Review;* April, 1983.

# THE TAX REDUCTION PROGRAMME AND INVESTMENT INCENTIVES

## A. Tax legislation and cuts in personal income tax

The 1981 Economic Recovery Tax Act (ERTA) made across-the-board cuts in income tax rates and introduced an Accelerated Cost Recovery System (ACRS) for capital allowances, together worth $169 billion in tax remission in FY 1985 (4½ per cent of GNP). Subsequent legislation has recouped over a third of these lost revenues, notably via the Tax Equity and Fiscal Responsibility Act (TEFRA) of 1982 and the Social Security Amendment Act (Text Table 7)[21]. The net effect of discretionary tax changes has thus been to reduce the tax burden by 2¾ percentage points ($106 billion at FY 1985 levels of income). The 1984 Deficit Reduction Act (DEFRA) is also expected to raise $16 billion in FY 1986, through various tax base and compliance measures (Text Table 8). However, since fiscal drag has automatically raised tax rates by 1¼ percent of GNP between FY 1981 and FY 1985, the overall impact has been a relatively small cut in government revenues equal to 1½ per cent of GNP ($63 billion) between 1981 and 1985.

The statutory income tax cuts were phased in three instalments, a 5 per cent cut in rates effective October 1 1981, 10 per cent July 1 1982, and 10 per cent July 1 1983, *making a 23 per cent cut in all* $(1 - [.95 \times .90 \times .90] = 0.23.)$ But since inflation had moved average income earners into a higher tax bracket by 1984, effective marginal tax rates have only fallen from 28 to 25 per cent of family income for those on median incomes (Diagram 7). The operative tax reduction has thus been 11 per cent. Similarly, because of fiscal drag the *average* rate of personal income tax has actually been reduced by 1½ percentage points (from 13¾ to 12¼ per cent of personal income) between 1980 and 1984, compared with the 3 per cent discretionary change arising from the difference between 1980 and 1985 tax law.

## B. Corporate income tax and investment incentives

*Tax cuts and corporate cash flow*

So far as business fixed investment is concerned, ERTA contained three principal provisions.

*i)* It raised depreciation allowances by shortening the depreciable lives of assets and allowing accelerated depreciation;

*ii)* It extended the investment tax credit (ITC) to some short-term assets not previously covered; and

*iii)* It introduced "lease back" provisions which permitted firms with insufficient profits to transfer (i.e. trade in) tax depreciation allowances.

TEFRA and DEFRA subsequently reversed some of these changes. TEFRA eliminated the additional acceleration of depreciation schedules that ERTA had proposed to bring in in 1985 and 1986, and instituted a basis adjustment of 50 percent of the ITC (i.e. firms receiving a 10 percent ITC would be able to depreciate only 95 percent of the asset). TEFRA also limited the transfer of benefits between taxpaying corporations and those with no current tax liability, by repealing "safe harbor leasing". The Deficit Reduction Act further curtailed the benefits of ACRS by lengthening tax lives for real property

117

from 15 to 18 years. As a result, in FY 1985 the net impact on revenues was put at $11.2 billion, or 4½ per cent of corporate profits[22]. In contrast to the income tax case, inflation has actually reinforced the downward trend: whereas high inflation raised the effective tax rate by increasing the tax base faster than true economic profit, lower inflation has reversed this (Diagram 7). The average rate of tax on corporate profits has been halved, from 44 per cent in 1980 to 22 per cent in 1984, so that tax reform has been less important for cutting company tax liabilities than has the deceleration of inflation[23]. According to flow of funds statistics, the depreciation allowances given by the tax system now exceed true ("economic") depreciation. The difference between tax allowances and true depreciation (known as the "capital consumption adjustment") increased significantly between 1980 and 1984. For non-financial corporate businesses there was a shift from a negative $14¼ billion (the tax system inadequately allowing for true depreciation) to a positive $54½ billion. Applying the statutory marginal tax rate of 46 per cent to this difference implies a tax remission of $30 billion, which would have reduced the corporate financing gap from $75 to $45 billion in 1984[24].

Corporate tax reform, and lower inflation, have therefore helped to improve company cash flow by raising the post-tax profits earned on existing assets. This has raised equity valuations and increased the value of working capital relative to sales. Despite the continuing trend towards greater "leverage" (seen in the rising debt/equity ratio – see Section III of the text), which has exposed company balance sheets to greater short-term risk, this would have been beneficial to new investment for several reasons. It would have raised the value of existing assets relative to price of new (thus giving a relative price advantage to new); it would have improved the allocation of saving to profitable enterprises; and it would have improved the creditworthiness of the corporate sector.

### Effective marginal rates

However, since firms base their investment decisions on the expected post-tax return of their new assets, not on the current tax rate levied on existing assets, it is the marginal tax rate on new investment that is more relevant to investment decisions than the average rate[25]. This determines the pre-tax rate of return required by companies before they will invest in *new* assets. According to the Congressional Budget Office, effective marginal corporate tax rates have fallen significantly, from 35 per cent to 16 per cent, the greatest impact being on equipment expenditures, where they have been zero or negative since 1981 (see Diagram 7). ERTA radically reduced marginal effective tax rates to a low of 15 per cent in 1982, or only about one-third of the top statutory tax rate. The Tax Equity and Fiscal Responsibility Act (TEFRA) partially reversed this, and together with the provision for longer tax lives for real property in the Deficit Reduction Act had the effect of raising the 1985 marginal tax rate by 8 percentage points. But since this has been more than offset by falling inflation expectations, the net effect has still been a reduction in the rate from 19 per cent to 16½ per cent between 1983 and 1985. This will have improved post tax rates of return and enabled investors to pay more for credit, thus possibly contributing to the increase in pre-tax rates of interest.

### Required rates of return and the "user cost" of capital

The *effective* marginal rate of tax describes the wedge between pre- and post-tax returns resulting from the combined effect of statutory corporate tax rates, inflation, depreciation and investment incentives. Its significance for investment behaviour is probably best evaluated in a "cost of capital" framework, which measures the rate of return companies need to receive, after tax, in order to justify expenditure on a given investment project. The standard formulation of the neoclassical user cost of capital is:

$$c = q[(r(1 - t) + d) * (1 - k - t*Z)]/(1 - t)$$

where $c$ is the real cost of capital, per dollar of investment (which is equated in equilibrium with the present value of the net income stream generated by the asset); $q$ is the relative price of capital goods; $r(1 - t)$ is the after tax cost of funds (taken under equity finance as a measure of opportunity cost of reinvesting); $d$ is the true economic depreciation rate on new assets; $k$ is the rate of the investment tax credit; $t$ is the statutory corporate income tax rate, and $Z$ is the present discounted value (in dollars of the year of investment) of depreciation deductions stemming from the investment.

The last term on the right hand side summarises the effect of the corporate tax system, where $(k + t^*Z)$ is the value of the tax concession given by the government to the company. It can be seen that if $(k + t^*Z)$ equals the statutory corporate tax rate t then $(1 - k - t^*Z)/(1 - t) = 1$ and the corporate tax system is then neutral, because the after tax return is the same as the pre-tax one and the effective marginal tax rate is zero. (This approximates, if interest payments are tax-deductible, to the government taking a 46 per cent stake in the investment and receiving 46 per cent of profits as tax; this means the company's return is $.54y/.54I = y/I$, where $y$ is the yield on investment I). If $(k+t^*Z)$ is less than t, the corporate tax serves as a disincentive to invest and the marginal effective tax wedge is positive, since the last term is greater than $t$. If the present value of allowances is greater than $t$, the corporate tax provides a subsidy to investment and marginal effective tax rates are negative; that is, the price of capital is lower than it would be if there were no corporate tax.

A more general specification of the cost of capital would need to take account of inflation in reducing the cost of borrowing funds under debt finance, where the real interest rate is $r(1 - t) - p'$ and $p'$ is expected inflation. Since the tax system allows nominal interest payments to be offset against tax, inflation enables borrowers to derive capital gains from the depreciation in the real value of outstanding debt. In this case, a tax system which allows economic depreciation and interest deductibility actually gives a net subsidy to investment (since only real interest payments should be allowable). On the other hand, it should also be remembered that inflation raises the effective corporate tax rate because it reduces the present value of depreciation allowances and artificially expands the tax base. Thus, in Table 16, the real value of investment allowances increases as the rate of inflation falls[26].

# DEREGULATION AND PRODUCTIVITY IN THE TRANSPORT AND COMMUNICATIONS SECTORS

## The economics of "hubbing"

Economies of vehicle size characterise most types of transportation. For example, a 20 per cent increase in productivity can be achieved by using double instead of single-trailer trucks, while similar efficiency gains can be realised by using articulated rather than standard buses. In aviation, as Diagram A-1 shows, the cost was 15 to 30 cents per available seat mile (ASM) for a commuter aircraft such as the Metro II in 1978, 5 to 10 cents for a B-737 jet and less than 5 cents for a B-747 jet. These economies of aircraft size have meant that two or more carriers can offer competitive service economically between any pair of cities only over the most heavily travelled routes. However, following deregulation airlines were able to realize significant productivity gains by shifting from linear railroad-like routes to sunbursts of routes emanating from various hubs[27]. The increased use of hub-and-spoke operations stems from the limited demand for many city-pair services combined with the economies of aircraft size. It allowed airlines to take advantage of the aircrafts' economies of scale and reduced costs by collecting passengers from various origination points at the hub airports, reshuffling them among planes, and sending them off again to their final destinations. Since most markets do not

*Diagram A-1.* **Scale economy issue: aircraft level 1978**

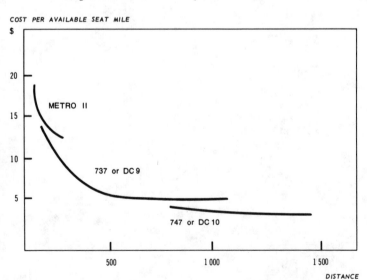

*Diagram A-2.* **Post-deregulation: the economics of hubbing**

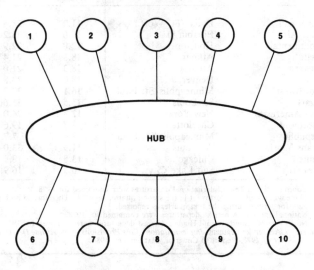

ASSUME : 20 PASSENGERS EACH CITY·PAIR

SCOPE OF OPERATIONS PERMITS FIRM TO TAKE ADVANTAGE
OF ECONOMIES OF SCALE OF AIRCRAFT SIZE

have enough traffic to support frequent non-stop jet service, the hub-and-spoke system discourages route abandonments and encourages services to places that would otherwise be unprofitable. In Diagram A-2, for example, passengers from Cities 1-5 can be given one stop service to Cities 6-10 by gathering 120 passengers at each originating city (20 of whom want to go to the hub city, and 20 to each of the Cities 6-10). Five jets could economically deliver the full scope of services. In contrast, if jet aircraft provided non-stop services, this would entail load factors of only 20 to 30 per cent, and hence much higher fares.

Table A-10 quantifies the greater use of hubbing in aviation. In 1983, most of the regulated airlines had 20 per cent of their domestic flights departing from their lead city, which normally served as their major hub; in contrast, none of them had this level of concentration in 1978. Between 1978 and 1983 American Airlines had more than doubled the percent of its domestic departures from Dallas, as had TWA from St. Louis. The strategy was adopted by the local carriers as well, such as Frontier, Ozark and Piedmont. Moreover, with open entry, many local airlines were well positioned to augment their regional monopolies by geographically extending their hub-and-spoke systems. The expansion of U.S. Air (then called Allegheny) after deregulation vividly illustrates this strategy. After deregulation, it began to branch out from its traditional service area to a variety of places including several sunbelt destinations. Within six months after passage of the Airline Deregulation Act, it had established services to Phoenix, Houston, New Orleans and several Florida cities out of its principal hub at Pittsburgh. Since passengers prefer to use a single carrier through to their destination, US Air became the leading airline in these long-haul markets to and from Pittsburgh.

Following deregulation, trucking also developed a significant hub-and-spoke type of route structure. In the case of less-than-truckload (LTL) freight, cargo from several originating points are consolidated at major terminal hubs and redistributed among trucks for shipment to their various destinations. This practice is appropriate for motor freight transportation because economies of vehicle size are significant, while the cost and time of re-routing shipments are not excessive and are not likely to

Table A.10. **The growth of airline "hubbing"**

| Airline | Leading hub city in 1983 | Per cent of airline's domestic departures at hub | |
|---------|--------------------------|:---------:|:---------:|
| | | 1978 Q2 | 1983 Q2 |
| American | Dallas/Ft. Worth | 11.2 | 28.6 |
| U.S. Air | Pittsburgh | 16.0 | 23.2 |
| Continental[1] | Houston | 12.8 | 22.9 |
| Delta | Atlanta | 18.3 | 21.4 |
| Eastern | Atlanta | 18.3 | 21.0 |
| Frontier | Denver | 18.0 | 33.8 |
| Northwest[2] | Minneapolis/St. Paul | 16.1 | 20.7 |
| Ozark | St. Louis | 15.5 | 35.6 |
| Pan American[3] | New York | 12.3 | 24.0 |
| Piedmont | Charlotte | 3.7 | 19.6 |
| Republic[4] | Minneapolis/St. Paul | 3.4 | 7.7 |
| Trans World | St. Louis | 11.9 | 33.0 |
| United | Chicago | 13.8 | 18.9 |
| Western | Salt Lake City | 10.3 | 16.9 |

1. Continental and Texas International departures were combined for 1978.
2. There was a strike at Northwest in the second quarter of 1978. Therefore in both years data for service during the first quarter is reported.
3. National and Pan American departures were combined for 1978.
4. North Central, Southern and Hughes Airwest departures were combined for 1978.
*Source:* CAB Service Segment, *Implementation of the Provisions of the Airline Deregulation Act of 1978,* Report to Congress, 31st January 1984.

reduce traffic substantially. As in aviation, the adoption of hub-and-spoke type of operations for LTL service has also preserved service on many routes[28]. Small and medium sized firms, in particular, stand to gain strong economies by developing joint distribution networks in the case of short and intermediate-haul shipments. Some scale economies have also been realised by centralizing repair, administrative and other services. However, these have not conferred monopoly power, since firms cannot raise prices much above costs without losing business to nearby competitors who can easily expand their operations. Nevertheless, since entry is not as free as in the airlines, post-decontrol incentives have led to several mergers of trucking firms, that sought to obtain the full range of benefits afforded by these economies of scope[29].

Under regulation, no railroad had an integrated national route structure, and few rail carriers could service a majority of their customers from origin to destination. Nearly 70 per cent of all rail shipments were interline movements involving two or more carriers[30]. There were hubs, such as Chicago, where rail routes converged and cars were shuffled among trains and carriers, but these hubs were often congested. Moreover, the fixed railroad tracks imposed a basic linearity on rail transport. In such a network, routes that were not profitable were likely to be abandoned (if the ICC would permit it). Thus, it was argued that the coordination of rail with other types of transport – such as barge and trucking – could provide the same economies in rail that hubbing had provided in aviation[31]. For example, abandoned freight routes could eventually receive rail service through the development of coordinated rail-truck hub-and-spoke types of operation where trucks would connect with the rail service. Recently, the ICC has begun to encourage such operations by easing restrictions on intermodal ownership and mergers between railroads, barge companies, and van lines.

## Economies of scale in the telecommunications industry

In contrast to transportation, which had not been able to achieve efficient delivery systems because of regulatory restrictions, the telephone system had been able to develop a co-ordinated and integrated delivery network. Transitional problems have arisen because of continued efforts by the FCC to charge access fees on a usage sensitive basis, which tends to discriminate against volume users, by causing access prices for large firms and long-distance companies to be well above incremental costs. Large users are now moving to supply their own services, "bypassing" the local exchanges in order to internalize the benefits of their lower costs. For example, Boeing Company is considering building its own private 70 000-line network in Seattle, in effect making the aerospace company the twenty-fifth largest phone company in the U.S.[32]. Its decision would cause Pacific Northwest Bell Telephone Co. to lose millions of dollars in annual revenues, and would force it to raise its rates to its remaining customers, who would have to cover the network's fixed costs without Boeing's help. Regulators are encouraging the removal of this traffic by continuing their efforts to impose high prices on large users in order to benefit smaller users. In addition, emerging technological developments, such as cellular mobile radio, are threatening to erode the natural monopoly attribute of the local exchange. Should this occur, the regulatory scheme for the local telephone companies would lose its economic rationale.

Furthermore, increasing returns to scale at the local level of delivery are leading to whole new sets of economic arrangements such as shared-tenant services within buildings or clusters of buildings, in order to achieve the necessary economies of scale for PBXs (private branch exchanges) and LANs (local area networks for interactive computer networks). These new arrangements allow users to "bypass" the local exchanges. The local operating companies are trying to respond by finding ways to take advantage of these innovations, but they have been hampered by the new restrictions resulting from divestiture. In August 1984 for example, the Justice Department rejected Ameritech's plan for involvement in such service, because one of its significant components – routing calls according to least costs – would result in Ameritech's determining the choice of long-distance carrier in violation of the consent decree issued by the Court as part of the AT&T divestiture. Customers also face substitution possibilities regarding the number of network lines to be connected and the total telecommunications messages to be sent. The choice between Centrex and PBX, for example, is a choice about how many exchange lines to have for a given pattern of calling.

# FEDERAL ADMINISTRATIVE DEREGULATION

Deregulatory efforts have not been limited to ending regulation for major industries, such as airlines, trucking and telecommunications. Perhaps as important as these highly publicized actions have been efforts to stem the proliferation of new rules and regulations issued by the various federal agencies and departments[33] and to foster more competition at the state and local level. Until the mid-1960s most federal regulatory actions were "economic", i.e. they were aimed at controlling monopoly power, market collusion, restraint-of-trade, and anti-competitive behaviour, or in the case of financial regulations at promoting financial stability. But in the late 1960s concern over environmental issues, occupational hazards, auto safety and other consumer issues led to the creation of special regulatory agencies such as the Environmental Protection Agency, Consumer Product Safety Commission, Occupational Safety and Health Administration, and to the mushrooming of new "social" rules and regulations dealing with these issues.

By the mid-1970s it became evident that these new "social" regulations were imposing significant costs on the economy and that many of the older "economic" regulations were either no longer necessary or were creating other distortions. As part of an anti-inflationary programme, President Ford directed regulatory agencies to prepare "inflation impact statements" to accompany new rules and regulations, which were to be reviewed by the "Council on Wage and Price Stability" (which was part of the Council of Economic Advisors); it was here that the early steps toward airline deregulation were taken. President Carter extended the process by requiring issuing agencies and departments to conduct cost-benefit analyses of new, major regulations and by establishing a regulatory review group in the White House. However, this had little effect in slowing the issuance of new regulations since the review group lacked power to impose effective sanctions on agencies that did not comply with their recommendations.

Subsequently, in 1981, President Reagan issued an Executive Order[34] that required all federal agencies and departments to have their cost benefit analyses approved by the OMB (Office of Management and Budget) before publishing the proposed regulation. If it did not meet the cost-benefit test of being the most cost effective way of dealing with the problem, it was returned to the issuing agency for reconsideration. In January 1985, President Reagan broadened the OMB's watchdog authority by issuing another Executive Order which required each federal agency and department to publish a regulatory programme in advance, listing all significant regulatory actions that it planned to initiate during the coming year, the purpose being to forestall uneconomic regulatory action before they got started. The OMB also received broad authority to review existing rules and regulations on a continuous basis. This centralization of control in the OMB has substantially slowed the issuance of new regulations over the past several years. In 1981 to 1982 the new special task force on deregulation also selected the 125 most costly rules and modified them at an estimated savings of $25 billion.

Moreover, the Congress recently passed the "Paperwork Reduction Act" which has given the OMB broad power to approve and disapprove any federal form used for collecting information or conducting business with the general public (approval being granted only for a three-year period). This applied to all federal agencies and departments, including the independent agencies such as the Federal Reserve System, Security and Exchange Commission, Federal Trade Commission, etc. It had been estimated that 2 billion hours were required each year for the country to complete paperwork required by the Federal government, with the bulk of it related to federal taxation and government procurement. The

OMB estimates that it has been able to reduce this required time by 0.5 billion hours or 25 per cent, with most of the "easy" savings having been achieved.

Besides the OMB, there are several other agencies that have played leading roles in deregulation. The FTC (Federal Trade Commission) has responsibility for enforcing anti-trust and restraint-of-trade legislation, as well as the unfair and deceptive advertising provisions of the various legislation pertaining to internal trade. In addition, the FTC's staff of 100 or so economists work actively with other federal agencies and local governments on fostering increased competition, forestalling uneconomic regulations and initiating lawsuits to end illegal monopolistic or collusionary activities. For example, the FTC is often invited to make statements or give testimony at Congressional or public hearings dealing with new legislation, rules and regulations. Although the Federal Government lacks authority to sue state governments, the FTC has sued city and local governments to end anti-competitive activity such as allowing local taxi monopolies. It has also co-operated with the Justice Department to end restraint-of-trade practices by local professional organizations and business groups, such as doctors, dentists and lawyers. The Justice Department, along with the FTC, has also played a major role in enforcing the anti-monopoly and restraint-of-trade provision of the various anti-trust acts. It has played the key role in the recent break up of AT&T. The Federal Reserve System has been given the key responsibilities for supervising and implementing the various financial deregulations required by Congress.

# CALENDAR OF MAIN ECONOMIC EVENTS

## 1984

*January*

In his State-of-the-Union message, the President commissioned a Treasury study into tax reform and simplification.

The President submitted his FY 1985 budget proposals to Congress, calling for a "downpayment" cut in the federal deficit through various expenditure reductions and tax "loophole" closures, together yielding $100 billion over three years beginning 1st October, 1985.

*February*

The Federal Reserve announced 1984 growth target ranges for monetary and credit aggregates ½ to 1 percentage point below those set for 1983.

The Federal Reserve replaced the lagged with a contemporaneous reserve requirement system.

*March*

The "flash" estimate of real GNP growth for Q1, 1984 was an unexpectedly strong 7.2 per cent (annual rate). (This was revised up in subsequent months to 10.1 per cent).

Reflecting strong loan demands, banks raised their prime lending rate to 11½ per cent from 11 per cent.

*April*

The Democratic-controlled House approved a tax bill raising $49 billion over three years.

Reflecting concern over unusual strength of the economy, the Federal Reserve raised the discount rate to 9 per cent from 8½ per cent.

Banks raised their prime lending rate to 12 per cent.

*May*

The Republican-controlled Senate passed a $140 billion package for reducing the federal deficit.

Liquidity problems at Continental Illinois Bank caused uneasiness in financial markets and provoked a sharp yield differential between private and Treasury money market instruments.

Banks raised their prime rate to 12½ per cent.

*June*

House and Senate conferees agreed to a $63 billion "downpayment" reduction in the federal deficit over three years, to be achieved through $50 billion increases in various taxes (mostly on liquor and cigarettes) and $13 billion cuts in domestic expenditure (largely Medicare). This was subsequently approved by both Houses of Congress and signed by the President. No agreement was reached on planned defence outlays.

The "flash" estimate for second quarter GNP growth was announced at 5.7 per cent (and revised up in subsequent months to 7.1 per cent).

In line with rising market rates, banks raised their prime lending rate to 13 per cent.

*July*

The Federal Reserve reaffirmed the 1984 monetary and credit target ranges announced in January.

*August*

The "Mid-Session Review of the 1985 Budget", prepared by the Office of Management and Budget, lowered its FY 1984 budget deficit estimate by $3.5 billion to $187 billion.

*September*

The "flash" GNP estimate for the third quarter was announced at 3.6 per cent (and revised down in subsequent months to 1.6 per cent).

Banks cut their prime lending rate to 12¾ per cent.

*October*

In a budget compromise between House and Senate, the real growth of defence expenditure was agreed at 5 per cent for FY 1986, compared to an original White House request of 13 per cent and a Democrat proposal of 3.5 per cent. This implied a cumulative reduction of $150 billion over three years from the Administration's baseline projection.

Reflecting weakening economic activity and slackening credit demands, banks reduced the prime rate on two occasions to 12½ per cent and then to 12 per cent.

*November*

The U.S. Treasury reported its tax reform and simplification proposals to the President. The package included a lowering of corporate tax rates from 46 to 33 per cent and simplification of individual tax rates to 3 bands ranging from 15 to 35 per cent. It also recommended a reduction in depreciation allowances, the elimination of most tax credits, a curtailment of personal deductions and the closure of other tax loopholes.

The Federal Reserve lowered the discount rate to 8½ per cent from 9 per cent and banks trimmed the prime rate to 11¾ per cent.

*December*

The fourth quarter "flash" GNP estimate was 2.8 per cent, subsequently revised up to 4.3 per cent.

The Federal Reserve lowered the discount rate further to 8 per cent and banks cut the prime rate to 11.5 per cent.

# 1985

*January*

The prime rate was reduced further to 10.5 per cent.

*February*

The President submitted his FY 1986 budget proposals to the Congress calling for a cut in the federal deficit to $144 billion by FY 1988, to be achieved by a 42 per cent cut in expenditures (other than defence, social security and debt service) from their 1988 current services level. A 5.9 per cent increase in defence authority was requested for FY 1984 and a $180 billion deficit was projected for FY 1986.

The Federal Reserve announced its monetary and credit target ranges for 1985, which were modified only slightly from those set for 1984.

As fourth quarter GNP growth was revised upward, the dollar reached all-time highs against most currencies.

*March*

The Senate Budget Committee and the President agreed on a package of major spending cuts.

Some 69 privately insured thrift institutions in Ohio were temporarily closed by the Governor following a "rush" on the banks by the public.

The "flash" GNP estimate for the first quarter was 2.1 per cent (later revised down to 0.3 per cent) and GNP growth for the fourth quarter of 1984 was revised sharply up.

In testimony to the House Budget Committee, Chairman Volcker announced the Federal Reserve was no longer easing.

*May*

The U.S. Republican-controlled Senate approved a $56 billion deficit reduction package for FY 1986 that had the approval of the President. The package included deferment of the cost-of-living adjustment for social security benefits and no increase in real defence outlays.

The House passed an alternative Democratic-backed plan that would cut the FY 1986 deficit by $56 billion, but which included a nominal defence freeze and no reduction in social security.

The President unveiled his "Tax Revision Plan".

As first quarter GNP was revised downward, the Federal Reserve reduced the discount rate to 7.5 per cent and banks lowered the prime rate to 10 per cent.

*June*

The "flash" GNP estimate for the second quarter was given as 3.1 per cent (later revised down to 1.9 per cent).

Banks further reduced their prime lending rate to 9.5 per cent, the lowest level since October 1978.

*July*

The Federal Reserve reaffirmed for 1985 the broader monetary and credit target ranges that were announced in January; however, it rebased the M1 target to the 1985Q2 level and widened the range to 3 to 8 per cent. It also announced tentative targets for 1986 of 4 to 7 percent for M1 and 6 to 9 per cent for M2 and M3.

*August*

The Senate and House Conference Committee agreed to a compromise budget resolution that maintained a $55½ billion reduction in the FY 1986 deficit (measured with respect to the Administration's Budget baseline).

*September*

The "flash" GNP estimate for the third quarter was 2.8 per cent (revised to 3.3 per cent in the October "preliminary" estimate).

The finance ministers of the Group of Five countries agreed to take more forceful action to lower the dollar exchange rate.

*October*

The Senate adopted a Balanced Budget and Emergency Deficit Control Bill, as an amendment to the annual Debt Ceiling Bill. This proposes to eliminate the federal deficit by FY 1991.

*November*

The House passed its own version of a balanced budget amendment, and a House-Senate Conference Committee began discussing a reconciliation bill.

# NOTES AND REFERENCES

1. For in-depth analyses of the issues discussed in this Annex, see OECD *Employment Outlook,* (annual).

2. Employment estimates based on establishment data (industrial payroll survey) differ from those derived from household data (current population survey). As the terms imply, the establishment data are based on surveys of companies' payrolls, whereas the household data are collected through interviews of individuals. Because of its broader coverage, the household survey is more comprehensive since it picks up employment by small firms. The establishment survey, however, provides better information on industrial breakdowns, wages, benefits, etc.

3. See Janet L. Norwood, "Labour Market Contrasts: United States and Europe", *Monthly Labor Review,* August 1983; Joyanna Moy, "Recent Labor Market Developments in the U.S. and Nine Other Countries", *Monthly Labor Review,* January 1984; and Constance Sorrentino, "International Comparison of Labor Force Participation, 1960-1981", *Monthly Labor Review,* February 1983.

4. Michael Urquhart "Employment Shift to Services: Where Did It Come From", *Monthly Labor Review,* April 1984. Also Ronald Kutscher and Jerome Mark, "The Service-Producing Sector: Some Common Perceptions Reviewed", *Monthly Labor Review,* April 1983.

5. Richard Devens, *et. al.* "Employment and Unemployment in 1984: A Second Year of Strong Growth in Jobs", *Monthly Labor Review,* February 1985.

6. The analysis in this section relies substantially upon OECD, *Employment Outlook,* September 1984 and 1985, and OECD *Economic Outlook,* June 1985, Chapter 3 "Employment and Unemployment".

7. While this analysis holds for OECD-Europe as a whole, it should be noted that not all European countries experienced a similar real wage problem and that they often varied substantially in adjusting to changing labour market conditions. Also, the Japanese experience differed significantly from that of OECD-Europe.

8. Admittedly, the relation between wage flexibility and youth unemployment is complicated by differences in social systems, industrial structures, employee attitudes as well as size and characteristics of competing labour groups. For a more in-depth analysis of these issues, see "Do Relative Wage Levels Affect Youth Employment?" OECD *Employment Outlook* 1984.

9. See "Moving In and Out of Unemployment: the Incidence and Patterns of Recurrent Unemployment in Selected OECD Countries", OECD *Employment Outlook* 1985.

10. See "The Determinants of Working Hours", OECD *Employment Outlook* 1983.

11. See "Employment in Small and Large Firms: Where Have The Jobs Come From?" OECD, *Employment Outlook* 1985.

12. Most union-management agreements would involve a written contract. However, normally the contract will specify only wages and work conditions, not the number of employees to be hired. Unions have frequently found it difficult to hold employers to their contracts, especially if they are experiencing financial difficulties. In some cases the Court has forwarded the idea of an implied contract – such as stated in employees' handbooks – but these usually involve internal procedures of transfers, promotions, etc. (especially as they relate to "equal opportunity" for women and

130

minorities), not wage levels or employment rights. Normally, some "due process" is required in dismissing a civil service employee, unless it is part of a general layoff. For a more extensive discussion of the legal aspects of hiring and firing, see Jack Stieber, "Most U.S. Workers May Still Be Fired Under The Employment-at-Will Doctrine", *Monthly Labor Review,* May 1984 (Conference Papers).

13. See Janet Norwood, *op. cit.*

14. See Ellen Sehgal "Occupational Mobility and Job Tenure in 1983", *Monthly Labor Review,* October 1984.

15. Richard Devens, *et al. op. cit.*

16. For example, Massachusetts, which accounts for one half of the region's employment, had 14 per cent of its jobs in textile, apparel and leather in 1947, but only 4 per cent in 1975. Total manufacturing employment fell 21 per cent in Massachusetts compared to a 19 per cent increase nationwide. See Susan E. Shank, "Changes in Regional Unemployment Over The Last Decade", *Monthly Labor Review,* March 1985.

17. See for example, Ann C. Orr and James A. Orr, "Job Cuts are Only One Means Firms Use to Counter Imports", *Monthly Labor Review,* June 1984 (Conference Papers).

18. See Marvin H. Koster, "Disinflation in the Labor Market", *Essays on Contemporary Economic Problems: Disinflation,* American Enterprise Institute, 1983 to 1984.

19. This section draws heavily on Chapter III of the OECD, *Employment Outlook,* 1985. Also see Chapters III and IV of the OECD, *Employment Outlook* 1984.

20. This is confirmed by BLS analysis of labour-intensity – i.e., labour hours per unit of output – in those industries where capital is less important or more difficult to measure. As exhibited in the second column of Table A-9, service industries dominate the most labour intensive industries.

21. Other legislation affecting tax receipts included the Highway Revenue Act (1982), the Interest and Dividends Tax Compliance Act (1983) and Railroad Retirement Revenue Act (1983). Collectively, these added $1.8 billion to receipts in FY 1984.

22. According to the latest CBO estimates under pre-ERTA law company tax revenues would have been $73.7 billion. ERTA reduced this by about $30 billion. TEFRA recovered $15½ billion by eliminating "safe harbour" leasing (though finance leasing still remains). DEFRA recouped a further $3½ billion. Current law will thus raise $62½ billion.

23. See CBO, "Revising the Corporate Income Tax", May 1985. The average corporate income tax rates shown in Diagram 7 are based on corporate tax liabilities and *economic* profits as measured by the Bureau of Economic Analysis. Economic profits include adjustments for depreciation and inventories. At the same time, it should be noted that the range of rates to which corporations are subject is so wide that there is virtually a different tax rate for every company (*Ibid.* p. 3). A recent study of non-financial corporations found that a quarter paid no tax, while 15 per cent had average tax rates over 30 per cent.

24. This substantially exceeds the figure of $11 billion cited as the direct effect of the various tax acts on company tax liability (see above), and can be interpreted as the combined effect of lower inflation and accelerated depreciation on company finances.

25. The effective marginal tax rate is a calculation of the tax rate that a firm could expect to pay over the lifetime of a new investment. It takes into account all the taxes that a firm would expect to pay on the income from an asset, as well as all the tax credits and depreciation deductions that accompany it. As income taxes and deductions occur in future years, they are adjusted to take into account the time value of money; that is, they are discounted back to the present. In technical terms, the rate is the ratio of the present value of taxes to the present value of income from a particular asset. The marginal effective tax rate estimates shown in Diagram 7 are based on equity-financed fixed assets (equipment and structures), taking account only of the tax rules for depreciation and the tax credit. The calculations are sensitive to assumptions about future inflation and interest rates and alternative assumptions might yield quite different tax rate levels.

26. Because tax depreciation allowances are restricted to the original cost of the asset (i.e., are not indexed for inflation), a nominal rate of return is used in discounting the present value of $t^*z$. An increase in the expected rate of inflation will therefore reduce the value of depreciation allowances and vice versa. For a fuller discussion of the issues involved see C. R. Hulten, "Tax Policy and the Investment Decision", *AER*, May 1984.

27. E.E. Bailey, D.R. Graham and D.P. Kaplan, *Deregulating the Airlines*. Cambridge, Mass.: MIT Press, 1985.

28. See S.A. Morrison and C. Winston, "Transportation Route Structures under Deregulation," *American Economic Review*, Vol. 75, May 1985, pp. 57 to 61.

29. See J.S. Wang Chaing, *Economics of Scale and Scope in Multiproduct Industries: A Case Study of the Regulated U.S. Trucking Industry*, Ph.D. Dissertation, MIT, July 1981.

30. See R.G. Harris and T.E. Keeler, "Determinants of Railroad Profitability: An Econometric Study" in K. Boyer and W. Shepherd, eds., *Essays in Honor of James R. Nelson*, Michigan State University Press, 1981, pp. 37 to 53.

31. See, Morrison and Winston *(op. cit.)*.

32. Reported in *Business Week*, 3rd December 1984.

33. Federal agencies and departments often have broad rule-making powers – both explicit and implicit – granted to them by Congress in enabling legislation. However, in promulgating new rules and regulations, the issuing agency must generally follow certain procedures to allow adequate time for all interested parties to review and criticize them. Proposed rules and regulations are initially published in the Federal Register to elicit public comment and significant proposals are frequently subject to public hearings where "uninterested" groups such as The Federal Trade Commission, public interest groups and economic or industrial experts as well as parties directly affected by the proposals are invited to make statements and give testimony. If approved, the new rules and regulations acquire the authority of law. However, they can be challenged in the law courts on several grounds: if they are not "supported on a rational basis", i.e., if there is no real need for them or if the same end could be achieved in a more effective or equitable way; if they are "arbitrary and capricious"; if they have been promulgated with improper procedures, or if they go beyond the authority of the underlying statute. Each quarter, the new rules and regulations are broken down by subject matter and published in the "Code of Federal Regulations".

34. It should be noted that Executive Orders generally apply only to the federal agencies and departments under the direct control of the President not the "independent" agencies, such as the Federal Reserve System, Security and Exchange Commission, etc. Although the President normally plays the key role in appointing the heads of these independent agencies, he normally lacks the authority to dismiss them once their appointments have been approved by Congress.

**Selected background statistics**

| | Average 1975-84 | 1975 | 1976 | 1977 | 1978 | 1979 | 1980 | 1981 | 1982 | 1983 | 1984 |
|---|---|---|---|---|---|---|---|---|---|---|---|
| **A. Percentage change from previous year at constant 1972 prices** | | | | | | | | | | | |
| Private consumption | 3.4 | 2.2 | 5.6 | 5.0 | 4.5 | 2.7 | 0.5 | 2.0 | 1.3 | 4.8 | 5.3 |
| Gross fixed capital formation | 4.2 | -12.2 | 9.4 | 13.6 | 9.9 | 3.8 | -7.1 | 3.1 | -6.8 | 9.7 | 18.0 |
| Residential | 3.8 | -12.5 | 21.3 | 18.6 | 2.8 | -5.2 | -20.3 | -5.5 | -15.0 | 41.7 | 12.2 |
| Non-residential | 4.6 | -12.1 | 5.3 | 11.7 | 12.9 | 7.4 | -2.4 | 5.5 | -4.7 | 2.5 | 19.8 |
| GNP | 2.8 | -1.2 | 5.4 | 5.5 | 5.0 | 2.8 | -0.3 | 2.5 | -2.1 | 3.7 | 6.8 |
| GNP price deflator | 6.9 | 9.3 | 5.2 | 5.8 | 7.4 | 8.6 | 9.2 | 9.6 | 6.0 | 3.8 | 3.8 |
| Industrial production | 2.6 | -8.9 | 10.7 | 5.9 | 5.8 | 4.4 | -3.6 | 2.6 | -8.1 | 6.4 | 10.7 |
| Employment | 1.9 | -1.1 | 3.4 | 3.7 | 4.4 | 2.9 | 0.5 | 1.1 | -0.9 | 1.3 | 4.1 |
| Compensation of employees (current prices) | 9.5 | 6.1 | 11.3 | 11.2 | 12.9 | 12.1 | 9.7 | 10.4 | 5.6 | 6.5 | 9.5 |
| Productivity (GNP/employment) | 0.8 | -0.1 | 1.9 | 1.8 | 0.6 | -0.1 | -0.8 | 1.4 | -1.3 | 2.4 | 2.6 |
| Unit labor costs (Compensation/GNP) | 6.6 | 7.4 | 5.6 | 5.4 | 7.5 | 9.0 | 10.0 | 7.7 | 7.9 | 2.7 | 2.5 |
| **B. Percentage ratios** | | | | | | | | | | | |
| Gross fixed capital formation as % of GNP at constant prices | 14.6 | 13.1 | 13.6 | 14.7 | 15.3 | 15.5 | 14.4 | 14.5 | 13.8 | 14.6 | 16.2 |
| Stockbuilding as % of GNP at constant prices | 0.4 | -0.5 | 0.6 | 1.0 | 1.1 | 0.5 | -0.3 | 0.7 | -0.7 | -0.2 | 1.5 |
| Foreign balance as % of GNP at constant prices | 1.9 | 2.6 | 2.0 | 1.6 | 1.7 | 2.5 | 3.4 | 2.9 | 2.0 | 0.8 | -0.9 |
| Compensation of employees as % of GNP at current prices | 60.2 | 60.1 | 60.3 | 60.1 | 60.1 | 60.3 | 60.8 | 59.7 | 60.7 | 60.1 | 59.3 |
| Direct taxes as percent of household income | 13.9 | 12.5 | 13.2 | 13.7 | 13.9 | 14.4 | 14.5 | 14.8 | 14.5 | 13.7 | 13.4 |
| Household saving as percent of disposable income | 6.5 | 8.8 | 7.1 | 6.1 | 6.2 | 6.0 | 6.2 | 6.9 | 6.4 | 5.2 | 6.3 |
| Unemployment as percent of total labour force | 7.7 | 8.3 | 7.7 | 7.0 | 6.1 | 5.8 | 7.2 | 7.6 | 9.7 | 9.6 | 7.5 |
| **C. Other indicator** | | | | | | | | | | | |
| Current balance (billion dollars) | -14.9 | 18.1 | 4.2 | -13.5 | -14.3 | 1.0 | 3.0 | 5.3 | -9.0 | -41.6 | -102.0 |

Table A. **National product and expenditure**

Seasonally adjusted, percentage changes from previous period, annual rates, 1972 prices

| | 1974-1983 % p.a. | 1974 | 1975 | 1976 | 1977 | 1978 | 1979 | 1980 | 1981 | 1982 | 1983 | 1984 |
|---|---|---|---|---|---|---|---|---|---|---|---|---|
| Private consumption | 2.8 | -0.7 | 2.2 | 5.6 | 5.0 | 4.5 | 2.7 | 0.5 | 2.0 | 1.3 | 4.8 | 5.3 |
| Public expenditure | 1.4 | 2.7 | 1.9 | 0 | 1.5 | 2.0 | 1.3 | 2.2 | 0.9 | 2.0 | -0.3 | 3.5 |
| Gross fixed investment | 1.2 | -8.2 | -12.2 | 9.4 | 13.6 | 9.9 | 3.8 | -7.1 | 3.1 | -6.8 | 9.7 | 18.0 |
| Residential | -1.5 | -22.6 | -12.5 | 21.3 | 18.6 | 2.8 | -5.2 | -20.3 | -5.5 | -15.0 | 41.7 | 12.2 |
| Non-residential | 2.2 | -1.7 | -12.1 | 5.3 | 11.7 | 12.9 | 7.4 | -2.4 | 5.5 | -4.7 | 2.5 | 19.8 |
| Final domestic demand | 2.2 | -1.2 | -0.1 | 4.9 | 5.5 | 4.8 | 2.6 | -0.4 | 2.0 | 0.2 | 4.4 | 6.8 |
| Stockbuilding[1] | -0.1 | -0.4 | -1.5 | 1.2 | 0.4 | 0.2 | -0.6 | -0.8 | 1.1 | -1.4 | 0.5 | 1.9 |
| Total domestic demand | 2.1 | -1.6 | -1.6 | 6.1 | 5.9 | 5.0 | 2.0 | -1.2 | 3.1 | -1.2 | 5.0 | 8.7 |
| Exports of goods and services | 3.7 | 11.5 | -4.5 | 6.3 | 2.5 | 12.2 | 15.4 | 8.8 | 0.7 | -7.8 | -5.6 | 4.7 |
| Imports of goods and services | 4.5 | -1.3 | -11.5 | 18.6 | 7.4 | 13.0 | 6.2 | -0.2 | 7.0 | 1.3 | 7.6 | 27.0 |
| Foreign balance[1] | 0 | 1.0 | 0.4 | -0.5 | -0.3 | 0.1 | 0.9 | 0.9 | -0.4 | -0.9 | -1.2 | -1.8 |
| GNP | 2.0 | -0.6 | -1.2 | 5.4 | 5.5 | 5.0 | 2.8 | -0.3 | 2.5 | -2.1 | 3.7 | 6.8 |

| | 1984 levels (1972 $ billions) | 1983 | | | | 1984 | | | | 1985 | |
|---|---|---|---|---|---|---|---|---|---|---|---|
| | | Q1 | Q2 | Q3 | Q4 | Q1 | Q2 | Q3 | Q4 | Q1 | Q2 |
| Private consumption | 1 062 | 2.6 | 10.0 | 3.8 | 6.8 | 4.6 | 7.9 | 0.6 | 3.6 | 5.2 | 4.9 |
| Public expenditure | 302 | -8.1 | -2.6 | -0.5 | -4.3 | 1.0 | 18.6 | 5.4 | 5.9 | 0.3 | 3.7 |
| Gross fixed investment | 265 | 11.1 | 22.7 | 21.9 | 23.4 | 20.8 | 16.4 | 9.3 | 5.3 | -0.1 | 12.6 |
| Residential | 60 | 64.4 | 78.5 | 31.6 | 4.3 | 20.8 | 1.3 | -4.5 | -5.9 | 5.5 | 6.1 |
| Non-residential | 205 | 0.2 | 9.5 | 18.9 | 30.6 | 20.5 | 21.4 | 13.7 | 8.5 | -1.5 | 14.4 |
| Final domestic demand | 1 630 | 1.4 | 9.1 | 5.4 | 6.9 | 6.3 | 11.1 | 2.9 | 4.3 | 3.4 | 5.9 |
| Stockbuilding[1] | 25 | 2.2 | 2.8 | 1.8 | 1.6 | 6.2 | -2.8 | 2.5 | -3.4 | 0.6 | -2.6 |
| Total domestic demand | 1 654 | 3.7 | 12.3 | 7.4 | 8.7 | 12.9 | 7.9 | 5.4 | 0.9 | 3.9 | 3.2 |
| Exports of goods and services | 146 | 4.5 | -3.4 | 14.1 | -1.7 | 11.5 | -0.6 | 7.7 | -0.8 | -8.9 | -15.2 |
| Imports of goods and services | 161 | 9.9 | 31.2 | 22.0 | 32.3 | 47.1 | 8.1 | 55.4 | -28.3 | 32.2 | -0.7 |
| Foreign balance[1] | -15 | -0.3 | -2.5 | -0.4 | -2.6 | -2.6 | -0.8 | -3.8 | 3.3 | -3.6 | -1.3 |
| GNP | 1 639 | 3.3 | 9.4 | 6.8 | 5.9 | 10.1 | 7.1 | 1.6 | 4.2 | 0.3 | 1.9 |

1. Changes as a percentage of previous period GNP.
Source: *Survey of Current Business*, US Department of Commerce.

Table B. Labour market (s.a.)

| | 1975 | 1976 | 1977 | 1978 | 1979 | 1980 | 1981 | 1982 | 1983 | 1984 | 1984 Q3 | 1984 Q4 | 1985 Q1 | 1985 Q2 |
|---|---|---|---|---|---|---|---|---|---|---|---|---|---|---|
| **1. Numbers of persons, millions** | | | | | | | | | | | | | | |
| Population of working age[1][2] | 153.2 | 156.1 | 159.0 | 161.9 | 164.9 | 167.7 | 170.1 | 172.3 | 174.2 | 176.4 | 176.6 | 177.1 | 177.5 | 177.9 |
| Civilian labour force[1] | 93.6 | 96.2 | 99.0 | 102.2 | 105.0 | 107.0 | 108.7 | 110.2 | 111.5 | 113.5 | 113.8 | 114.2 | 115.2 | 115.2 |
| Unemployment[1] | 7.9 | 7.4 | 7.0 | 6.2 | 6.1 | 7.7 | 8.3 | 10.7 | 10.7 | 8.5 | 8.4 | 8.2 | 8.4 | 8.4 |
| Employment[1] | 85.8 | 88.8 | 92.0 | 96.0 | 98.8 | 99.3 | 100.4 | 99.5 | 100.8 | 105.0 | 105.3 | 106.0 | 106.7 | 106.8 |
| Employment[3] | 76.9 | 79.4 | 82.5 | 86.7 | 89.8 | 90.4 | 91.2 | 89.6 | 90.2 | 94.5 | 94.9 | 95.8 | 96.6 | 97.3 |
| Federal government | 2.7 | 2.7 | 2.7 | 2.8 | 2.8 | 2.9 | 2.9 | 2.7 | 2.8 | 2.8 | 2.8 | 2.8 | 2.8 | 2.9 |
| State and local | 11.9 | 12.1 | 12.4 | 12.9 | 13.2 | 13.4 | 13.3 | 13.1 | 13.1 | 13.2 | 13.2 | 13.3 | 13.3 | 13.3 |
| Manufacturing | 18.3 | 19.0 | 19.7 | 20.5 | 21.0 | 20.3 | 20.2 | 18.8 | 18.4 | 19.4 | 19.7 | 19.7 | 19.6 | 19.4 |
| Construction | 3.5 | 3.6 | 3.9 | 4.2 | 4.5 | 4.3 | 4.2 | 3.9 | 3.9 | 4.3 | 4.4 | 4.4 | 4.5 | 4.6 |
| Other | 40.4 | 41.9 | 43.8 | 46.3 | 48.4 | 49.5 | 50.8 | 51.0 | 51.9 | 54.7 | 54.9 | 55.6 | 56.4 | 57.1 |
| **2. Percentage change from previous period (s.a.a.r.)** | | | | | | | | | | | | | | |
| Population of working age[1][2] | 2.0 | 2.0 | 1.8 | 1.8 | 1.8 | 1.7 | 1.4 | 1.3 | 1.1 | 1.2 | 1.1 | 1.2 | 0.9 | 1.0 |
| Civilian labour force[1] | 1.8 | 2.7 | 2.9 | 3.3 | 2.7 | 1.9 | 1.6 | 1.4 | 1.2 | 1.8 | 0.8 | 1.5 | 3.5 | 0.1 |
| Employment[1] | -1.1 | 3.4 | 3.7 | 4.4 | 2.9 | 0.5 | 1.1 | -0.9 | 1.3 | 4.1 | 1.2 | 2.5 | 3.0 | 0.1 |
| Employment[3] | -1.7 | 3.2 | 3.9 | 5.1 | 3.6 | 0.7 | 0.8 | -1.7 | 0.7 | 4.7 | 3.9 | 4.0 | 3.3 | 2.9 |
| Federal government | 0.9 | -0.5 | -0.2 | 0.9 | 0.7 | 3.4 | -3.3 | -1.2 | 1.3 | 1.2 | 2.0 | 2.2 | 1.4 | 4.0 |
| State and local | 4.3 | 1.7 | 2.2 | 4.2 | 2.0 | 1.5 | -0.9 | -1.2 | 0 | 0.6 | 2.2 | 2.2 | 0.1 | 1.5 |
| Manufacturing | -8.7 | 3.7 | 3.6 | 4.2 | 2.6 | -3.6 | -0.6 | -6.9 | -1.8 | 5.3 | 2.1 | 1.1 | -3.4 | -2.7 |
| Construction | -12.3 | 1.4 | 7.7 | 9.8 | 5.5 | -2.6 | -3.6 | -6.8 | 1.1 | 10.1 | 6.7 | 4.7 | 11.8 | 9.9 |
| Other | 1.0 | 3.8 | 4.5 | 5.7 | 4.5 | 2.4 | 2.5 | 0.5 | 1.7 | 5.3 | 4.8 | 5.5 | 6.1 | 4.6 |
| **3. Unemployment rates** | | | | | | | | | | | | | | |
| Total | 8.5 | 7.7 | 7.0 | 6.1 | 5.9 | 7.2 | 7.6 | 9.7 | 9.6 | 7.5 | 7.5 | 7.2 | 7.3 | 7.3 |
| Married men | 5.1 | 4.2 | 3.5 | 2.8 | 2.7 | 4.2 | 4.3 | 6.5 | 6.5 | 4.6 | 4.5 | 4.4 | 4.4 | 4.3 |
| Females | 9.3 | 8.6 | 8.2 | 7.1 | 6.8 | 7.4 | 7.9 | 9.4 | 9.2 | 7.6 | 7.6 | 7.4 | 7.6 | 7.5 |
| Youths | 20.0 | 19.0 | 17.8 | 16.3 | 16.1 | 17.8 | 19.6 | 23.2 | 22.4 | 18.9 | 18.6 | 18.4 | 18.5 | 18.3 |
| **4. Activity rate[4]** | 65.8 | 66.8 | 68.1 | 69.9 | 70.7 | 69.9 | 69.8 | 68.4 | 68.7 | 70.8 | 70.9 | 71.1 | 71.6 | 71.4 |

1. Household survey.
2. Non-institutional population aged 16 and over.
3. Non-agricultural payroll.
4. Employment as percentage of population aged from 16 to 64.
Source: Monthly Labor Review. Department of Labor.

136

Table C. Costs and prices
Percentage changes from previous period, s.a.a.r.

| | 1975 | 1976 | 1977 | 1978 | 1979 | 1980 | 1981 | 1982 | 1983 | 1984 | 1984 Q3 | Q4 | 1985 Q1 | Q2 |
|---|---|---|---|---|---|---|---|---|---|---|---|---|---|---|
| **Rates of pay** | | | | | | | | | | | | | | |
| Major wage settlements[1] | 8.7 | 8.1 | 8.0 | 8.2 | 9.1 | 9.9 | 9.5 | 6.8 | 4.0 | 3.7 | 4.8 | 2.8 | 2.8 | 3.2 |
| Hourly earnings index[2] | 8.3 | 7.2 | 7.5 | 8.2 | 8.0 | 9.0 | 9.1 | 6.8 | 4.7 | 3.4 | 3.1 | 3.2 | 3.4 | 3.3 |
| Wages and salaries per person | 6.5 | 6.7 | 6.5 | 7.8 | 8.7 | 9.1 | 8.9 | 6.0 | 4.4 | 4.4 | 4.7 | 3.8 | 4.7 | 6.0 |
| Compensation per person | 7.3 | 7.6 | 7.2 | 8.2 | 8.9 | 9.2 | 9.2 | 6.5 | 5.1 | 5.1 | 4.9 | 4.2 | 5.1 | 5.9 |
| **Productivity** | | | | | | | | | | | | | | |
| Hourly, non-farm business | 1.8 | 3.2 | 2.1 | -0.1 | -0.7 | -0.3 | 1.5 | -0.3 | 3.4 | 2.7 | -1.1 | 2.3 | -3.3 | 1.1 |
| Per employee, non-farm business | 0.6 | 3.3 | 1.7 | -0.6 | -1.3 | -1.3 | 1.4 | -1.5 | 4.0 | 3.6 | -1.9 | 1.5 | -4.1 | 0.4 |
| Per employee, whole economy | -0.1 | 1.9 | 1.8 | 0.6 | 0 | -0.8 | 1.4 | -1.3 | 2.4 | 2.6 | 0.3 | 1.7 | -2.6 | 1.8 |
| **Unit labour costs** | | | | | | | | | | | | | | |
| Hourly, non-farm business | 7.4 | 4.8 | 5.1 | 8.0 | 10.8 | 11.2 | 7.7 | 8.1 | 1.3 | 1.4 | 4.9 | 1.3 | 8.5 | 2.2 |
| Whole economy | 7.4 | 5.6 | 5.4 | 7.5 | 9.0 | 10.1 | 7.6 | 7.9 | 2.7 | 2.5 | 4.6 | 2.4 | 8.0 | 4.0 |
| **Prices** | | | | | | | | | | | | | | |
| GNP deflator | 9.2 | 5.2 | 5.8 | 7.4 | 8.7 | 9.2 | 9.6 | 6.0 | 3.8 | 3.8 | 4.0 | 2.8 | 5.4 | 2.6 |
| Private consumption deflator | 7.6 | 5.2 | 5.8 | 7.0 | 9.0 | 10.2 | 8.7 | 5.9 | 3.7 | 3.2 | 4.3 | 2.4 | 3.2 | 2.8 |
| Consumer price index | 9.2 | 5.7 | 6.5 | 7.6 | 11.3 | 13.5 | 10.4 | 6.2 | 3.2 | 4.3 | 3.7 | 3.5 | 3.3 | 4.2 |
| Food | 8.5 | 3.1 | 6.3 | 10.1 | 10.9 | 8.5 | 7.8 | 4.0 | 2.1 | 3.9 | 3.2 | 3.2 | 3.4 | -0.3 |
| Wholesale prices | 9.2 | 4.6 | 6.1 | 7.8 | 12.5 | 14.1 | 9.1 | 2.0 | 1.3 | 2.4 | -0.9 | 0.4 | -2.2 | 0.4 |
| Crude products | 0.4 | 2.9 | 3.2 | 12.0 | 17.0 | 11.0 | 8.0 | -2.9 | 1.4 | 2.2 | -4.7 | -1.7 | -12.6 | -13.2 |
| Intermediate products | 10.5 | 5.2 | 6.5 | 6.8 | 12.6 | 15.4 | 9.3 | 1.4 | 0.6 | 2.5 | -0.5 | 0.4 | -1.7 | 0.5 |
| Finished products | 10.8 | 4.4 | 6.5 | 7.8 | 11.1 | 13.5 | 9.3 | 4.0 | 1.7 | 2.1 | 0.1 | 0.4 | 0.7 | 2.2 |

1. Total effective wage adjustment in all industries under collective agreements in non-farm industry covering at least 1 000 workers, not seasonally adjusted.
2. Production or non-supervisory workers on private non-agricultural payrolls.
Source: Monthly Labor Review, Bureau of Labor Statistics, Department of Labor; Survey of Current Business, US Department of Commerce.

Table D. **Household income and expenditure**

OECD definitions

| | 1975 | 1976 | 1977 | 1978 | 1979 | 1980 | 1981 | 1982 | 1983 | 1984 |
|---|---|---|---|---|---|---|---|---|---|---|
| *$ billion* | | | | | | | | | | |
| Wages and salaries | 806 | 890 | 983 | 1 106 | 1 238 | 1 357 | 1 493 | 1 569 | 1 659 | 1 804 |
| Other labour income | 125 | 146 | 169 | 195 | 221 | 243 | 272 | 296 | 326 | 369 |
| Compensation of employees | 931 | 1 036 | 1 152 | 1 301 | 1 458 | 1 600 | 1 765 | 1 864 | 1 985 | 2 173 |
| Property income, etc. | 266 | 287 | 321 | 370 | 430 | 472 | 564 | 596 | 627 | 728 |
| Current transfers received | 178 | 194 | 208 | 224 | 250 | 298 | 337 | 376 | 405 | 417 |
| *less:* Consumer debt interest | 24 | 27 | 31 | 37 | 45 | 50 | 54 | 58 | 65 | 78 |
| Total income | 1 351 | 1 491 | 1 650 | 1 857 | 2 092 | 2 319 | 2 612 | 2 777 | 2 951 | 3 240 |
| *less:* Direct taxes | 281 | 324 | 368 | 421 | 489 | 541 | 625 | 657 | 678 | 743 |
| Disposable income | 1 071 | 1 167 | 1 283 | 1 436 | 1 604 | 1 778 | 1 987 | 2 121 | 2 274 | 2 498 |
| Consumers expenditure | 976 | 1 084 | 1 204 | 1 346 | 1 507 | 1 668 | 1 849 | 1 985 | 2 156 | 2 342 |
| Savings | 94 | 83 | 78 | 90 | 97 | 110 | 137 | 136 | 118 | 156 |
| *Percentage changes from previous period (s.a.a.r.)* | | | | | | | | | | |
| Wages and salaries | 5.3 | 10.4 | 10.5 | 12.5 | 11.9 | 9.6 | 10.1 | 5.1 | 5.8 | 8.7 |
| Other labour income | 11.9 | 17.2 | 15.3 | 15.4 | 13.2 | 10.2 | 12.1 | 8.5 | 10.2 | 13.3 |
| Compensation of employees | 6.1 | 11.3 | 11.2 | 12.9 | 12.1 | 9.7 | 10.4 | 5.6 | 6.5 | 9.5 |
| Property income, etc. | 4.9 | 7.7 | 12.0 | 15.2 | 16.2 | 9.8 | 19.5 | 5.7 | 5.2 | 16.2 |
| Current transfers received | 26.2 | 9.0 | 7.0 | 7.7 | 11.8 | 18.9 | 13.3 | 11.5 | 7.7 | 2.9 |
| Total income | 8.3 | 10.3 | 10.7 | 12.5 | 12.7 | 10.8 | 12.6 | 6.3 | 6.3 | 9.8 |
| *less:* Direct taxes | 1.9 | 15.3 | 13.6 | 14.5 | 16.0 | 10.7 | 15.6 | 5.0 | 3.3 | 9.5 |
| Disposable income | 10.1 | 9.0 | 9.9 | 12.0 | 11.7 | 10.9 | 11.7 | 6.8 | 7.2 | 9.9 |
| Consumers expenditure | 9.9 | 11.0 | 11.1 | 11.8 | 11.9 | 10.7 | 10.9 | 7.3 | 8.6 | 8.6 |
| Savings ratio[1] | 8.8 | 7.1 | 6.1 | 6.2 | 6.0 | 6.2 | 6.9 | 6.4 | 5.2 | 6.3 |
| Consumer price deflator | 7.6 | 5.1 | 5.8 | 7.0 | 9.0 | 10.2 | 8.7 | 5.9 | 3.7 | 3.2 |
| Real disposable income | 2.3 | 3.6 | 3.9 | 4.6 | 2.5 | 0.6 | 2.8 | 0.8 | 3.4 | 6.5 |
| Real consumers expenditure | 2.2 | 5.6 | 5.0 | 4.5 | 2.7 | 0.5 | 2.0 | 1.3 | 4.8 | 5.3 |
| Non-durables | 1.6 | 4.7 | 3.6 | 3.3 | 2.5 | 0.7 | 1.5 | 0.6 | 3.7 | 4.6 |
| Services | 3.3 | 4.3 | 4.9 | 4.8 | 3.7 | 2.7 | 2.3 | 2.5 | 3.4 | 3.3 |
| Durables | 0.3 | 12.3 | 9.1 | 6.4 | 0.2 | -6.6 | 2.5 | -0.3 | 12.1 | 13.1 |

1. Savings as percentage of disposable income.
*Source:* Survey of Current Business, US Department of Commerce.

## Table E. Monetary indicators

| | 1975 | 1976 | 1977 | 1978 | 1979 | 1980 | 1981 | 1982 | 1983 | 1984 | 1984 Q3 | 1984 Q4 | 1985 Q1 | 1985 Q2 |
|---|---|---|---|---|---|---|---|---|---|---|---|---|---|---|
| **Monetary aggregates** *(percentage changes from previous period s.a.a.r.)* | | | | | | | | | | | | | | |
| M1 | 4.7 | 5.6 | 7.6 | 8.0 | 7.9 | 6.3 | 7.1 | 6.6 | 11.2 | 6.9 | 4.6 | 3.3 | 10.9 | 10.6 |
| M2 | 9.3 | 12.9 | 12.7 | 8.5 | 8.3 | 8.1 | 9.5 | 9.5 | 12.6 | 7.6 | 7.0 | 9.4 | 12.6 | 5.4 |
| M3 | 8.3 | 10.8 | 12.2 | 12.0 | 11.0 | 9.3 | 11.9 | 11.2 | 10.0 | 9.7 | 9.9 | 11.5 | 11.1 | 5.3 |
| **Velocity of circulation** | | | | | | | | | | | | | | |
| GNP/M1 | 5.43 | 5.71 | 5.92 | 6.18 | 6.40 | 6.56 | 6.88 | 6.70 | 6.48 | 6.72 | 6.73 | 6.79 | 6.71 | 6.61 |
| GNP/M2 | 1.60 | 1.57 | 1.55 | 1.61 | 1.67 | 1.68 | 1.72 | 1.63 | 1.56 | 1.61 | 1.61 | 1.60 | 1.58 | 1.57 |
| GNP/M3 | 1.38 | 1.38 | 1.37 | 1.38 | 1.39 | 1.39 | 1.39 | 1.30 | 1.27 | 1.29 | 1.28 | 1.27 | 1.25 | 1.25 |
| **Federal Reserve Bank reserves** *($ billion)* | | | | | | | | | | | | | | |
| Non-borrowed | 24.4 | 24.7 | 25.4 | 26.6 | 26.4 | 28.0 | 29.8 | 31.2 | 34.1 | 34.0 | 31.1 | 33.9 | 38.8 | 40.1 |
| Borrowed | 0.2 | 0.1 | 0.5 | 0.9 | 1.3 | 1.4 | 1.4 | 1.1 | 1.0 | 3.7 | 7.1 | 4.6 | 1.4 | 1.3 |
| Total | 24.5 | 24.8 | 25.8 | 27.4 | 27.8 | 29.4 | 31.1 | 32.3 | 35.1 | 37.8 | 38.1 | 38.5 | 40.2 | 41.4 |
| Required | 24.3 | 24.6 | 25.6 | 27.2 | 27.6 | 29.1 | 30.8 | 31.9 | 34.6 | 37.1 | 37.5 | 37.8 | 39.4 | 40.6 |
| Excess | 0.2 | 0.2 | 0.2 | 0.2 | 0.2 | 0.3 | 0.3 | 0.4 | 0.5 | 0.7 | 0.6 | 0.7 | 0.8 | 0.8 |
| Free (excess – borrowed) | 0 | 0.1 | –0.2 | –0.7 | –1.1 | –1.0 | –1.0 | –0.7 | –0.5 | –3.0 | –6.4 | –3.9 | –0.6 | –0.5 |
| **Interest rates (%)** | | | | | | | | | | | | | | |
| Federal funds rate | 5.8 | 5.0 | 5.5 | 7.9 | 11.2 | 13.4 | 16.4 | 12.3 | 9.1 | 10.2 | 11.4 | 9.3 | 8.5 | 7.9 |
| Discount rate[1] | 6.2 | 5.5 | 5.5 | 7.5 | 10.4 | 11.8 | 13.4 | 10.9 | 8.5 | 8.8 | 9.0 | 8.5 | 8.0 | 7.7 |
| Prime rate[2] | 7.9 | 6.8 | 6.8 | 9.1 | 12.7 | 15.3 | 18.9 | 14.9 | 10.8 | 12.1 | 13.0 | 11.8 | 10.5 | 10.2 |
| 3 month Treasury Bills | 5.8 | 5.0 | 5.3 | 7.2 | 10.1 | 11.4 | 14.0 | 10.6 | 8.6 | 9.5 | 10.3 | 8.8 | 8.2 | 7.5 |
| AAA rate[3] | 8.8 | 8.4 | 8.0 | 8.7 | 9.6 | 11.9 | 14.2 | 13.8 | 12.0 | 12.7 | 13.0 | 12.3 | 12.3 | 11.6 |
| 10 year Treasury Bonds | 8.0 | 7.6 | 7.4 | 8.4 | 9.4 | 11.5 | 13.9 | 13.0 | 11.1 | 12.4 | 12.9 | 11.7 | 11.6 | 10.8 |

1. Rate for Federal Reserve Bank of New York.
2. Prime rate on short-term business loans.
3. Corporate bonds, AAA rating group, quoted by Moody's Investors Services.
*Source :  Federal Reserve Bulletin,* Board of Governors of the Federal Reserve System.

| | 1971 | 1972 | 1973 | 1974 | 1975 |
|---|---|---|---|---|---|
| Exports, fob[1] | 43 319 | 49 381 | 71 410 | 98 306 | 107 088 |
| Imports, fob[1] | 45 579 | 55 797 | 70 499 | 103 811 | 98 185 |
| Trade balance | −2 260 | −6 416 | 911 | −5 505 | 8 903 |
| Services, net[2] | 4 528 | 4 475 | 10 110 | 14 652 | 13 846 |
| Balance on goods and services | 2 268 | −1 941 | 11 021 | 9 147 | 22 749 |
| Private transfers, net | −1 117 | −1 109 | −1 250 | −1 017 | −906 |
| Official transfers, net | −2 585 | −2 745 | −2 631 | −6 168 | −3 707 |
| Current balance | −1 434 | −5 795 | 7 140 | 1 962 | 18 136 |
| Long-term capital (excluding special transactions) | −9 105 | −5 126 | −7 888 | −6 469 | −17 926 |
| a) Private[3] | −6 711 | −3 740 | −6 180 | −7 136 | −15 968 |
| b) Official | −2 393 | −1 386 | −1 708 | 667 | −1 958 |
| Basic balance | −10 539 | −10 921 | −748 | −4 507 | 210 |
| Non-monetary short-term private capital[4] | −1 118 | −659 | −1 271 | −182 | 1 130 |
| Non-monetary short-term official capital | – | – | – | – | – |
| Errors and omissions | −9 779 | −1 879 | −2 654 | −1 458 | 5 897 |
| Balance on non-monetary transactions | −21 436 | −13 459 | −4 673 | −6 147 | 7 237 |
| Private monetary institutions short-term capital | −9 029 | 2 406 | −572 | −2 325 | −10 267 |
| a) Assets[5] | −2 368 | −2 199 | −5 047 | −18 333 | −11 175 |
| b) Liabilities[5][6] | −6 661 | 4 605 | 4 475 | 16 008 | 908 |
| Net transactions of monetary authorities | −30 465 | −11 058 | −5 245 | −8 472 | −3 028 |
| Liabilities to foreign official monetary agencies[7][8] | 27 400 | 10 352 | 5 090 | 9 940 | 3 877 |
| Use of IMF credit | – | – | – | – | – |
| Special transactions | – | – | – | – | – |
| Miscellaneous official accounts | – | – | – | – | – |
| Allocation of SDR's | 717 | 710 | – | – | – |
| Change in reserves (+ = increase) | −2 349 | 4 | −158 | 1 467 | 849 |
| a) Gold | −866 | −547 | – | – | – |
| b) Currency assets | −382 | 1 | −182 | 30 | 317 |
| c) Reserve positions in IMF | −1 350 | −153 | 33 | 1 265 | 466 |
| d) Special drawing rights | 249 | 703 | −9 | 172 | 66 |

1. Excluding military goods.
2. Services include reinvested earnings of incorporated affiliates.
3. Including:
   a) Direct investment financed by reinvested earnings of incorporated affiliates;
   b) Investments by foreign official agencies in US corporate stocks and in debt securities of US Government corporations and agencies, private corporatio and State and local governments.
   c) Investment by international financial institutions and private foreign residents in US Treasury bonds and notes.
   d) Until 1977, US banks' long-term assets and liabilities.
   e) Until 1978, US non-banking concerns' long-term assets and liabilities to unaffiliated foreigners.
4. Including investments by international financial institutions and private foreign residents in US Treasury bills and certificates and, since 1979, U non-banking concerns' long-term assets and liabilities to unaffiliated foreigners.
5. Including US banks' long-term assets and liabilities since 1978.
6. Excluding liabilities held by foreign official monetary agencies.
7. Excluding liabilities to IMF and investments by foreign official agencies in US corporate stocks and in debt securities of US Government corporations a agencies, private corporations and State and local governments.
8. Including liabilities to BIS.
Source: Survey of Current Business, US Department of Commerce.

**ECD basis**

dollars

| 1976 | 1977 | 1978 | 1979 | 1980 | 1981 | 1982 | 1983 | 1984 |
|---|---|---|---|---|---|---|---|---|
| 114 745 | 120 816 | 142 054 | 184 473 | 224 269 | 237 085 | 211 198 | 200 257 | 220 343 |
| 124 228 | 151 907 | 176 020 | 212 028 | 249 781 | 265 086 | 247 667 | 261 312 | 327 778 |
| −9 483 | −31 091 | −33 966 | −27 555 | −25 512 | −28 001 | −36 469 | −61 055 | −107 435 |
| 18 688 | 21 198 | 23 626 | 32 241 | 34 488 | 41 129 | 35 328 | 28 142 | 16 986 |
| 9 205 | −9 893 | −10 340 | 4 686 | 8 976 | 13 128 | −1 141 | −32 913 | −90 449 |
| −917 | −859 | −843 | −921 | −1 044 | −919 | −1 161 | −1 012 | −1 355 |
| −4 080 | −3 759 | −4 264 | −4 730 | −6 033 | −5 914 | −6 897 | −7 638 | −9 845 |
| 4 208 | −14 510 | −15 446 | −964 | 1 899 | 6 294 | −9 199 | −41 563 | −101 649 |
| | | | | | | | | |
| −13 179 | −10 456 | − 8 056 | −15 241 | −1 694 | 12 038 | 13 505 | 4 927 | 37 138 |
| −13 592 | −8 162 | −5 872 | −11 455 | 2 855 | 17 446 | 19 265 | 9 742 | 42 266 |
| 413 | −2 294 | −2 184 | −3 786 | −4 549 | −5 408 | −5 760 | −4 815 | −5 128 |
| −8 971 | −24 966 | −23 502 | −16 205 | 205 | 18 332 | 4 306 | −36 636 | −64 510 |
| −2 028 | −2 369 | −2 409 | −1 420 | 4 124 | 1 249 | 10 289 | −1 294 | 12 630 |
| − | − | − | | − | − | − | − | − |
| 10 543 | −2 022 | 12 540 | 25 403 | 24 982 | 22 275 | 32 916 | 9 331 | 30 015 |
| −456 | −29 357 | −13 371 | 7 778 | 29 311 | 41 856 | 47 511 | −28 599 | −21 865 |
| | | | | | | | | |
| −8 247 | −4 330 | −17 465 | 6 394 | −36 095 | −42 047 | −45 148 | 23 668 | 20 234 |
| −19 006 | −10 676 | −33 356 | −26 213 | −46 838 | −84 175 | −111 070 | −25 391 | −7 337 |
| 10 759 | 6346 | 15 891 | 32 607 | 10 743 | 42 128 | 65 922 | 49 059 | 27 571 |
| | | | | | | | | |
| −8 703 | −33 687 | −30 836 | 14 172 | −6 784 | −191 | 2 363 | −4 931 | −1 631 |
| | | | | | | | | |
| 11 262 | 34 065 | 30 103 | −14 181 | 13 784 | 4 272 | 2 602 | 6 125 | 4 761 |
| − | − | − | − | − | − | − | − | − |
| − | − | − | − | − | − | − | − | − |
| − | − | − | 1 139 | 1 152 | 1 093 | − | − | − |
| 2 558 | 375 | −732 | 1 133 | 8 154 | 5 176 | 4 965 | 1 195 | 3 132 |
| − | 118 | 65 | 65 | − | − | − | − | − |
| 268 | −158 | 4 683 | −257 | 6 471 | 861 | 1 040 | −3 305 | 1 156 |
| 2 212 | 294 | −4 231 | 189 | 1 667 | 2 492 | 2 552 | 4 435 | 995 |
| 78 | 121 | −1 249 | 1 136 | 16 | 1 823 | 1 372 | 65 | 979 |

# BASIC STATISTICS :
## INTERNATIONAL COMPARISONS

| | Units | Reference period[1] | Australia | Austria |
|---|---|---|---|---|
| **Population** | | | | |
| Total . . . . . . . . . . . . . . . . . . | Thousands | 1984 | 15 540 | 7 552 |
| Inhabitants per sq.km . . . . . . . . . . . . . . . . | Number | | 2 | 90 |
| Net average annual increase over previous 10 years . . . . | % | | 1.3 | 0.0 |
| **Employment** | | | | |
| Total civilian employment (TCE)[2] . . . . . . . . . . . | Thousands | 1984 | 6 471 | 3 235 |
| *of which:* Agriculture . . . . . . . . . . . . . . . . | % of TCE | | 6.2 | 9.4 |
| Industry . . . . . . . . . . . . . . | % of TCE | | 28.1 | 38.1 |
| Services . . . . . . . . . . . . . . | % of TCE | | 65.7 | 52.5 |
| **Gross domestic product (GDP)** | | | | |
| At current prices and current exchange rates . . . . . . . | Billion US$ | 1984 | 173.7 | 64.5 |
| Per capita . . . . . . . . . . | US$ | | 11 178 | 8 535 |
| At current prices using current PPP's[3] . . . . . . . . . | Billion US$ | 1983 | .. | 75.6 |
| Per capita . . . . . . . . . . . . | US$ | | .. | 10 010 |
| Average annual volume growth over previous 5 years . . . | % | 1984 | 2.6 | 1.6 |
| **Gross fixed capital formation (GFCF)** . . . . . . . . . . . . . | % of GDP | 1984 | 21.8 | 21.8 |
| *of which:* Machinery and equipment . . . . . . . . . . . | % of GDP | | 9.3 (83) | 10.2 |
| Residential construction . . . . . . . . . . . . | % of GDP | | 3.7 (83) | 5.1 (8 |
| Average annual volume growth over previous 5 years . . . | % | | 1.3 | −0.9 |
| **Gross saving ratio[4]** . . . . . . . . . . . . . . . . . . . . . . . | % of GDP | 1984 | 20.3 | 24.1 |
| **General government** | | | | |
| Current expenditure on goods and services . . . . . . . . | % of GDP | 1984 | 17.1 | 18.5 |
| Current disbursements[5] . . . . . . . . . . . . . . . . . | % of GDP | 1983 | 32.4 | 45.5 |
| Current receipts . . . . . . . . . . . . . . . . . | % of GDP | 1983 | 32.6 | 46.6 |
| **Net official development assistance** . . . . . . . . . . . . . . | % of GNP | 1983 | 0.49 | 0.23 |
| **Indicators of living standards** | | | | |
| Private consumption per capita using current PPP's[3] . . . | US$ | 1983 | 6 287 * | 5 716 |
| Passenger cars, per 1 000 inhabitants . . . . . . . . . . | Number | 1983 | .. | 306 (8 |
| Telephones, per 1 000 inhabitants . . . . . . . . . . . . | Number | 1983 | 540 | 460 |
| Television sets, per 1 000 inhabitants . . . . . . . . . . | Number | 1983 | .. | 300 (8 |
| Doctors, per 1 000 inhabitants . . . . . . . . . . . . | Number | 1983 | .. | 1.7 (8. |
| Infant mortality per 1 000 births . . . . . . . . . . . . | Number | 1983 | 9.6 | 11.9 |
| **Wages and prices** (average annual increase over previous 5 years) | | | | |
| Hourly earnings in manufacturing . . . . . . . . . . . . | % | 1984 | 14.9 (83) | 5.7 |
| Consumer prices . . . . . . . . . . . . . . . . . . . | % | 1984 | 9.0 | 5.5 |
| **Foreign trade** | | | | |
| Exports of goods, fob* . . . . . . . . . . . . . . . . | Million US$ | 1984 | 23 856 | 15 720 |
| as % of GDP . . . . . . . . . . . . . . . . . . . . | % | | 15.3 | 23.4 |
| average annual increase over previous 5 years . . . . . . | % | | 5.1 | 0.4 |
| Imports of goods, cif* . . . . . . . . . . . . . . . . | Million US$ | 1984 | 23 424 | 19 596 |
| as % of GDP . . . . . . . . . . . . . . . . . . . . | % | | 15.1 | 29.2 |
| average annual increase over previous 5 years . . . . . . | % | | 7.2 | −0.6 |
| **Total official reserves[6]** . . . . . . . . . . . . . . . . . . . . . | Million SDR's | 1984 | 7 869 | 5 070 |
| As ratio of average monthly imports of goods . . . . . . | Ratio | | 4.1 | 3.2 |

* At current prices and exchange rates.
1. Unless otherwise stated.
2. According to the definitions used in OECD *Labour force Statistics.*
3. PPP's = Purchasing Power Parities.
4. Gross saving = Gross national disposable income *minus* Private and Government consumption.
5. Current disbursements = Current expenditure on goods and services *plus* current transfers and payments of property income.
6. Gold included in reserves is valued at 35 SDR's per ounce.
7. Including Luxembourg.
8. Included in Belgium.
9. Including non-residential construction.

# EMPLOYMENT OPPORTUNITIES

## *Economics and Statistics Department*

## OECD

A.     **Administrator.**   A number of economist positions may become available in 1985 in areas such as monetary and fiscal policy, balance of payments, resource allocation, macroeconomic policy issues, short-term forecasting and country studies. *Essential* qualifications and experience: advanced university degree in economics; good knowledge of statistical methods and applied econometrics; two or three years experience in applied economic analysis; command of one of the two official languages (English and French). *Desirable* qualifications and experience also include: familiarity with the economic problems and data sources of a number of Member countries; proven drafting ability; experience with the estimation, simulation and implementation of computer-based economic models; some knowledge of the other official language.

B.     **Principal Administrator.**   A number of senior economist positions may become available in 1985 in areas such as monetary and fiscal policy, balance of payments, resource allocation, macroeconomic policy issues, short-term forecasting and country studies. *Essential* qualifications and experience: advanced university degree in economics; extensive experience in applied economic analysis, preferably with a central bank, economics/finance ministry or institute of economic research; good knowledge of statistical methods and applied econometrics; command of one of the two official languages (English and French) and proven drafting ability. *Desirable* qualifications and experience also include: experience in using economic analysis for formulating policy advice; familiarity with a number of OECD economies; experience in using econometric models; good knowledge of the other official language.

These positions carry a basic salary (tax free) from FF 171 284 or FF 211 318 (Administrator) and from FF 242 960 (Principal Administrator), supplemented by further additional allowances depending on residence and family situation.

Initial appointment will be on a two or three year fixed-term contract.

Vacancies are open to both male and female candidates from OECD Member countries. Applications citing reference "ECSUR", together with a detailed curriculum vitæ in English or French, should be sent to:

> Head of Personnel
> OECD
> 2, rue André-Pascal
> 75775 PARIS CEDEX 16
> France

# OECD SALES AGENTS
## DÉPOSITAIRES DES PUBLICATIONS DE L'OCDE

**ARGENTINA – ARGENTINE**
Carlos Hirsch S.R.L., Florida 165, 4° Piso (Galería Guemes)
1333 BUENOS AIRES, Tel. 33.1787.2391 y 30.7122

**AUSTRALIA – AUSTRALIE**
D.A. Book (Aust.) Pty. Ltd.
11-13 Station Street (P.O. Box 163)
MITCHAM, Vic. 3132. Tel. (03) 873 4411

**AUSTRIA – AUTRICHE**
OECD Publications and Information Center
4 Simrockstrasse 5300 Bonn (Germany). Tel. (0228) 21.60.45
Local Agent/Agent local :
Gerold and Co., Graben 31, WIEN 1. Tel. 52.22.35

**BELGIUM – BELGIQUE**
Jean De Lannoy, Service Publications OCDE
avenue du Roi 202, B-1060 BRUXELLES. Tel. 02/538.51.69

**CANADA**
Renouf Publishing Company Limited/
Éditions Renouf Limitée Head Office/Siège social – Store/Magasin :
61, rue Sparks Street,
OTTAWA, Ontario KIP 5A6. Tel. (613)238-8985. 1-800-267-4164
Store/Magasin: 211, rue Yonge Street,
TORONTO, Ontario M5B 1M4. Tel. (416)363-3171
Regional Sales Office/
Bureau des Ventes régional :
7575 Trans-Canada Hwy., Suite 305,
SAINT-LAURENT, Québec H4T 1V6. Tel. (514)335-9274

**DENMARK – DANEMARK**
Munksgaard Export and Subscription Service
35, Nørre Søgade
DK 1370 KØBENHAVN K. Tel. +45.1.12.85.70

**FINLAND – FINLANDE**
Akateeminen Kirjakauppa
Keskuskatu 1, 00100 HELSINKI 10. Tel. 65.11.22

**FRANCE**
OCDE, 2, rue André-Pascal, 75775 PARIS CEDEX 16
Tel. (1) 45.24.82.00
Librairie/Bookshop : 33, rue Octave-Feuillet,
75016 PARIS. Tél. (1) 45.24.81.67 ou (1) 45.24.81.81
Principal correspondant :
13602 AIX-EN-PROVENCE : Librairie de l'Université.
Tél. 42.26.18.08

**GERMANY – ALLEMAGNE**
OECD Publications and Information Center
4 Simrockstrasse 5300 BONN Tel. (0228) 21.60.45

**GREECE – GRÈCE**
Librairie Kauffmann, 28 rue du Stade,
ATHÈNES 132. Tel. 322.21.60

**HONG-KONG**
Government Information Services,
Publications (Sales) Office,
Beaconsfield House, 4/F.,
Queen's Road Central

**ICELAND – ISLANDE**
Snaebjörn Jónsson and Co., h.f.,
Hafnarstraeti 4 and 9, P.O.B. 1131, REYKJAVIK.
Tel. 13133/14281/11936

**INDIA – INDE**
Oxford Book and Stationery Co. :
NEW DELHI-1, Scindia House. Tel. 45896
CALCUTTA 700016, 17 Park Street. Tel. 240832

**INDONESIA – INDONÉSIE**
PDIN-LIPI, P.O. Box 3065/JKT., JAKARTA, Tel. 583467

**IRELAND – IRLANDE**
TDC Publishers – Library Suppliers
12 North Frederick Street, DUBLIN 1 Tel. 744835-749677

**ITALY – ITALIE**
Libreria Commissionaria Sansoni :
Via Lamarmora 45, 50121 FIRENZE. Tel. 579751/584468
Via Bartolini 29, 20155 MILANO. Tel. 365083
Sub-depositari :
Ugo Tassi
Via A. Farnese 28, 00192 ROMA. Tel. 310590
Editrice e Libreria Herder,
Piazza Montecitorio 120, 00186 ROMA. Tel. 6794628
Agenzia Libraria Pegaso,
Via de Romita 5, 70121 BARI. Tel. 540.105/540.195
Agenzia Libraria Pegaso, Via S. Anna dei Lombardi 16, 80134 NAPOLI.
Tel. 314180.
Libreria Hoepli, Via Hoepli 5, 20121 MILANO. Tel. 865446
Libreria Scientifica, Dott. Lucio de Biasio "Aeiou"
Via Meravigli 16, 20123 MILANO Tel. 807679
Libreria Zanichelli
Piazza Galvani 1/A, 40124 Bologna Tel. 237389
Libreria Lattes, Via Garibaldi 3, 10122 TORINO. Tel. 519274
La diffusione delle edizioni OCSE è inoltre assicurata dalle migliori librerie nelle città più importanti.

**JAPAN – JAPON**
OECD Publications and Information Center,
Landic Akasaka Bldg., 2-3-4 Akasaka,
Minato-ku, TOKYO 107 Tel. 586.2016

**KOREA – CORÉE**
Pan Korea Book Corporation,
P.O. Box n° 101 Kwangwhamun, SÉOUL. Tel. 72.7369

**LEBANON – LIBAN**
Documenta Scientifica/Redico,
Edison Building, Bliss Street, P.O. Box 5641, BEIRUT.
Tel. 354429 – 344425

**MALAYSIA – MALAISIE**
University of Malaya Co-operative Bookshop Ltd.
P.O. Box 1127, Jalan Pantai Baru
KUALA LUMPUR. Tel. 577701/577072

**THE NETHERLANDS – PAYS-BAS**
Staatsuitgeverij, Verzendboekhandel,
Chr. Plantijnstraat 1 Postbus 20014
2500 EA S-GRAVENHAGE. Tel. nr. 070.789911
Voor bestellingen: Tel. 070.789208

**NEW ZEALAND – NOUVELLE-ZÉLANDE**
Publications Section,
Government Printing Office Bookshops:
AUCKLAND: Retail Bookshop: 25 Rutland Street,
Mail Orders: 85 Beach Road, Private Bag C.P.O.
HAMILTON: Retail: Ward Street,
Mail Orders, P.O. Box 857
WELLINGTON: Retail: Mulgrave Street (Head Office),
Cubacade World Trade Centre
Mail Orders: Private Bag
CHRISTCHURCH: Retail: 159 Hereford Street,
Mail Orders: Private Bag
DUNEDIN: Retail: Princes Street
Mail Order: P.O. Box 1104

**NORWAY – NORVÈGE**
Tanum-Karl Johan a.s
P.O. Box 1177 Sentrum, 0107 OSLO 1. Tel. (02) 80.12.60

**PAKISTAN**
Mirza Book Agency, 65 Shahrah Quaid-E-Azam, LAHORE 3.
Tel. 66839

**PORTUGAL**
Livraria Portugal, Rua do Carmo 70-74,
1117 LISBOA CODEX. Tel. 360582/3

**SINGAPORE – SINGAPOUR**
Information Publications Pte Ltd,
Pei-Fu Industrial Building,
24 New Industrial Road N° 02-06
SINGAPORE 1953. Tel. 2831786, 2831798

**SPAIN – ESPAGNE**
Mundi-Prensa Libros, S.A.
Castelló 37, Apartado 1223, MADRID-28001. Tel. 431.33.99
Libreria Bosch, Ronda Universidad 11, BARCELONA 7.
Tel. 317.53.08, 317.53.58

**SWEDEN – SUÈDE**
AB CE Fritzes Kungl Hovbokhandel,
Box 16 356, S 103 27 STH, Regeringsgatan 12,
DS STOCKHOLM. Tel. 08/23.89.00
Subscription Agency/Abonnements:
Wennergren-Williams AB,
Box 30004, S104 25 STOCKHOLM. Tel. 08/54.12.00

**SWITZERLAND – SUISSE**
OECD Publications and Information Center
4 Simrockstrasse 5300 BONN (Germany). Tel. (0228) 21.60.45
Local Agents/Agents locaux
Librairie Payot, 6 rue Grenus, 1211 GENÈVE 11. Tel. 022.31.89.50

**TAIWAN – FORMOSE**
Good Faith Worldwide Int'1 Co., Ltd.
9th floor, No. 118, Sec. 2,
Chung Hsiao E. Road. TAIPEI. Tel. 391.7396/391.7397

**THAILAND – THAILANDE**
Suksit Siam Co., Ltd., 1715 Rama IV Rd,
Samyan, BANGKOK 5. Tel. 2511630

**TURKEY – TURQUIE**
Kültur Yayinlari Is-Türk Ltd. Sti.
Atatürk Bulvari No : 191/Kat. 21
Kavaklidere/ANKARA. Tel. 17 02 66
Dolmabahce Cad. No : 29
BESIKTAS/ISTANBUL. Tel. 60 71 88

**UNITED KINGDOM – ROYAUME-UNI**
H.M. Stationery Office,
P.O.B. 276, LONDON SW8 5DT.
(postal orders only)
Telephone orders: (01) 622.3316, or
49 High Holborn, LONDON WC1V 6 HB (personal callers)
Branches at: EDINBURGH, BIRMINGHAM, BRISTOL,
MANCHESTER, BELFAST.

**UNITED STATES OF AMERICA – ÉTATS-UNIS**
OECD Publications and Information Center, Suite 1207,
1750 Pennsylvania Ave., N.W. WASHINGTON, D.C.20006 – 4582
Tel. (202) 724.1857

**VENEZUELA**
Libreria del Este, Avda. F. Miranda 52, Edificio Galipan,
CARACAS 106. Tel. 32.23.01/33.26.04/31.58.38

**YUGOSLAVIA – YOUGOSLAVIE**
Jugoslovenska Knjiga, Knez Mihajlova 2, P.O.B. 36, BEOGRAD.
Tel. 621.992

Les commandes provenant de pays où l'OCDE n'a pas encore désigné de dépositaire peuvent être adressées à :
OCDE, Bureau des Publications, 2, rue André-Pascal, 75775 PARIS CEDEX 16.

Orders and inquiries from countries where sales agents have not yet been appointed may be sent to:
OECD, Publications Office, 2, rue André-Pascal, 75775 PARIS CEDEX 16.

69131-11-1985

**OECD PUBLICATIONS**
2, rue André-Pascal
**75775 PARIS CEDEX 16**
No. 43369
(10 86 02 1) ISBN 92-64-12769-0
ISSN 0376-6438

●

*PRINTED IN FRANCE*